ussia

T553943

D0421361

00 9600473

THE MEDIA IN RUSSIA

Anna Arutunyan

Open University Press

Open University Press
McGraw-Hill Education
McGraw-Hill House
Shoppenhangers Road
Maidenhead
Berkshire
England
SL6 2QL

email: enquiries@openup.co.uk
world wide web: www.openup.co.uk

and Two Penn Plaza, New York, NY 10121—2289, USA

First published 2009

Copyright © Anna Arutunyan 2009

A catalogue record of this book is available from the British Library

ISBN-13: 978-0-33-5228898(pb) 978-0-33-5228904(hb)
ISBN-10: 0-33-5228895(pb) 0-33-5228888-7(hb)

Typeset by Kerrypress, Luton, Bedfordshire
Printed in Great Britain by Bell and Bain Ltd, Glasgow

The **McGraw·Hill** Companies

CONTENTS

For my daughter, Mary

ACKNOWLEDGEMENTS

This book would not have been possible without Ivan Zassoursky, who got me into writing it in the first place, and through whom I came to know Brian McNair. I am indebted to Brian's patience and trust in this endeavour. This book would also not have been possible without my former editor at *The Moscow News*, Anthony Louis, who encouraged me to write and helped with invaluable suggestions and edits. I would also like to thank Anne Fisher for her help (at the last minute).

My thanks go to Professor Rafael Ovsepyan for starting me off on the right track, and to Marina Petrushka for her advice on research and getting sources for some of the toughest parts of the book. Robert Bridge and the team an *The Moscow News* have been very supportive, and Mikhail Samardak even advised with the art. I'm grateful for the historic opportunity that working on this book has presented me.

Finally, I would like to thank my family: my husband, Mikhail, who not only supported me in the logistics of juggling a job, a book and a small child, but encouraged, advised and even edited in the months that this book was in progress; and my daughter Mary, who was a baby when this book was being written. None of this, of course, would have been possible without the tremendous support from the rest of our family.

INTRODUCTION

- **Messianic snobbery: towards a populist media?**
- **Mouthpiece of the state: the challenges of a viable emancipation**
- **The spread of advertising**
- **Book structure and overview**

Today, two decades after perestroika began, Russia stands once again at a crossroads on its quest for self-identification. The world continues to watch in suspense as it anticipates which path Russia looks poised to take: western integration, or rebirth as an alternative world power. Recent developments in Russia's media have shown it to be both a victim of Russia's strenuous politics and a reflection of the country's historical path. The media in Russia has been confronted with the same challenges and paradoxes of democracy that plagued the nation as a whole throughout the 1990s and that bear their fruit today. Thus, the aim of this book is to offer an introduction to the Russian media in its struggle to become the Fourth Estate, focusing in particular on its development in the post-Soviet era.

This book will explore the Russian media along two vectors, delving into its 300-year history (time) in order to weigh in on its current landscape (space). It is not a history, but neither is it merely a descriptive almanac of the various Russian media and their roles. Given that readers are acquainted with Russia to some degree through current events, it is inevitable that they have also formed some picture of where its media stands. This book will flesh out that image and give some perspective on the main challenges that the Russian media has struggled with in the past and which continue to shape its present and future.

In its centuries-long legacy of relations with the rest of the world, Russia has taken on the role of a promising, but misguided, and often menacingly boisterous, student. Since the fall of communism, each time the international spotlight falls on Russia, the first question that usually comes to the minds of many westerners is, 'Is Russia reverting back to its totalitarian ways?' Because free speech is the cornerstone of a free nation, that question has been inevitably directed, first and foremost, at Russia's media. Thus, for the last two decades, the question has been framed, 'Is the Russian state once again clamping down on the media and curtailing free speech?'

While the purpose of this book is not political, any honest and sober description of the Russian media cannot avoid that question, simply because it is the first and frequently the only one that is being asked about the Russian media. Framed in this way, however, it begs one of two answers, both of which would give an equally biased picture of where Russia's media stands.

The first answer would argue that yes, the Russian state is indeed clamping down on the media, here are the myriad ways it is doing so, and here are the dangers this clampdown will bring. Through this prism, the explanation fails to address Russia's media on its own terms, trying instead to assess it based on a rigid, western paradigm that presupposes the media as an inherently free 'adversary' of the state, while the definition of 'free media' also falls under an equally rigid, western understanding of the term.

However, the second answer, that the Russian state is *not* clamping down on its press, would place us in an even trickier position. The arguments in favour of this point of view would inevitably fall into one of two categories: either defending the actions of the state based on its allegedly beleaguered position and a need to act in the interests of the people, or blaming the critics by arguing that Russia's media is being judged according to double standards, since western media, subordinate as it is to advertising and business interests, is actually no 'freer'. Both of these arguments, which have been used both in Soviet Russia's political doctrine (and are being rehashed by today's government) and by critics of the West at home, are logically and historically suspect.

Instead of answering a reductive question and compounding the misconception, a greater and more worthwhile challenge is to formulate the right question. One of the underlying problems of this task is the tendency to define Russia and Russian issues using comparisons to an echelon, in this case, the West, and measuring its media according to the standard, 'western' idea of a 'free' media. Both of these concepts are notoriously hazy, but if we wish to explore the Russian media and its prominent issues head-on, we will not be able to avoid them.

What is the West, and can Russia ever become a part of it? In the purely geographical sense, of course it cannot. For all purposes, however, the West has come to stand for a number of industrialized democracies with high standards of living, chiefly the USA, Europe, Canada, Australia and Japan. Because Russia long ago entered the path to industrialization and has stumbled upon the path of democratization, it has inadvertently measured itself according to those standards. So has the West, with western European nations 200 years ago issuing virtually the same critiques of Russian society as they continue to do today. We will leave that discussion aside, using it only as a comparison to how Russia's media is viewed.

The same applies to Russia's media. However, adequately defining a 'free and independent' media would possibly take up an entire book on its own. For Russia's purposes, we will understand a free and independent media as a system that effectively spreads information through all sectors of society, a system where state involvement, if any, cannot be such that it alters, in any considerable way, the nature of the information that is being spread. The questions that should be asked are: to what extent has Russia ever had a free and independent media and to what extent does its current, post-1990 media landscape represent a free and independent press? Finally, to what extent is that media capable of representing and impacting on society? These are no trivial questions, and they will underpin our discussion of where the Russian media stands today and how its origins inform its current condition, focusing in particular on its current, post-1990 travails.

First, it is important to examine two reoccurring concerns that, taken together, are unique to the Russian media. The first characteristic is the messianic nature of Russian writing as a whole, and Russian journalism in particular. The second revolves around the absolutist role of the Russian state, not as a force that *dictates to and curtails* the media, but as one that, a priori, *creates and sustains* the media, whether loyal or oppositionist. As we explore the media, we will see that these characteristic concerns not only persist throughout its history, they also re-emerge as challenges to its current development. As we see how the 'liberation' of the press in 1990 negated neither the presence nor the effects of these characteristic aspects, we will come to a better understanding of the kinds of questions we should be asking about where the Russian media – and even Russia as a whole – is headed.

Messianic snobbery: towards a populist media?

The Russian intelligentsia likes to welcome guests and foreigners with a self-depreciating saying: 'A poet in Russia is more than a poet'. In its ever more sardonic variations, this famous phrase has become, 'The man of letters is bigger than a man of letters', or even 'The writer in Russia is bigger than Russia'. The original meme was immortalized in a poem by Yevgeny Yevtushenko,[1] but it easily encompasses Russians' attitude not just towards their literature, but towards the written word as a whole. This attitude has been particularly vexing for the journalist. Not regarded with quite as much respect as the writer, the vaunted 'engineer of the human soul' (an apt but daunting description, considering it came from Joseph Stalin in an address to the nation's top writers in 1932),[2] nevertheless the journalist was, by the very nature of his profession, charged with the responsibility of informing the masses. In Russia this task was made even more gargantuan by the vast chasm historically separating the literate elites and the illiterate masses. Aided and abetted by a culture that lauded only its quickest and sharpest pens, not necessarily those who actually got around to *informing* the public of newsworthy events, the Russian journalist developed his share of messianic snobbism.

Perhaps the most apt characterization of the journalist's role in Russia was given by Vladimir Lenin, who outlined party propaganda as the chief *raison d'être* of the media in an essay published in 1905: 'Newspapers must become the organs of the various party organizations, and their writers must by all means become members of these organizations. Publishing and distributing centers, bookshops and reading rooms, libraries and similar establishments — all must be under party control.'[3] While this much is probably already known by Russia-watchers, it should not be interpreted as Lenin's own innovation, as a state of affairs that suddenly came into being at the turn of the twentieth century. Instead, Lenin was, to a large extent, describing not so much how things should be under the dictatorship of the proletariat, but how things had been in Russia at least for the past several decades, if not centuries.

Lenin's call for party-led journalism should not be confused with the partisan journalism that was a feature of the nineteenth-century European press. In many ways, the Russian press of the time would appear similarly 'partisan' in the sense that it represented 'parties' or camps, and its content swayed heavily towards the didactic. The glaring difference, however, was the lack of a 'party' system in Russia. Europe's partisan newspapers, particularly those of Great Britain, reflected the political processes and debates of existing parties. They were the extension, in other words, of a democratic process. In Russia, meanwhile, there were no legal political 'parties', in the western sense of the word, to take advantage of the media by using it as a press organ. Instead, throughout the nineteenth century, there were 'camps' (the Russophiles and the westernizers, for example) and various marginalized or outright illegal parties, all of them equally removed from the political process.

Indeed, the primary feature of the printed word in Russian culture was its underlying didactic and messianic principle, and a press need not necessarily be partisan to be didactic. Even at those times when it was purely informative, Russian journalism was still inherently didactic due to the near monopoly that first the Church, then the state, had on the printed word from the very start (we should remember that there were no newspapers in Russia before the eighteenth century). Peter the Great's efforts to westernize his country were indeed messianic in nature. His launching of the first newspaper, *Vedomosti*,[4] in 1702 was messianic in the sense that he was building upon an important aspect of his westernizing mission, and he was the one who would deliver Russia from its backwardness: Russia would have a newspaper, like other European countries. With the media founded on this top-down model originating with the state, it was inevitable that adversaries of the state would also be bound by an opposite, but equally messianic, information paradigm.

However, elements of messianic journalism are not unique to Russia; after all, the whole idea of investigative reporting can arguably be called messianic. Still, the messianic nature of Russian journalism in its early years was characterized not by what it had, but by what it lacked: the idea of information as commodity, of facts being valued in and of themselves.

Russian textbooks on the history of journalism and the media say little about mass circulation newspapers and tabloids. One reason is that this particular journalistic medium appeared relatively late, in the end of the nineteenth century, due in part to low literacy rates and the resultant lack of a mass readership. Another reason, however, is that this mass of written content provided little for media historians and critics to analyse. Whereas a newspaper essay by Chekhov or Chernyshevsky is not only a sample of Russian journalism at its best, but also offers sharp insight into contemporary polemics, the same could hardly be said of a news blurb in a provincial newspaper about the installment of a street lamp at the town's busiest intersection. Since the Russian analytical tradition, grounded in Marxism and Hegelian dialectics, was characterized by a propensity to describe events as a struggle between two adversaries, there was little room for journalists to ponder how two inches of text about a street lamp could also impact society – particularly by helping to get street lamps installed in other places.

The Russian press did include news items from the start; after all, Peter the Great's *Vedomosti* was a newspaper in the classical sense of the word. But news items were rarely a feature in and of themselves. Instead, they were treated by most serious publications either as secondary additions or as platforms for discussion. According to American scholar Louise McReynolds, Russian newspapers eventually did commodify the news, but much later than newspapers did in the West; furthermore, this period of commodified news was short-lived, since it was hijacked by the exclusively political objectives of Bolshevism. In the meantime, the distaste with which the elite treated (and, in many cases, continues to treat) commodified news rubbed off on its treatment of all news circulated by mass print vehicles. This led to a split in the newspaper medium between serious periodicals discussing news that concerned the elite, and cheap tabloids devoted to developments concerning the majority of citizens.

These issues play deeply into how journalists define themselves as herald bearers of a free press and a fourth estate that can impact policy and bring about social change. Reporting on community events, gathering locally-important news and building the kind of information network that could benefit grassroots initiative was valued far less than revealing the misdeeds and cover-ups of those on high, challenging the authorities in their most controversial endeavours, and, indeed, simply *provoking* authority. Thus, instead of fortifying the press as a fourth estate, these issues all had the opposite effect of reinforcing the absolutism that circumscribed the press and highlighting the press's own vulnerability.

Mouthpiece of the state: the challenges of a viable emancipation

In 2004, President Vladimir Putin was asked at a Kremlin press conference about free press in Russia. He responded with one of the cutting *bon mots* for which he had already become notorious in his four years of power: 'There is a phrase in a famous Italian film – "a real man should always try, while a real woman should always resist" '.[5] Interestingly, Putin did not indicate which role the press should take. Nevertheless, the comment was later reprinted by journalists and media scholars with certain interpretive additions: 'the government, as a man, should try, while the press, as a woman, should resist'.[6] *Moskovsky Komsomolets* columnist Alexander Minkin even openly accused the president of condoning rape and alluded to the phrase in subsequent columns.[7]

Since we only have the official *Rossiyskaya Gazeta* as the source of the original quote, there is no telling for certain what exactly Putin said, let alone what he could have actually meant. What is noteworthy here is the readiness with which journalists interpreted the phrase to their own disadvantage. After all, it would be equally logical to see the press as trying to uncover information, and the government as resisting leaks. Indeed, according to the official report, Putin later clarified his remark: 'the government always tries to reduce criticism, while the media finds everything it can to get the government to see its mistakes'. If that was actually what Putin said, then the defensive role appears to fall on the government, not on the press.

Whatever the president was trying to say, the manner in which the phrase was reprinted shows the extent to which journalists have internalized their subordinate role. They can hardly be blamed, for, in the 300 years of the Russian mass media's existence, that media has been, with few exceptions, directly dependent on the state in terms of funds, means of production and even editorial initiative.

The defining feature of Russian journalism is that it emerged from its start in 1702 as a top-down, government-sponsored endeavour. Whereas private periodicals had already been published for centuries in Europe, Russian society at that time had simply not yet got around to establishing any sort of grassroots, private publications. To a large extent, society was still grounded in feudalism by the government's grip on all methods of production and its hold on much of the country's infrastructure. That feudalism, characterized by mass illiteracy among the serfs, prevented the development of any mass readership for newspapers or magazines.

Peter's *Vedomosti* did not just serve to launch the nation's media. In effect, the newspaper laid the foundation for an entire journalistic tradition, establishing the newspaper as an extension of the government, with its primary purpose rooted in propaganda. While commercial publications in other countries developed gradually, based on models offered by private periodicals, in Russia they were begun as a result of government efforts, seemingly as an afterthought, not by direct initiative from below. Furthermore, the czar's government held a monopoly on reformist efforts, which led to a sort of Catch-22 of reform: the good intentions behind the many instances when Russia's leaders actually did take the task of fostering a viable media and a fourth estate into their own hands were completely negated in practical terms, since the very act of top-down fostering ran counter to the whole purpose of the fourth estate, which was to foster civil society from the *bottom*. Therefore, it was only rarely that the Russian media succeeded in impacting political and social change without prodding from the government. Two of the most prominent successes are Emperor Alexander II's liberal reforms and Mikhail Gorbachev's policy of glasnost, or openness, in the media. In both cases, however, journalists succeeded precisely because the country's leaders were open to change and dialogue themselves.

The pivotal point in the history of the Russian media, as we shall see in this book, was Gorbachev's 1990 decree eliminating party control of media outlets and allowing non-party groups and individuals to establish and release their own publications. This was not the only attempt to do away with preliminary censorship, but it was by far the most successful, ushering in an entirely new era when newspapers and television were given unbridled freedom to discuss events and criticize policy. Also, the birth of the new media of the 1990s coincided with the birth of a new nation. In 1991, the Soviet Union fell apart and the Communist Party tumbled from power, leading to the creation of the Russian Federation.

New or not, it was nevertheless a media that spoke and wrote in the same language, and, more importantly, relied on the same Soviet-era broadcasting, printing and distribution infrastructure. Through this language and infrastructure, Russia's post-Soviet media inherited the same cultural traditions and the same dependence on the state that governed the preceding 300 years of journalism. Contemporary media's struggle with that legacy, and its consequences, will be the focus of this book.

The spread of advertising

One important feature of any media system that is absent from this book is advertising and public relations (PR). It is crucial to stress that this absence does not imply a minimal role for advertising in the Russian media; quite the opposite. In fact, it is precisely the importance of the sphere of advertising and PR that convinced me that this book does not offer sufficient space to discuss it as it deserves. A brief numerical overview, however, may be in order. It should also be mentioned that readers may have the misleading impression that Russian advertising and PR were born concomitant to the breakup of the Soviet Union. This is not the case. Rather, these industries flourished in the 1990s, but this development simply reflects the enormous post-collapse influx of capital and so is comparable to similar surges in other media. Another problem that complicates an adequate treatment of the subject is the notoriously murky advertising climate that developed in the 1990s, particularly on television.

One issue related to advertising that warrants mention in this section, however, is consumption. With consumption remaining strong in Russia regardless of market indicators, Russians demonstrate unique consumption patterns that deserve separate research. As a result, their attitudes towards – and, hence, the effectiveness of – advertising is influenced by a legacy of social trends, including the 'shopping deficit' of the Soviet

Union, which, market analysts say, is still being compensated for to this day. In the current economic climate, oil exports finance both a predilection for consumption (fuelled by low taxes and relatively high levels of disposable income) and the introduction of newer brands in a similarly booming retail market. The Russian advertising market, meanwhile, has proved to be the fastest growing in the world.[8] In September 2008 it was valued at $7.4 billion, according to the Association of Communication Agencies of Russia. Since 2000, it has been growing at a rate of up to 60 per cent. While this figure was lower than what Gallup forecasted in 2005, that it was 'only' up 20 per cent from the previous year indicated that market growth was slowing down for the first time since 2000.

While this book is not the place to lay out a formal causal relationship between the booming advertising market and Russian spending habits, some figures indicating the social standing, net worth and influence of each medium are noteworthy. According to TNS Gallup,[9] in 2006 Russia occupied the twelfth spot worldwide in advertising expenditure, trailing Canada and Australia (the first and second spot were occupied by the USA and Japan, respectively). In 2005, television accounted for over 46 per cent of advertising, while newspapers held just 5.8 per cent and magazines 11.6 per cent. In contrast, the print media, which witnessed a steady surge of advertising during the 1990s, would see its share of total advertising shrink by 2005 to 4.2 per cent for newspapers and 10 per cent for magazines. By 2010, advertising shares of other media are predicted to shrink, giving way to the expanding presence of television and the internet. By 2010, their advertising shares are forecasted to increase to 56.6 per cent and 4.9 per cent, respectively. In real terms, however, newspaper advertising is growing at a similar rate as television advertising, according to the Russian Association of Communication Agencies.

The bigger realm of PR is an even more serious issue for Russia. Given how its media has for centuries served propaganda, the sudden emergence of commercial PR to a large extent incorporated the know-how of government propaganda, forging a uniquely Russian PR culture. In spite of, or perhaps because of, this, the Russian government's efforts to form an effective PR policy have also notoriously failed, even though it commissioned the US-based Ketchum Inc. as its chief PR consultant. A policy of secrecy, silence and excessive caution still reigns, where open discussion could easily improve the standing of the Russian government in the West, something that was illustrated during the August 2008 military conflict in Georgia over the pro-Russian separatist republics of Abkhazia and South Ossetia. While Russia's internal propaganda rallied the Russian population and proved a general success on the home front, it quickly began losing the global information war precisely because of its lack of PR, while rival President Mikhail Saakashvili of Georgia, with his fluent English and US advisers, used PR to his full advantage.

Book structure and overview

The purpose of *The Media in Russia* is not to provide a comprehensive history, but rather to acquaint readers with the Russian national media's unique characteristics and to provide an interpretive framework of cultural and historical phenomena affecting each medium's development. The book approaches this subject less from an academic perspective than from the point of view of the needs of a broad general readership. I will weigh in on my own 10 years of experience working in the Russian media as a reporter and journalist, and outline how the population, the media consumer, relates to what is being shown on television, printed in newspapers and broadcast over the radio. The first three chapters give a general overview, while the remainder of the book is devoted to particular mediums: the press, television, cinema, radio and the internet.

Chapter 1 gives readers a sense of the social impact of the media in today's Russia. It sketches out the particular challenges facing the various media and, most importantly, compares their relative audience impact. I will also identify and describe the most prominent television channels, radio stations and newspapers, so that readers will be familiar with them and ready to encounter them in subsequent chapters. Using surveys, ratings and polls, the chapter presents Russia's media playing field not from the point of view of media critics, but from the point of view of the audience, analysing to what extent Russians trust their media, what they prefer to read and watch, and where they get their news. The concept of news will also be introduced in this chapter, highlighting the differences between Russian news and news agencies and their European counterparts. A comparative overview of each media will spell out the chief issues to be addressed in subsequent chapters.

Chapter 2 explores one of the central themes in this book: control, ownership and power in the Russian media. Unlike other chapters, it focuses heavily on the current situation and its development throughout the 1990s. It will define the problem of media independence and analyse how the media's financial dependence on the government impacted on the ability of the Russian media as a whole to reinvent itself as a viable mediator between the government and the public. The turmoil of the 1990s, with President Boris Yeltsin's struggles to build a democracy and implement liberal economic reforms, dealt a serious blow to the nation's free press by plunging media outlets into free market conditions in which many were simply not prepared to survive. Within a few years, media outlets were bought out or taken over by politicized capital. During the second half of the 1990s, the oligarchs used their media assets – which included leading newspaper and television stations – as their primary weapons in vicious muckraking campaigns against each other and against Yeltsin's ailing government. Such media campaigns are no novelty in developing countries. In Russia, however, their sheer intensity and the closeness with which they followed the only brief period of unbridled media freedom that Russia had ever known, served to shatter illusions among the public – and among journalists themselves – that the media was finally free in Russia and could go on to forge a meaningful and lasting fourth estate. It is in this context that we need to understand the efforts to rein in the most influential media outlets through takeovers by state-affiliated monopolies, efforts which occurred throughout Vladimir Putin's presidential administration. The government's role in these takeovers is undisputed, but their intent and purpose are less clear.

Chapter 3 delves into the historic meaning of freedom for the Russian media. The chapter outlines Russia's status in terms of media freedom, security for journalists and censorship. It will directly address the question of whether Russia has ever had a free press. It will also explore the different meanings of censorship and how they play out in the Russian media, for example, by attempting to differentiate issues of security from direct government clampdowns. An important section of the chapter deals with the history of Russian censorship, based on research presented in a book by Russian media scholar Grigory Zhirkov. This historic context will be presented not as a simple linear development, but as a testament to the inherent journalistic legacy that plays into the Russian media today. Parallels can be drawn from many historical periods to the specific problems that the Russian media continues to deal with to this day. Readers will then be able to identify the origins of some of the current conflicts regarding media freedom in past instances, when the Russian press was given considerable liberties, only to see those liberties taken away.

The chapter will also examine the current security issues facing journalists, pointing to an abundance of threats that reporters continue to face in Russia, not necessarily because of any direct government clampdown, but due to issues of corruption and crime. The chapter will also offer specific examples of the circumstances under which journalists have been harassed. Journalists frequently fall prey to corrupt business and government interests, but they remain doubly vulnerable due to an extremely malleable justice system that protects neither the country's journalists, nor the entire population as a whole, from embedded corruption. Legal aspects of control are also explored as readers are introduced to current media law and what it entails.

Chapter 4 tackles the oldest journalistic traditions by examining the origins of Russia's print media. As the oldest medium, print journalism can be credited with laying out the framework, the ideals and the controversies inevitably inherited by newer media like radio and television. The history of Russian journalism combines the two main paradoxes that form the cornerstone of this book: that the state-led, top-down nature of Russian newspapers hampered their ability to bridge the gap between the government and the people as a whole, while the flourishing of independent, literary journalism, while fostering criticism and dissidence, only widened the gap dividing the people into mass readers and elites. In modern-day Russia, these clashes have created a dilemma already familiar around the world: is it possible to make a newspaper both serious and influential on the one hand, and popular and profitable on the other?

Focusing on several modern newspapers, including the tabloid *Moskovsky Komsomolets* and the once influential *Moskovskie Novosti*, the chapter will explore the origins of this dilemma and how it plays out today. In particular, it will spotlight *The Moscow News*, Russia's oldest running English language newspaper, and will follow its development from a 1930s PR stunt to its de facto status as a translation of *Moskovskie Novosti* in the 1990s, to its renewal in 2007 under the auspices of the state-run RIA Novosti news agency.

Chapter 5 devotes itself to film and television. Since much of the conflict over ownership and control of this powerful media resource is discussed in Chapter 2, this chapter will focus more on content. It will identify the origins of modern television, both Russian and foreign, in the early twentieth-century works of avant-garde filmmakers like Dziga Vertov and Sergei Eisenstein. They transformed filmmaking into a powerful tool, regardless of the format (news or propaganda) in which it was used. The chapter will then track the development of Soviet television programming from the 1930s through to the present day, analysing changing attitudes towards quality. At the heart of Soviet television programming was its propagandistic and educational function, which, during the years when broadcasting was live, established some of the best traditions in television. Older generations, especially, tend to regard 'classic' Soviet television much more favourably than today's programming. Early programming was primarily aimed at educating the public about various professions and the successes of the state, while frequently showcasing role models in a talk-show format that grew immensely popular throughout the 1960s.

With its primary function as a powerful, demonstrative tool of communist propaganda, the use of television as spectacle began emerging early on. The 'spectacle', defined by Ivan Zassoursky, one of the prominent young media experts in Russia today, reached its pinnacle during the 1990s, when even political news was presented in such a way as to entertain and shock rather than inform. The power of television to impact history is evident in the role it played during the 1991 coup and its subsequent use during the first Chechen War, the presidential election and the media wars towards the end of the decade. The chapter closes with a description of contemporary entertainment programming that addresses the questions of quality standards and the absence of an independent regulating body. Since this type of regulation falls on the government, it is often difficult to distinguish between political motivations and quality concerns; tellingly, the job of warning television stations of infraction is carried out by none other than the prosecutor general.

Chapter 6 discusses radio, Russia's most underestimated medium. At once totalitarian and egalitarian, the early Soviet government used it to target the illiterate masses and thus bridge a gap that the printed media had failed to overcome. As a medium that did not require literacy to be effective, radio continued to surpass television in sheer size of audience, even after televisions became common in Soviet homes. Unhampered by the expenses associated with television broadcasting and print media production and distribution, in the current media landscape radio easily shirks government regulation even as it retains the potential to reach thousands of listeners. The chapter will cover the history of the medium in Soviet Russia, paying special attention to the legacy of Yuri Levitan, the famous announcer from the 1940s and onward. This chapter will juxtapose the central role of radio with the pluralism it helped foster when rock music burst onto the scene during perestroika. While television entertainment was of little or no political value during the 1980s and early 1990s, rock was a political statement in and of itself, arguably as powerful as the newly-liberated newspapers in its potential to criticize the government and rally the like-minded. The sudden launch of FM radio and a variety of music formats quickly allowed Russian radio to catch up with its western counterparts. The re-emergence of talk radio and the staying power of news radio stations like Ekho Moskvy mean that radio as a medium can be both popular and influential.

The final chapter deals with the internet – perhaps the most promising medium in terms of its ability for creating networks and forging a semblance of civil society. The Russian internet suffers from the same paradox as print media: despite a host of online news sites and magazines, despite a closely-knit, sophisticated web culture and a lively, politicized blogosphere, so far it has little standing in the population as a whole. While the number of internet users has surged and continues growing steadily, it still makes up but a fraction of the population. Meanwhile, among those who use it, very few regard it as a source of news, information or analysis, using it mainly to chat, send email and play games. Chapter 7 will examine this paradox by delving into the roots of the Russian internet, from its beginning in the mid-1990s to the present day. A special section is devoted to the peculiar hold that Livejournal has taken on the country's educated elite, not so much as a social networking tool, but as a source of news analysis and self-expression.

The book concludes with a look at where Russia's media may be headed, and what course the paradoxes outlined here may take: what chances does Russia's media have of forging a lasting civil society, how are those processes playing out, and which media are involved in taking Russian journalism to new heights?

1 THE CURRENT MEDIA PLAYING FIELD

- **The old Russian media vs. the new**
- **Forms of media and their roles**
- **The news in transformation**
- **Beyond authoritarianism and towards a fourth estate**

During the last century, two factors played a determining role in the state of Russian mass media: the authoritarian model that dominated all spheres of life and subverted information for purposes of propaganda, and the parallel rapid rise of electronic media. If censorship and government control have at some point been a feature of media development all over the world, in Russia this legacy had a particularly profound and lasting effect, considering that it was the government itself that frequently played a progressive role in forging its national media, by creating and bolstering outlets that it would then use to control public opinion. If Marshall McLuhan's famous 'the medium is the message' still rings true in Russia, where the surge of electronic media came particularly fast and where its development was particularly dynamic, then another paradigm, 'the government is the message', also applies in a tradition where any halfway successful outlet is either launched by the government or eventually made subservient to it. Combined with the near-sacred status traditionally occupied by the written word, this legacy goes hand in hand with Russian journalism's penchant for ideology and propaganda, regardless of who the organ serves. And while a number of relatively information-oriented newspapers had begun to appear prior to the Bolshevik revolution, it was the legacy of the journalist as an instrument of propaganda that persevered. In this environment, the rise of electronic media like radio, cinema and television – which, due to their very nature, could serve as powerful tools in manipulating mass consciousness – were instrumental in grounding these traditions into an electronic infrastructure. But new media also played a dramatic role in fundamentally transforming the purpose and function of mass media in a place that touted itself as a nation of readers.

Before we can begin exploring the state of mass media today, we must look at what Russians themselves understand by the term 'mass media' and how that term is defined legally. Both definitions – popular and legislative – differ somewhat from the meanings ascribed to this concept in the West.

A pivotal point, as we shall see in later chapters, was President Mikhail Gorbachev's declaration in 1990 that anyone could establish a mass medium. In order to understand what this means, we need to keep in mind how mass media in Russia was stipulated in the law before and after this crucial point in time. Prior to the 1990 law on mass media, only government and party-affiliated organs could start up their own publication. This meant, essentially, that a citizen of the Soviet Union could not start a newspaper. All that changed with Gorbachev's decree, which meant that any citizen could found a newspaper or other publication. But the decree did not change the mindset that was formed of a restrictive legal understanding of what mass media is, and who – and how – it is to be founded by.

Indeed, according to current legislation, not everyone can establish a newspaper. In fact, in order for a media outlet to exist at all, an application for registration, which, among other information, must include sources of financing, must be filed with the Press Ministry. The current law states, for instance, that

> A notification about the receipt of an application with the indication of its date shall be sent to the founder or the person authorized by it. The application shall be subject to consideration by the registration body within a month since the said date. A mass medium shall be deemed to be registered upon the issue of a registration certificate.[1]

Besides the legal effects that this law has on the state of media ownership, it also inevitably helps define mass media in Russia as a whole. On the surface, there is the linguistic difference. What we refer to as 'mass media' can be expressed in two ways in Russian: the direct transliteration, or mass media, which is less common, and *sredstva massovoi informatsii* (SMI) – literally, 'instruments of mass information'. The latter is more commonly used both in the legal sense and in layman's terms. And while the classic, dictionary definition differs little from that of the western expression, first coined in 1920, SMI is associated with a much narrower scope – possibly reflecting the restrictions laid out in the legislation. In other words, if the English word 'media' encompasses news, entertainment, the internet, video, DVD and even other forms of communication, SMI, while it formally encompasses all those things as well, is more frequently used to pertain to journalists and journalism – whether in print outlets, television, radio or the internet.

The old Russian media vs. the new

In a country where the printed word has traditionally held a revered status, its newly-acquired freedom in 1990 plunged the Russian media into a sea of uncontrolled competition with the new electronic media, this time without the safety net that Soviet control used to provide. When the fall of the communist regime issued Russian newspapers, in effect, a carte blanche, they had only one direction to go in: reveal everything that had been censured by the Party in the years past. Readership, which was always large in the Soviet years, remained so and even increased in the early 1990s (depending on the publication). But in the following years, with much of the printed press unable to sustain itself in free market conditions and suffering from a crisis of genre and identity, newspaper readerships plummeted. As it did so, it created new ideological and informational vacuums which were quickly becoming filled by newer, more powerful media – television, radio and the internet. In his 2004 assessment of the economic playing field of the Russian media, Semyon Gurevich wrote:

> The television market is developing the fastest. Using its unique capabilities of presenting its audience with visual information, television has quickly usurped some of the most important functions of the press and pushed it into the information field where television's capabilities were limited.[2]

This did not mean, however, that newspapers stopped developing. The 1990 media law caused the number of periodicals to surge dramatically, and it continues to grow to this day. But this growth pertained not so much to a development of each separate publication as to the rise of specialized periodicals – indeed, a niche that was not fully exploited during the years of the Soviet Union.

Russia's identity as a nation of readers peaked during the Soviet Union period, when the communist government achieved virtually 100 per cent literacy nationwide through its education reforms. But with the introduction of the free market in the 1990s this began to change as more and more Russians began to get their news, entertainment and information from television. And while this change had been noticed for decades in the West, in Russia – where it was more pronounced, more sudden, and more drastic – the change occurred virtually overnight. In her look at audience patterns for printed media, Russian media scholar Irina Fomicheva registered the following shift:

> The irregularity of contact between the press and its audience led to a shifting of roles in the mass information system. By the beginning of the 1990s newspapers lost their leading status as sources of information in general and in particular as sources of practical information to television and radio. Television became a leader not only in the cities (where this process began earlier) but also in the provinces.[3]

Before we can begin to explore in depth each of these media and the challenges they face, we must understand what each of them means for the Russian media consumer. The purpose of this chapter, therefore, is to paint a picture of the information world that the Russian media consumer currently inhabits. Only by understanding how Russians themselves see their media and perceive the information around them – including the prejudices and distrust that they harbour towards the journalistic profession as a whole and certain media in particular – can we begin to get a clear sense of the nuances and contradictions that set the Russian media apart from that of the rest of the world.

Forms of media and their roles

The printed press

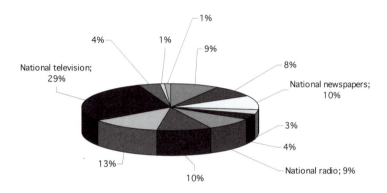

Figure 1.1 Where Russians get their news[4]

The unique power of the printed word in the Russian media has relegated its press – newspapers and printed periodicals – to a special status of traditional influence. It is because of this that some of the most pivotal changes in the Russian media during the 1990s revolved around both the wane of the newspaper and the transformation of the concept of news and journalism.

To understand some of the recent and historical processes that have impacted this transformation, we should look at the types of publications that exist in Russia at the beginning of the twenty-first century. To do this, it is useful to pinpoint two parameters that distinguish publications today – their *scope* and their *genre*.

The scope of a publication refers to the location of its target audience – i.e. whether a newspaper is *national*, *regional* or *district-level*. Polls show that this is a very important factor in terms of readership.

Russian periodicals can be categorized into two genres: the *mass circulation periodical* and what journalism scholar Lyudmila Resnyanskaya calls the *quality publication*. As of 2006, ratings show that national 'quality' publications – the 'serious' periodicals that are often quoted in the West, such as *Kommersant* and *Izvestia* – are read by very few people nationwide in comparison to national mass circulation periodicals. And while this is a typical situation for newspapers around the world, the difference in readership between mass circulation periodicals and 'serious' publications in Russia actually underlines the struggle of the independent media to make any meaningful impact in politics and society. Resnyanskaya gives the following definition of a mass circulation newspaper:

> The standard of a 'mass circulation newspaper' includes a financial model that counts on a large audience with various tastes and interests ... The functions of informing and entertaining become top priority. The aesthetics of a mass circulation, universal newspaper are built on simplification, banalization of political, economic and social issues, heightened interest in pop culture, scandals, and exploiting 'boulevard' themes. Post-Soviet mass publications, having staked on entertainment, sensationalism ... increasing the amount of information on health, family relations, free time, travel, and advice, conform to such 'standards of quality'. As interpreted by mass publication newspapers, the world of the reader is quite comfortable, understandable, not burdened by social and political collisions, not contradictory, while the events are usually fast-paced.[5]

Resnyanskaya identifies the three leading newspapers in this category as the *Argumenty i Facty* weekly, and the tabloid dailies *Moskovsky Komsomolets* and *Komsomolskaya Pravda*. These publications, with a long Soviet legacy, work as 'attention grabbers'. As for quality publications, this group:

> Traditionally includes analytical publications, either universal-themed or specialized. Periodicals of this level have a different quality in comparison to mass publications. The target audience of quality publications primarily includes elite groups that are interested in exchanging information on issues that affect all of society ... This type of publication, being an instrument of information and analysis, plays the role of an uninvolved observer, a rational critic, and an energetic mediator between the government and society ... [6]

Resnyanskaya identifies several Soviet-era newspapers as conforming to this model: *Trud*, *Izvestia* and *Moskovskie Novosti*. During the 1990s, a number of other 'quality newspapers' appeared – the leading titles in this category being *Nezavisimaya Gazeta* and *Kommersant*.

Those familiar with the American press might be tempted to allude to examples of the difference between, for instance, *The New York Times* and *The New York Daily News*. But in Russia's case, this would be very misleading. Take, for instance, *Kommersant* and *Komsomolskaya Pravda*. Both are national publications, meaning that they are theoretically available all over Russia, and not just in Moscow. However, travelling outside of Moscow or the Moscow region, it is very difficult to find a kiosk that will carry a copy of *Kommersant*.

Ratings underline this problem. As of July 2007, the top 50 newspapers in terms of average issue readership (AIR) did not include a single 'quality' publication as defined by Resnyanskaya. *Argumenty i Fakty* scored the highest rating, with 11.3 per cent AIR; *Komsomolskaya Pravda*'s weekly edition scored third place, with 8.7 per cent readership.[7]

TNS Gallup ratings, which PR experts describe as the most reliant gauge of a publication's popularity for advisers, paints a similar picture. By 2008, *Komsomoslaya Pravda* boasted the highest AIR among daily newspapers, with 2.25 million readers across Russia (the only daily to exceed that was *Iz ruk v ruki*, an advertisement catalogue). In contrast, among serious publications, the state-run official organ, *Rossiyskaya Gazeta* scored the highest, with 991,700 AIR. It was followed by *Trud* (435,700 AIR), *Izvestia* (424,900 AIR) and *Kommersant* (347,400 AIR).[8]

Television

The dominance of television was already visible soon after perestroika. Given the nature of the average Russian household, which has fewer television sets than in the West, this dominance is even more striking. According to a 1993 survey by the Russian Center for Public Opinion Research, more than twice as many people got their news from television as from newspapers. As a source of information about events in the country, television ranked first, with 86 per cent, followed by radio (43 per cent), then newspapers (28 per cent). Although Russians relied so heavily on television for their news, by the year 2000 only 60 per cent of households owned at least one television set.[9] We can compare this to the prevalence of television in the nation most notorious for its TV watchers – the USA. There, 99 per cent of households own at least one television set. But a far larger segment of the US population gets its news from newspapers than in Russia. Compared to Russia, just 52 per cent of Americans watch TV news, while 34 per cent of Americans read a newspaper.[10]

What is even more significant is that in 1993 most Russians, unlike Americans, did not have access to cable news. Historically, the Soviet era, until the 1980s, provided Russians with four television channels. These were Channel 1 (the 'first programme' or 'first button'), Channel 2 (the all-Union programme), Channel 3 (regional programming) and Channel 4 (educational). Much of the population in the provinces, however, had access only to Channels 1 and 2. Channel 5 was available in St Petersburg.

In the 1990s, this framework remained the same despite the surge of private capital. Today, although there is a larger number of available channels, the first five channels reflect the Soviet model, even in name: the first channel, after being renamed ORT in the early 1990s, is back to being called Channel 1. It is state-owned and still the most watched station nationwide. Channel 2 is now called Rossiya and is also state-owned. Channel 3 is owned by the Moscow government and covers local news, while Channel 4 was bought by Vladimir Gusinsky and, as NTV, became the founding block of his media empire. NTV became the first and most acclaimed independent television station in Russia before it was taken over by the state-owned Gazprom.

Despite the appearance of new channels that are predominantly geared towards entertainment (STS, TNT, REN-TV, DTV), television ratings[11] reflect the descending order of the channels themselves, illustrating to what extent tradition and the Soviet legacy still determine popularity (see

Figure 1.2). Another rating,[12] which can serve as a better gauge of trust towards and the pervasiveness of certain television channels, examines the popularity of each television channel separately as opposed to relative to other television channels (see Figure 1.3).

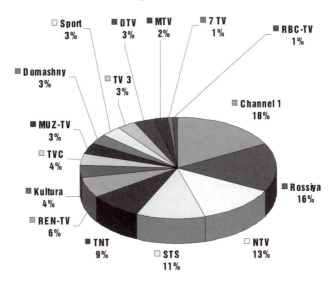

Figure 1.2 Television station ratings: audience share

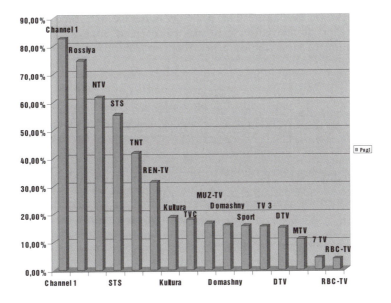

Figure 1.3 Television station ratings: audience preferences

It is difficult to measure how much trust Russians actually have in such a pervasive medium as television. But despite the undisputed preference for television by Russian media consumers, Russians tend to display a condescending attitude towards television content, and do not appear to trust the medium any more than they trust newspapers. What may serve as a gauge of the general distrust is the frequent animosity that can be gleaned from the treatment of television by media analysts and political technologists.

Radio

Combining some of the troubles and advantages of print media and television, radio – a symbolic medium of the twentieth century – remains surprisingly influential across Russia and the former Soviet Union. Partially due to Russia's size and, until recently, to the limited access to television, radio remains the chief source of information for much of the population, particularly in remote regions. It is influential both as a source of political information and in its use for entertainment, particularly for 'background music'. As such, it rivals the influence of television. Indeed, Yassen Zassoursky, Russia's premier journalism scholar and a rector of Moscow State University's journalism department, identifies radio as the most 'open' information source.

While radio fails to rival television in terms of sheer political influence, recent Moscow-based studies suggest that in some cases radio can garner an audience that is even larger than that of television. Moreover, in contrast to television, Russia's radio boasts popular stations that are not only 'independent' politically but sometimes vehemently oppositionist. In Moscow alone, nearly 74 per cent of survey respondents say they listen to the radio during the day.[13] The political influence of radio, while much less than that of television, can still be deemed considerable. From a political point of view, the data presented in Figure 1.4 is notable.

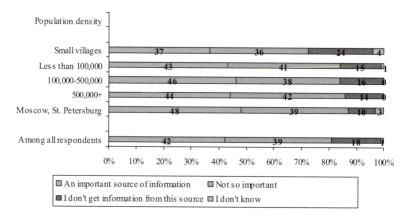

Figure 1.4 Is radio an important or not so important source of political information during election campaigns? Importance of radio as a source of information based on population density[14]

Radio in Russia can be classified, much like the print media and television, both according to scope and genre. Musical subgenres, however, are broad and hard to classify on the current radio scene. Like the print media, radio stations in Russia are classified as all-national or federal stations, regional stations and local or municipal stations.

- *National* stations broadcast over the entire population. They include state-run stations like Radio Russia, which has the largest radio audience in the country (41 per cent of men and 49 per cent of women listen to it), and Radio Mayak, which holds third place for audience size.
- *Regional* radio stations broadcast over a region or *oblast*, as well as over a large city.
- *Local* radio stations are broadcast over small towns and residential areas.

Like other media, radio stations are also classified not only by their broadcast scope and audience, but by what they broadcast. Journalism scholar Lyudmila Bolotova identifies *universal* radio stations, *information* radio stations and *musical-entertainment* radio stations.[15]

Despite the general popularity of musical entertainment, the nation's historical, state-run universal station, Radio Russia, remains the most popular, echoing a similar situation in television. A typical example of the Soviet legacy of universal broadcasting, Radio Russia, much like the BBC, has traditionally broadcast news, talk shows, music, sociopolitical and analytical programmes, as well as plays. In the words of Bolotova, it has been able to retain the best of national radio broadcasting.

Information radio stations offer frequent and in-depth news broadcasts, featuring talk shows that are more geared to current events than universal radio stations like Radio Russia. The most popular example is the state-run Radio Mayak. Launched in 1964, it still personifies Soviet news radio despite a modern overhaul. Currently it airs news every 15 minutes and offers listeners a wide variety of interviews, benefiting from an extensive network of special correspondents around the country and abroad.

Since its launch in 1990, the independent, commercially-owned Ekho Moskvy radio station has been another leader in Russian information radio. Bolotova calls it the only real commercial information radio station, and despite its current ownership by the state-owned Gazprom gas giant, it remains one of the few vocal critics of the political regime.

By far the more dynamic segment of national radio has been the music/entertainment category, which burst on the scene in the early 1990s with music that predominantly targeted young audiences. Despite the popularity of Radio Russia, the music/entertainment category still remains the most widely listened to.

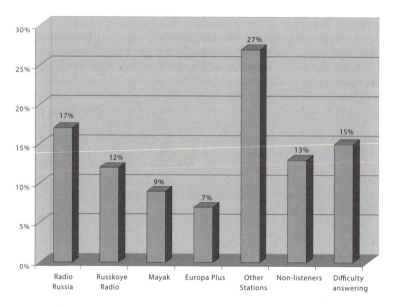

Figure 1.5 Radio station ratings: audience preferences[16]

As we can see from Figure 1.5, while Radio Russia is favoured by 17 per cent of respondents, the number two leading radio station was Russkoye Radio, a widely popular musical station launched in 1995. As the first station to broadcast only popular music in Russian, it witnessed phenomenal success, and after over a decade of broadcasting remains the most popular commercial music station in Russia. Europa Plus, the preferred station of 7 per cent of respondents, also broadcasts predominantly in the music/entertainment category, mostly focusing on international adult contemporary entertainment. According to the same poll, music, news and sport make up the most widely listened-to programming in Russian radio broadcasting, explaining both the popularity of Radio Russia and the music/entertainment stations.

In this context, it would be illustrative to return to the significance of Ekho Moskvy as a unique information radio station, in some sense a beacon that helped launch independent broadcasting in Russia. While Bolotova identifies it as the 'unchanged leader of information broadcasting', given the polls cited, this 'leadership' is not reflected statistically in terms of audience size. The survey cited above shows that of the information radio stations, radio Mayak leads the way in popularity. This points to a peculiarly Russian dichotomy of popularity versus influence in the media sphere, much like in the printed media. In other words, the most popular outlets are not the most influential, while the most influential frequently have a much smaller audience. In that sense, we cannot measure the extent of Ekho Moskvy's leadership in terms of scope – instead, its significance lies in its legacy, credibility and pervasiveness as an oft-quoted source of news.

Launched in August, 1990 by the journalism faculty of the Moscow State University together with the USSR Association of Radio and the *Ogonek* magazine, Ekho Moskvy was, in the words of Yassen Zassoursky, not only the first independent radio station, but the first independent mass medium. As such, it reflected the dominant characteristics of other independent media even as it came under the ownership first of private capital, then the state-owned Gazprom: frequent quotability, particularly in the West, and relatively low ratings nationwide, particularly outside of Moscow and St Petersburg. The same inherent dissonance plagued the so-called 'quality' print media and, as we shall see later, the internet.

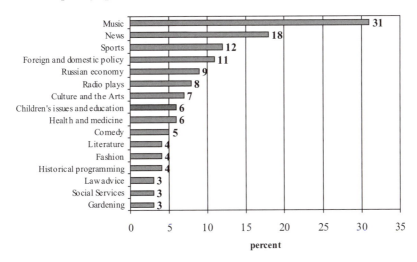

Figure 1.6 Thematic preferences of radio audiences[17]

Internet

At the start of the twenty-first century, the internet remains the most paradoxical media phenomenon in Russia. Even though the number of Russians with access to the internet continues to grow rapidly, it is still but a fraction of the population. Despite its impact, often touted in the western media, a strikingly small proportion of the population actually has access to it, let alone uses it as a source of information. The sheer success of online media projects launched in the late 1990s and the liveliness of its often politicized blogosphere were in fact limited to a narrow percentage of the population, predominantly the educated elite.

This paradox can be partially explained by a circumstance practically unique to Russia: the appearance of the internet coincided with unprecedented freedom of the press. Thus, the technology for a fundamentally new medium became available just in time for a new journalistic paradigm to sprout, a paradigm that did not entail control and sustenance from the government. The fact that online media were so cheap to sustain and so difficult to control spurred budding internet journalists into action.

The Russian internet's status as arguably the only true free medium, with a whole slew of successful, exclusive media outlets, is hampered by the fact that for a free medium it is still accessed by a far smaller proportion of the population than in the West. From the start, RuNet, as Russians frequently call their internet, was aggressively populated by primary news content sites with no print analogues, whereas in the West information sites are predominantly online versions of printed newspapers. Very frequently, this meant that the RuNet took over as a source of information where traditional media like print, radio and television lagged behind due to issues of freedom, independence and the logistics of infrastructure. On the one hand, this allowed Russia's internet to develop very rapidly despite a relatively small percentage of the population being able to access it. But on the other hand, it ironically played a role in restraining the development of the print media.

While we will look in depth at these paradoxes and contradictions in Chapter 7, it is helpful here to understand what place the internet actually holds among Russian media consumers, and how it is used in comparison to other sources of information. A comprehensive study by the All-Russian Center for Public Opinion Research in 2006 found that not only did a fraction of the Russian population actually use the internet, but their trust in and understanding of the internet as a medium was limited as well. According to the survey, when respondents were asked whether they used the internet and how often, a striking 76 per cent said that they did not use it at all. Figure 1.7 shows how the internet was used among those who did access it. Even

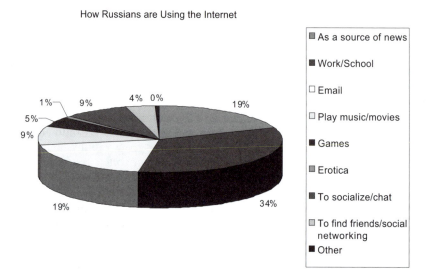

Figure 1.7 How Russians are using the internet

among the more affluent, cosmopolitan and younger respondents – the ones most likely to use the internet – 21 per cent to 27 per cent (depending on the category) characterized the internet as an 'important source of information during political campaigns'. But among those likeliest categories, between 40 and 53 per cent said they did not use it at all. This points to a perennial problem not just in Russian media but in its politics and civil society – when we do speak of any significant impact or transformation, it more often than not affects the elite exclusively, and only to a small extent the rest of the population. The Russian internet, it seems, is no exception.

The news in transformation

With the fall of the Iron Curtain, the appearance of the internet and freedom of the press, Russians became exposed to new concepts of news. And with a surge of independent news agencies, a new style of news presentation was adopted in a strikingly short period of time. The new presentation format frequently led to clashes in style and genre, particularly in the print media, which had to quickly adapt to a new format of news coverage.

At the heart of this new development was the transformation of the news agencies themselves. Before we can begin to explore the impact that independent news agencies had on the media in post-Soviet Russia, we must look at the origins of what made Russian news agencies – and hence, the Russian concept of news – unique.

In the West, news agencies appeared in the first half of the nineteenth century, facilitated by the electric telegraph. The giants of today – Agence France Presse, Associated Press in the USA, and Reuters, all came into being in the nineteenth century, originating with existing newspapers and syndicates. The style in which they presented their hard news was already a reflection of existing news presentation in newspapers, at least in the case of Associated Press, which had its roots in newspaper syndicates. According to Stuart Allan's *News Culture,* in Britain and the USA, as early as the middle of the nineteenth century,

> ... journalists were placing a greater emphasis on processing 'bare facts' in 'plain and unadorned English'. Each word of a news account had to be justified in terms of cost, which meant that the more traditional forms of news language were stripped of their more personalized inflections.[18]

Hence in the West, the process of carving out the concept of hard news had begun practically with the creation of the telegraph. From the start, hard news presentation was firmly rooted in the commercial aspects of private newspaper syndicates.

In Russia, the news agencies that had begun appearing around the same time floundered, while those that did survive ended up at the mercy of the government. Some newspapers, such as *Birzhevye Vedomosti,* had their own telegraph bureaus as early as 1862. By 1866, the Russian Telegraph Agency was launched, but pervasive censorship and state control continuously nipped its development. 'The agency had received permission to have its own bureau in various cities, to publish its telegram bulletins and sell them',[19] writes an official history published in 2000 by the Russian Education Ministry, in a testament to the kind of conditions in which news agencies were forced to compete. According to Louise McReynolds, Russia's media infrastructure at the time was no match for the western news system:

> In 1870, to avoid competition, Europe's Big Three news agencies – Reuters, Havas, and Wolff – formed a cartel, dividing the world into 'colonial' news territories. Russia came under the Germans' dominion, which effectively meant that the majority of news flowing into and out of Russia would be filtered through the Wolff Bureau. Additional stories came from European periodicals, but only after the time lag of publication and distribution. Russia's small and poorly funded private news agencies, which operated through a succession of twelve-year leases granted by the government, could not compete with the cartel.[20]

This state of affairs paved the way for the St Petersburg Telegraph Agency, which began to operate on 1 September 1904. As Russia's longest lasting major telegraph news agency, it was launched on direct order of the czar. This is but one example of how efforts at modernization and industrialization in Russia have inevitably come from the top, thus owing their livelihood to, and being controlled by, the government. The St Petersburg Telegraph Agency was the predecessor of what is now the partially state-owned news agency ITAR-TASS.

Characteristically, the origins of the agency did not lie in newspaper services or syndicates – instead it was directly initiated by the Finance Ministry, the Foreign Ministry and, even more tellingly, the Ministry of the Interior. Its champion, the reform-minded finance minister Sergei Witte, was himself a former journalist. Czar Nicholas II approved the agency with the purpose of 'report[ing] within the Empire and abroad on political, financial, economic, trade and other data of public interest'. Historically, however, the purpose of the agency seemed to have been an ill-fated quest by the government to both foster an effective news service and control it. As McReynolds puts it,

> The notion that public opinion could be influenced by the circulation of factual information resulted in the establishment of an official telegraph news agency, the St Petersburg Telegraph Agency (PTA). From the time its charter was issued in 1904 until the Bolsheviks took it over as their own in 1917, the PTA led a precarious existence trying to meet the ideal of its founders. It functioned, often unwillingly, as the central institution where

debates raged between advocates of the public's need and right to be informed and those who valued the autocratic ethos of disregarding that public's opinions.[21]

PTA would serve, under several names, as a blueprint for a highly centralized system of providing information during the Soviet period and afterwards. In 1918 the now-Bolshevik government renamed the agency the Russian Telegraph Agency (ROSTA), creating 'the central information agency of the whole Russian Socialist Federative Soviet Republic ... ' In 1925, it spawned the Telegraph Agency of the Soviet Union (TASS), the precursor to today's ITAR-TASS.

While news agencies were traditional extensions of the newspaper business in the West, their purpose in the Soviet Union was entirely different. Not only an instrument of propaganda, TASS doubled as an intelligence mechanism for the Supreme Soviet, its controlling founder. Its employees, frequently acting as simultaneous information sources for security and intelligence, obtained information that was destined for the analytical desks of the KGB. Conveniently, some of its unclassified information was distributed to news outlets inside the country.

A slightly different function was served by the Soviet Union's other major news agency, APN. Created by the Foreign Ministry in 1941 as Sovinformburo, it focused initially on issuing reports from the World War II front that were destined for radio, newspapers and magazines. In 1961, it was renamed Agentstvo Pechati 'Novosti' (Print Agency "News"), or APN, and shifted its priorities to foreign propaganda and the dissemination of information abroad. Indeed, according to its official statute, the purpose of the agency was 'spreading truthful information about the USSR abroad and familiarizing Soviet society with the life of people in foreign countries'. It was also involved in obtaining foreign intelligence. After the breakup of the Soviet Union, it transformed into RIA Novosti, a state-run news agency that apparently abandoned gathering intelligence. Its function shifted to news. Committed to the same principles of 'spreading truthful information' about Russia, it would go on to launch Russia's first English-language news channel, Russia Today, in 2005.

The deeply ingrained, pre-Soviet practice of direct government control of news agencies makes the explosion of independent news agencies like Interfax following 1990 all the more revolutionary. Used for so long as a direct instrument of propaganda (and intelligence), first by the Russian Empire and then by the Communist Party, the whole idea of news as hard facts was somewhat askew in the minds of many Russians. When Russia finally did get a free press in 1990, the journalists, severed from a predominantly authoritarian tradition by perestroika, didn't exactly know what to do with their freedom to report on the hard news as it happened. The idea of a *lede* – the first line stating the who, what, when and where of a news item – hardly existed. Hence, the initial concept of objectivity was initially understood to mean printing what had hitherto been suppressed or made taboo. The inevitable fetish for sensationalism that this approach sparked was hardly the best environment for fair and balanced reporting. Journalists understood, however, the pressing necessity of a new news format if there was to be any semblance of an unbiased exchange of information. In the light of the proliferation of independent news agencies, this need was all the more immediate.

One of the pioneers of the new style of news presentation was the *Kommersant* business daily, which targeted what was emerging as an educated and relatively affluent middle class. The newspaper itself grew out of the Fakt news agency, which was launched in 1987. It is telling to look at *Kommersant*'s interpretation of the new news ethic, in a mission statement that it laid out for itself:

> In order to understand what kind of revolution *Kommersant* accomplished, one should recall that journalism in the USSR was very different – from the headlines to the way the information was presented. In those times, every intern, even when writing about a fire at a poultry plant, strove to demonstrate the talent of a columnist. That was why news articles so often started off with a lyrical digression, with historical or philosophical allusions.[22]

Thus, nearly a century after it had done so in the West, the separation of fact from commentary had begun. This separation would remain, however, as little more than a vulnerable fine line, so superficial that it was frequently crossed, even by *Kommersant*'s best journalists.

Beyond authoritarianism and towards a fourth estate

As we explore in depth the history of each medium in Russia, we should keep in mind what the surveys can tell us about how Russians perceive their media world. Despite the country's widespread literacy and the traditional power of the spoken word, we have seen how print media has been floundering in post-Soviet Russia, while the power of electronic media – television and radio – is even more pervasive than in the West. The paradoxes pointed out in each respective medium reflect, on the one hand, the imprint that authoritarianism has left on Russian media, while on the other they reflect the ability of the media to continue to manipulate the masses, despite the population's general distrust of that media.

The legacy of authoritarianism has left a media that struggles with its own internal problems even in the liberated environment that it was given in the early 1990s. In the following chapters we will explore the origins of some of these paradoxes, and try to answer the questions raised in this chapter regarding the habits of Russian media consumers.

2   MEDIA AND POWER: OWNERSHIP IN THE AGE OF FREE MARKET

> - The structure of media ownership in Russia
> - The flourishing of news television and the demise of 'independent' channels
> - The media wars
> - Ownership in the printed press
> - Ownership vs. control

One of the cornerstones of glasnost, and indeed of the kind of democracy that was anticipated following the collapse of the Soviet Union in 1991, was a free and independent press. As Russia continues to struggle in forging an identity that is both anchored in the past and in synch with its role as a global player and a democracy, the question of whether Russia has an independent press has yet to be answered. The exuberant press culture that exploded in Russia in the late 1980s and early 1990s, as journalists rushed to unmask the atrocities of the Soviet regime, created an illusion of freedom and independence. But whether or not the press was ever free in Russia, it was hardly ever truly independent. Ultimately, control and ownership determine to what extent any national media is independent and hence free. In this chapter, we will first examine the system of interaction between the journalist, the media owner (the oligarch) and, ultimately, the state. We will then explore how this system first allowed independent news television to flourish and then inevitably sparked the media wars that led to its demise.

The structure of media ownership in Russia

One of the axioms of journalistic independence is that a journalist is free to write and publish inasmuch as he is granted a platform by the owner of a publication. Except for a few notable exceptions when journalists in Russia collectively owned their media, the journalist is normally dependent on the owner, who makes distribution possible and disseminates content produced by the journalist to the masses. This dependent status of the journalist remains practically the same whether the media is controlled by the state or owned 'independently' by media barons or private capital. The Russian media, incidentally, has suffered through the worst that both systems have to offer.

Under the Soviet system, a journalist and what he wrote was fully controlled by the Communist Party, which funded and hence controlled all publications, television and radio networks across the country. Without a private printing press, it was also the Communist Party that dictated the cost of printing, materials and distribution. The funds for each medium – newspaper, radio, television – were allotted directly by the Press Ministry in much the same way as ideology was dictated from above. To a certain extent, publications could allot a certain amount of profit from sales for their own budgets, but mostly the revenue generated by a publication went back into the Press Ministry, while a publication's budget was structured according to strict regulations stipulated from the top.

One exception to this system was advertising. While there were no 'commercials' in the Soviet media in the western sense of the word until late perestroika, paid public announcements on television and in newspapers were common. In fact, a 1968 law allowed regional newspapers to publish advertisements as long as the total advertising space took up no more than 25 per cent of the last page. Up to 30 per cent of the advertising revenue could be used in the newspaper's budget.[1]

Yakov Lomko, who edited *The Moscow News*, an English-language newspaper for foreigners, from 1960 to 1980, details the money trail at a time when publications essentially belonged to the state. Even while funded by the Press Ministry, newspapers were encouraged to make ends meet themselves.

> In communist times, there was self-financing. There was an opinion that all newspapers should be profitable. So we too aimed to get away from state subsidies, and I would sit and think how to get two tenths of a kopeck from the cost of each issue. For an advertisement of a foreign tobacco company, published in 30 issues, we got 26,000 pounds sterling. For this we were reprimanded by the Committee for Cultural Cooperation, which controlled all organizations connected with foreign countries. But the Central Committee of the Communist Party came to our aid. Part of the above-plan profit we directed towards building housing for our staff – 300–350sq. m. a year. We advertised our export organizations and would get an income of 110,000–120,000 rubles a year.[2]

But the fall of communist rule overturned this centralized system of control, while new media legislation only vaguely outlined the legal and financial interaction between owner, publisher, editor and journalist. Advertising – a conceptual and commercial novelty for the Russian market – proved even murkier. Based on the 1996 media law, up to 40 per cent of a newspaper's space, and up to 25 per cent of broadcasting time, could be used for advertising.

In describing the difference in control before and after 1990, it would be fitting to view the state as a media monopolist, with the Soviet media model manifested as an authoritarian, centralized, top-down system. It could be called instrumental in that the media is nothing more than an instrument in the hands of the state, the party and the government.[3] The importance of a centralized, instrumental system – and its impact on later 'independent' media – cannot be overstated. In the Soviet model, every medium was essentially an extension of the state – a vector from a single node that made the Russian media landscape resemble something like a spider's web. Peripheral (regional) nodes answered directly to a party centre, which in turn was controlled from Moscow. On the one hand, this highly centralized press infrastructure practically guaranteed an effective method of distributing information to rural areas that had no other means to establish a functioning press network. On the other, it is precisely this centralization that made local, grassroots media networking next to impossible.

The current Russian media system was born in June 1990, when President Mikhail Gorbachev's government passed a new media law that in effect not only abolished censorship, but introduced for the first time the freedom to found and register publications. A 1991 bill that outlawed the Communist Party and 'freed' the press it controlled left journalistic teams floundering on their own. The new laws changed the Russian media landscape in a pivotal way by abolishing the very thing that held it together – centralization. While censorship had already eased somewhat by the end of the 1980s, the new media law created the possibility of something simply unheard of during the Soviet era: creating a publication that was not subordinate to the government. The wide-reaching implications of this structural freedom should not be underestimated. While offering journalists a degree of freedom by allowing them to dictate their own editorial policy, this and subsequent media laws effectively cut off these very journalists from a vital support network.

Apart from greater freedom and seeming independence, the new opportunities created a fundamentally new problem of sustainability: 'A vertical, a pyramid, with the Communist Party Central Committee's *Pravda* at the top, down to the regional papers at the very bottom – all this disappeared'.[4] This affected the development of journalism in three separate ways.

- First, by cutting off a publication from the Soviet-era 'centre', the new system put a strain on the printing presses, which were now forced to function in a market system without the know-how or the materials to do so. This drove up prices, making newspaper printing, particularly in rural areas, a costly and cumbersome burden.
- Second, by taking on the burden of running a newspaper into its own hands, the editorial team found itself unable to thrive in a market-driven system. In an infrastructure that was not adapted to commercial exchange, expertise in advertising as well as its effect on a readership not accustomed to advertising meant that new publications struggled to sustain themselves.

- Third, the spirit of glasnost, freedom of the press, and the journalist's view of himself as an enlightened fourth estate ironically introduced a degree of chaos into the editorial habits of the emerging media. With journalistic 'ethics' – however totalitarian they were – habitually dictated and regulated, with content strictly controlled by a rigorous Soviet journalism school, the new journalists did away not just with censorship but with all rules.

In short, 70 years of communism and state-controlled media gave birth to a media system that completely lacked one of its most important components – an economic infrastructure. Democratic Russia found itself without information capital and a poor, economically unprotected press. Lack of investment and skyrocketing costs for paper, printing and distribution hindered the development of a sustainable press. Meanwhile, as newspapers raced for higher readership and circulation, lower standards became acceptable.

After decades of a relatively homogenous and monolithic system of media control throughout the communist era, Yassen Zassoursky identifies a number of control models that surfaced in succession with the start of perestroika.[5]

First, during perestroika (1986–90) the mechanisms of control, production, and distribution were much the same as during any other Soviet period, but journalists had greater editorial freedom. This model remained inherently instrumental. But while centralized Party control remained, the difference lay in the purpose. Whereas previously the media was the propaganda apparatus of the Communist Party, under Gorbachev it was an instrument of democratization.

Second, after a short, golden age of unbridled independence from government or corporate control, journalists came face to face with tough market realities in the period 1990–5. Publications were owned and controlled by 'journalistic collectives', but rising costs of paper, printing and distribution took their toll. The price of newspaper copies grew, while circulations plummeted. This era witnessed a transformation from a vertical system to a horizontal, pluralistic one where various independent newspapers and magazines sprouted all over the country, but had questionable scope, influence and, most importantly, sustainability. According to media expert Anna Kachkayeva, the first broadcast of NTV on Channel 4 in January 1994 served as a turning point, as a private channel took to the airwaves for the first time, paving the way for what she called a new system of propaganda.

The third 'model' is the rise of the oligarchs between 1995 and 1999. President Boris Yeltsin's government tried to help the fledgling free press with subsidies during the early 1990s, initially garnering him considerable support in the press – support that was not necessarily reflected at a popular level. But subsidies coming from a government that was on the verge of bankruptcy itself did not alleviate the situation, and publications turned to emerging private capital – banks and corporations. While the new media moguls did not appear to interfere in editorial decision-making in a significant way, that all began to change in the run-up to the 1996 presidential election. The desire of the corporate elite to re-install a business-friendly president was so great that the media owners joined efforts and enlisted their chief information resources to aid President Boris Yeltsin's re-election campaign. The abuse of the 'free press' for the sake of countering a perceived communist scare created a much distrusted oligarchy and forever compromised public trust in the media. In the media wars that ensued, oligarchs first used their resources to support the government and then turned against the Yeltsin administration. The results were disastrous: by 1998, the mounting smear campaigns forced a desperate Yeltsin into a frenzy of appointments, going through a handful of prime ministers by the end of the year. Whereas the government had full control of the media just over a decade before, by 1998 the political implications of the interference of the media barons in the government's work were destabilizing indeed. It heralded a return to the authoritarian model of journalism, with the sole difference that journalists now answered to businessmen rather than the Communist Party.

Finally, we have the 'return to a government' model (2000–present). Following the chaos of the media wars, President Vladimir Putin's administration made efforts to fortify government control of the media. Two key events characterized this epoch – the creation of the Ministry of Press, Broadcasting and Mass Communication, and the consolidation of VGTRK, the all-Russian state television and radio company, into a major holding with new channels and radio stations. Anna Kachkayeva notes another pivotal development that essentially put an end to 10 years of chaotic and unbridled media freedom: the NTV drama and the transfer of the independent channel into the hands of a government corporation.[6] The general trend, however, ran in tandem with rapid commercialization and conglomeration of publications and stations by media holdings. The new millennium was characterized by greater transparency of media control by private corporations as opposed to government ownership.

While the West has noted an increasingly authoritarian streak in press management under Putin, the current media playing field is still a far cry from the Soviet-style control model that some western observers speak of. In it, the oligarch still plays a key role as financier. The last decade has seen the oligarchs becoming increasingly tamer, with many opting to adopt a pro-Kremlin stance in their media to curry favour with the administration. In this case, while the owner does not directly dictate editorial content, the editor is frequently either like-minded or careful to remain within a set of unspoken boundaries of allowed criticism. Advertising, while growing robustly (particularly during the Putin years) continues to play a secondary role. The state does not act as a direct preliminary censor; rather, through its ownership of leading media outlets and television, it indirectly influences coverage. State-owned television producers normally resort to self-censorship and taboo, avoiding topics that can potentially generate a negative reaction or a suggestive phone call. Some media are known to have 'curators' within the presidential administration who consult on shaping editorial policy. Finally, the journalist and editor have more control over their work than it would appear under this kind of model. Apart from self-censorship, in some cases lack of commercial accountability and know-how actually render Russian journalists a lot more 'free' than their western counterparts.

The surge of private capital into what were former Party organs did not necessarily make them independent, as we shall see in this chapter. Rather, the lack of any fundamental system of private media and the lacuna of privately controlled media capital, provided for the chaos that the media wars of the 1990s would embody. That the Russian tradition lacked any major private media system to begin with meant that regardless of how well notions of freedom and independence were embraced, the government continued to play an important, if not determining, role in the sustenance of the press and, especially, television.

The flourishing of news television and the demise of 'independent' channels

It comes as little surprise that it was television that grew into a medium with enormous potential to influence the masses on the one hand and great vulnerability to corruption on the other. But apart from inherent aspects that endow the moving picture with the power to manipulate public conscience in ways the written word seldom can, it was the heavy presence of political capital and state involvement that made this influence so formidable in the politics of the mid- to late 1990s.

Russia's growing financial-industrial groups started entering the media market as soon as they amassed enough money to spend. By the mid-1990s, notable businesses like Vladimir Gusinsky's Most, Oleg Boiko's Olbi and Boris Berezovsky's Logovaz were investing considerable capital in new and exiting print and electronic outlets. Gusinsky launched the influential (and now defunct) *Segodnya* newspaper, while Berezovsky snapped up shares in ORT television. NTV television and *Ogonek* magazine, flush with funds from Gusinsky's flourishing media empire, re-emerged with a new identity on the media playing field.

Although Ovsepyan notes the considerable revenue from advertising for Russia's central television stations (most notably Ostankino, before it was renamed ORT and came under the de facto control of business tycoon Boris Berezovsky),[7] the role of media magnates Gusinsky and Berezovsky in forming the media playing field, and even determining to a large extent the political playing field of the late 1990s, cannot be underestimated. These and other oligarchs emerged not just as a financial force, but as a political power to be reckoned with by the government. Besides their personal connections within the Kremlin, these new bosses controlled television stations, thus wielding a power that would help shape Russia's politics for at least the next five years.

ORT: private or public?

The Ostankino television station is illustrative of the powerful tangle of politics, money and connections that shaped each outlet. Its fate was also typical of post-Soviet television in general. Primarily, it was power that would determine the independence of each television station, and Ostankino was no exception. Together with the second channel, the All-Russian State Television and Radio Broadcasting Company (VGTRK, later to become known as RTR), Ostankino was initially at the heart of a power struggle between Boris Yeltsin and Mikhail Gorbachev. Yeltsin, as president of the Russian Soviet Federated Socialist Republic (RSFSR), understood that his influence and power was dependent on the possibility of controlling his own television channel. Following tough negotiations with Soviet President Gorbachev, that finally happened in May 1992, when the RSFSR received the VGTRK and six hours of broadcasting per day. But Yeltsin did not stop there. That same year, he won control of Ostankino, which broadcast over the entire Soviet Union, thus consolidating his media influence not just as a republican leader, but as a national one, and ensuring his government a dominant position in the information field.

Ostankino was renamed ORT (Obshchestvennoye Rossiiskoye Televideniye), Public Russian Television in early 1995, following the establishment of the ORT Joint Stock Company Council of Trustees, which was chaired by President Boris Yeltsin himself. ORT was registered anew on 28 February 1995.[8]

Determining advertising revenue in Russian television – particularly in the chaotic days of the early 1990s – is next to impossible. In the early 1990s, 80 per cent of Ostankino's revenue came from non-government sources – mostly private, commercial companies and private sponsorship. By 1995, one minute of advertising on Ostankino could cost as much as $12 million. Still, by the end of 1994, the channel was bleeding red ink – it had no funds to sustain itself.[9] The murder of Ostankino director Vladislav Listyev in March of 1995 can be viewed as the apotheosis of Russian-style TV management of the 1990s. While motives for his death still remain shady, it is widely speculated that he was killed for financial and political reasons. An immensely popular anchor, Listyev came to head ORT in the early days of 1995, and immediately tried to put an end to shady business practices involving middlemen in procuring advertising for the channel. This kind of meddling, while not confirmed, was seen as one of the reasons he was targeted on 1 March. Russian media scholar Anna Kachkayeva writes of this period: 'The barbaric battles for advertising ended; wild and thievish, after the new law "On Advertising" the advertising market began taking on a more civilized character'.[10]

ORT, it has been said, in effect became the first major media privatization of its time, when a major television station in both scope and name (the significance of Channel 1 – the number one button across the country – is no small matter) was transferred into the hands of big business. However, ORT's 'privatization' was emblematic of how Soviet-era, state-owned channels evolved into independent television channels, and then back into the state channels that they are today. In the case of ORT, one of the major aspects that aided this revolution was the dubious nature of the privatization itself. Indeed, ORT was never a fully 'private' station, with up to 50 per cent government shares, according to various reports. Because of the nature of Berezovsky's relationship with the government, it is hard to establish to what extent the government actually controlled the station at any point in time. The station was essentially both private and state-owned at the same time.

ORT was to become Boris Berezovsky's central asset, and yet to this day the exact nature of his control of the channel is unclear. What is more important is that the Berezovsky clan is one of the best illustrations of the extent to which big business in Russia during the 1990s was interdependent with the government. And while we can argue that the government was just as dependent on oligarch money as the oligarchs were dependent on their Kremlin connections, in retrospect it is not surprising that not only ORT but other independent channels ended up under Kremlin control within the next decade.

The same month that Listyev was murdered, Sergei Blagovolin was appointed general director of this newly-privatized television station. Prior to his reassignment, he had headed the TV station's analytical centre. The nature of his appointment is illustrative of Berezovsky's behind-the-scenes control of his media holdings. Officially, Berezovsky became Blagovolin's deputy, but in reality he was instrumental in appointing the new general director himself: 'I telephoned Sergei and offered him to head the television company', Berezovsky recalled in an interview with *Kommersant-Vlast* magazine in 2005.[11] 'He agreed; it was a big deal, and played a very big role for ORT during its time of transition'. If this shows the conditional nature of Berezovsky's influence, then Blagovolin's other deputy is emblematic of the delicate power balance between private and state spheres of influence. The other deputy was Arkady Yevstafyev, head of the press service of the State Property Committee, and a solid member of the reformist Anatoly Chubais camp. Speaking to the *Kultura* weekly in 1998, Blagovolin described those delicate relations:

There are two schemes for television companies in the world: commercial TV, which mostly lives off of advertising, and state television, funded by tax payers (the most typically quoted example is the BBC in England). In Russia, unfortunately, this scheme is manifested in the fact that the government controls about 51 per cent [see Table 2.1] of shares while completely forgetting about its responsibilities before the company. While I was at ORT, Chubais was a state representative among our shareholders. Meanwhile, ORT did not receive any state funds, and [Chubais] did not take part in any of our activities.[12]

Table 2.1 Founders of the company Russian Public Television (24 January 1996)[13]

Founder	Share (%)
State Property Committee	36
State enterprise 'Television Technical Centre'	3
Russian State Television and Radio Company 'Ostankino'	9
ITAR-TASS	3
Joint stock company 'Association of Independent Television Companies'	3
Joint stock company 'Logovaz'	8
National Foundation for the Development of Sport	2
Bank 'Menatep'	5
Bank 'Natsionalny Kredit'	5
Bank 'Stolichny'	5
RAO Gazprom	3
Alfa-Bank	5
Obyedinenny Bank	8
Joint stock company 'Trading Company Mikrodin'	5

In the case of ORT, Blagovolin, despite Berezovsky's later comments, would play an essentially nominal role. These behind-the-scenes dealings would set out a strategy for the way that television companies in Russia would be managed for the rest of the 1990s. According to media analyst Ivan Zassoursky, the essence of this strategy of covert control was 'buying the workers rather than the enterprise'. Then the enterprise itself could be bought at a cheaper price. Berezovsky, for instance, would personally award salaries to the most important employees, in addition to the 'white' salary. This dual wage system also meant that less taxes had to be paid.[14]

If its privatization was murky, then ORT's return to state control appears more logical. In the spring of 1999, Russia's lower house of parliament, the State Duma, passed a law that in effect nationalized all of ORT's assets. It was no wonder that this law was heavily backed by ultra-nationalist Vladimir Zhirinovsky, a politician with a known penchant for patriotic escapades. The law stipulated that Channel 1 was now 'state property', meaning that any sale or transfer of its stock could only be regulated by a specific federal law. It also forbade the transfer of ORT stock to any foreign company or individual.

And then, in June 2000, shortly after the inauguration of President Vladimir Putin, Berezovsky officially revealed just how much of the channel he actually controlled. The business tycoon stated that he owned 49 per cent of ORT stock, and suggested that he was involved in negotiations to transfer his share to the government. These were followed by allegations from the Kremlin in August that ORT had an outstanding debt of $100 million to Vneshekonombank that should have been paid back in January. To pay back the debt, it was suggested that Berezovsky give up his share of the station.

If news coverage that was critical of the new Putin administration appeared to have played a major role in the April 2001 takeover of NTV, that same coverage comes in a different light in the case of ORT. Both stations – just as much as the print media in Russia – came out with varying degrees of criticism for the way the new president handled the sinking of the *Kursk* submarine in August 2000, in which the 118-man crew perished. When the *Kursk* sank the financial attack against Gusinsky and his Media-Most was well underway, and debt problems at ORT had long surfaced. However, that didn't keep ORT from broadcasting footage of angry relatives of the submarine victims. Following this coverage, the outspoken ORT anchor, Sergei Dorenko, was fired, while Berezovsky, in his last private meeting with Putin, was accused by the president of orchestrating yet another campaign to smear him.

Finally, in a deal still riddled with rumour and speculation, in January 2001 Berezovsky sold his 49 per cent share in the company to his partner Roman Abramovich, a co-owner of the Sibneft oil company. Abramovich, who in later years was to become not only Russia's richest man but also an oligarch notoriously loyal to the Kremlin, had just been elected governor of the far-east Chukotka region. The reported price of the deal was $150 million, and it was known in advance that Abramovich would transfer the assets to the government. He kept his word and, in July of that year, sold the shares to the state-owned Sberbank. Years later, in London, Berezovsky alleged that the Abramovich deal was a 'racket', and accused his former partner of forcing him to give up his shares.

Kachkayeva calls Berezovsky's relationship with ORT a 'rental' rather than an ownership, shedding light on the murky, speculative and oftentimes contradictory character of media empires like those of Berezovsky, where one could hardly draw a line between the government and private capital:

> Boris Berezovsky was essentially allowed to rent the chief state channel in the country since 1995. After Berezovsky was forced to give up control of ORT, it served to confirm yet again that ORT's status as a half-state-owned channel was a myth. How, under what conditions, did stock that was formally associated with Berezovsky-owned structures get transferred to other private owners? What banks are currently part of the ORT-KB consortium, what is the mythical OOO 'RastrKom 2002' or OOO 'Eberlink 2002'? Who stands behind them and why did these companies get 49 per cent of shares of the largest television station in Europe? There were no tenders, no reports of sales, except for rumours and unconfirmed information that his former partner, Roman Abramovich, paid Berezovsky an indemnity of $50 million ... Now belonging to a new elite in the interests of the government, Channel 1 has gone six years without paying back its $100 million debt ... The government, as a chief shareholder, pays timely interest on that loan.[15]

Following the sale of his stakes, a partner of Berezovsky's in the Aeroflot airline, Nikolai Glushkov, was arrested and charged with fraud in December 2000. Fearing legal action, Berezovsky soon left Russia, leaving a string of accusations and mounting extradition requests. He has been living in the UK ever since, and has become one of the most virulent and powerful critics of Vladimir Putin's regime.

The NTV legacy

The 2000–2001 takeover of NTV – which, with its pronounced opposition to the second Chechen military campaign, was a flagship of TV independence – was heralded as a political campaign by the new administration, in order to tighten its grasp on a media that 'needed to learn its place'. In many ways this was true – Alfred Kokh, then the director general of Gazprom Media (a subsidiary of the state-owned gas giant Gazprom) said as much when he admitted that the holding's bid for the channel was at least in part politically motivated. But to say that Gazprom's takeover of the independent TV station was nothing more than a Kremlin-hatched plan to impose censorship would be a dangerous oversimplification. Indeed, while singled out for its debt, it was not the only channel that owed millions of dollars. Like other channels, most notably ORT, NTV would see the state-owned Gazprom creeping into its financial sphere as it called back the TV station's enormous debt. NTV may have been oppositionist, but its financial and political independence was just as imaginary as that of ORT and other channels. Finally, ORT met a similar fate, a few months later, despite a year of loyalty to the Putin administration.

The 'attack' on NTV began in late 1999, when Vneshekonombank claimed that Gusinsky's Media-Most holding owed it money. The holding was allegedly overdue on loans interest. As of spring of 1999, Gazprom was a minority shareholder in Media-Most, with 14.3 per cent of shares. In addition, 48.5 per cent of shares had been mortgaged against loans for the holding.

A case illustrative of the intricate relationship between finances, politics and the government is the fate of Gusinsky, the ultimate owner of Media-Most and hence NTV itself. The NTV conflict turned political when the General Prosecutor's Office launched criminal investigations against Media-Most and Gusinsky personally in April 2000. Gusinsky was detained in June 2000 on accusations of fraud and embezzlement of funds. He was released a few days later on bail, while the next month prosecutors froze his assets and put all his property under arrest. But negotiations between Gazprom and Media-Most led to a secret agreement, dubbed 'Protocol 6', that stipulated a transfer of shares to Gazprom in exchange for guarantees that the prosecution of Gusinsky would be halted. Gusinsky was free to leave the country, and later that autumn made a statement that he gave up his shares under pressure. Protocol 6 was made public in an issue of the *Segodnya* daily, a newspaper controlled by Gusinsky. After Gusinsky fled the country, prosecutors issued an international arrest warrant. By January 2001, Gazprom Media chief Alfred Kokh announced that his company was now owner of a controlling share of NTV stock and intended to appoint a new board of directors. The new owners forced their way into the editorial offices in April 2001. The takeover served as a culmination of a property war in which the journalists were not spared. In late 2000, they came under pressure from prosecutors who threatened to press dubious libel charges. When the journalists protested publicly and appealed to Vladimir Putin, the pressure stopped, and Putin met with them. But no agreement was reached. 'NTV journalists were collateral damage in the war over the television station, in the attempt to install the right owners,' Yevgeny Kiselyov, the channel's general director and chief anchor, said in an interview, 'Putin saw me as a puppet of Gusinsky. He did not believe in the possibility of journalistic independence.'

These last developments caused a heated outcry. Journalists at the channel were outraged at what they perceived as an outright attack on press freedom. The editorial team split into two camps, one refusing to continue its work for a station controlled by a corporation that was partially owned by the government, and the other willing to accept the new owners as long as they did not meddle in editorial policy. What resulted was an MTV-style reality show, with TV anchors gathering to discuss their grievances with each other on the air. Amid the controversy revolving around the channel's takeover, this televised, reflective deconstruction caused ratings to skyrocket. In a notorious open letter, Alfred Kokh compared the team's fight for free speech to a soap opera.

Ironically, the transfer of power that occurred in 2001 did not signify serious curtailing of editorial freedom. Still, a part of NTV's editorial and production team, headed by Yevgeny Kiselyov, left the station and went to work for TV-6, a channel primarily geared towards entertainment and owned by Berezovsky. The rest remained at NTV. Boris Jordan, an American, was appointed by Koch to head the station on conditions of relative editorial freedom.

However it was perceived by the press, the NTV takeover did not herald censorship, as the journalists had feared. Editorially, its new owners did not keep the team from taking a flagrantly oppositionist stance in covering the October 2002 Nord-Ost hostage standoff. Still, Nord-Ost proved a turning point in the controversial issue of how the Russian media responded to terrorist attacks. Essentially, if the Kremlin was indeed pursuing a policy of strengthening its grasp on an out-of-control media, the Nord-Ost débâcle was the last straw. In January 2003, Gazprom Media shareholders sacked Jordan without giving any sort of explanation. Alexei Miller, who then headed Gazprom Media, appointed a pulmonary doctor, Nikolai Senkevich, to head the channel. Finally, by July 2004, the post of NTV's director general was given to Vladimir Kulistikov, a former manager at VGTRK. After having reined in ORT, following this lesser-known NTV reshuffle, there was only one truly independent television station left – TV-6.

TV-6: Berezovsky's last media asset

Besides ORT, Berezovsky's control had initially spread to another television channel, TV-6. In fact, if his official holdings in ORT constituted just
16 per cent, his ownership of the predominantly entertainment-oriented
Channel 6 constituted 75 per cent. Another 10 per cent belonged to
structures controlled by the mayor of Moscow, Yuri Luzhkov.

The identity of TV-6 as a news channel is tightly bound up with the
fate of NTV. Following the takeover of NTV in 2001, anchor Yevgeny
Kiselyov, together with a team of loyal journalists, joined TV-6, viewing it
as a safe haven for free journalism. And although the story of TV-6 was
far less publicized and its subsequent takeover less 'symbolic' than that of
NTV, it does show that the re-nationalization, as it has been called, of
Russia's television was far more nuanced than the current trend, which
views it through a prism of either state censorship or corrupt media
capital, would allow.

Unlike its predecessors, TV-6, it could be said, was targeted in the
prime of its life. Kiselyov's team turned the entertainment channel into a
station that offered high quality, professional news journalism that, when
coupled with the channel's penchant for entertainment programming,
increased ratings and, subsequently, profits. Indeed, this dynamic of
success did not reflect either ORT or NTV – and yet TV-6, too, was
reined in under a similar scheme.

Several months after acquiring a new team of journalists (who showed
strong oppositionist tendencies), the station encountered financial troubles. In September 2001, Lukoil-Garant, then a non-government pension
fund that controlled 15 per cent of shares in TV-6, filed a lawsuit asking
for a court order to close down the station, on claims that TV-6 was
carrying considerable losses. That very month, the Supreme Arbitration
Court ruled in favour of Lukoil-Garant, and by January 2002 the Press
Ministry revoked TV-6's licence, shutting down the station.

Ironically, the journalistic community interpreted the disappearance of
TV-6 in a diametrically different manner – for various reasons, many were
willing to take the conflict between non-government financial institutions
at face value, and forget about possible political motivations. Some
observers attributed this scepticism to a weariness with the sort of
emotional scandals that the takeover of Gusinsky's channel had sparked.
Another important reason was that the bitter pill of the closure of TV-6
was sweetened with the creation of TVC, a short-lived, questionably
independent station.

The lessons of re-nationalization

The question remains, however: what light, if any, does TV-6's takeover
shed on the idea of a transfer back to the type of government model
proposed by Yassen Zassoursky? The key difference is that the 'takeover'
was not orchestrated by any known government asset.

he similarity, however, was that TV-6 was controlled by Berezovsky, who by 2002 was well on his way to becoming the virulent critic of Putin's regime that he is today. A bigger question is what direct role President Putin may have had in reining in NTV and re-establishing state control at ORT. Putin is known to have a vindictive streak that could well have explained, in retrospect, an insistence on hounding first Gusinsky, then Berezovsky, out of Russia's media sphere. But the difference in relations between Putin and Berezovsky and Putin and Gusinsky – and a similar fate for their channels – reflects much more than the revenge Putin may have wanted on Berezovsky and Gusinsky. It illustrates the grey area that not only media owners but journalists themselves occupy in their relations with government officials. In what Andrew Jack describes as a 'classic Berezovsky appointment', the journalist Sergei Dorenko was recruited to ORT with the sole aim of 'assault[ing]' the 'principal rivals to the pro-Putin Unity party'. Dorenko would consult regularly about the channel's coverage of the elections, but he based his work largely on his own convictions – he was against Moscow Mayor Yuri Luzhkov and Prime Minister Yevgeny Primakov. Jack writes that Dorenko indeed had an axe to grind with Primakov:

> [Dorenko] told me he had first fallen out with Primakov in 1996 when he criticized the then foreign minister over the proposed Russia-NATO treaty. When Primakov – never a great fan of the media – became prime minister in 1998, he exacted revenge, insisted that if ORT wanted a $100 million rescue package from the state, Dorenko must be fired. The presenter's acerbic reports on cronyism in Luzhkov's administration triggered investigations against him by the Moscow mayor. He believed the Luzhkov-Primakov duo was a threat to both Russia and himself.[16]

In the landslide victory for Unity, Dorenko as a journalist played an important role in propelling Putin to power. That paved the way for the eventual takeover of NTV and the destruction of Gusinsky's empire.

Was there a common denominator that helped pave the way in all these television channels for an ultimate switch back to a government model? Or was their fate a personal whim of Vladimir Putin? Once again, a look at the inherently political nature of the private capital that controlled these media – and the structurally close proximity of media capital to the government – will help us answer that question. No development in recent Russian history illustrates that controversial proximity better than the media wars of the mid-1990s.

The media wars

The idea that the Putin administration launched a clampdown on Russia's free press during his first term in office oversimplifies both the political and the commercial media failures that took place during the Yeltsin era.

The commercial aspects of this problem were touched upon earlier in this chapter – they were identified early on, in the first years following the breakup of the Soviet Union. Today, Kachkayeva cites former press minister – and former oligarch – Mikhail Lesin, who pointed out that 'in ten years we have not formed a media market: we do not sell stock, we do not sell companies. They don't die out. Not a single media company has gone bankrupt'.[17] Meanwhile, media experts tend to identify only one period of true media freedom: the decentralization that went on between 1990 and 1995. During this period, the Russian media briefly became the fourth estate, in the sense that as a free institution it had the power to mould politics and society, arguably reflecting the will of the people.

Other liberal media experts point out, however, that as many media outlets were simply not prepared to compete with one another, the new, unbridled commercial freedom fuelled an unprecedented financial chaos that ended with the formation of a few nominal media empires, including those of Berezovsky and Gusinsky, in 1994. That year, incidentally, coincided with what some called the end of the 'golden age' of post-perestroika media freedom. Others identified the end of the golden era much sooner, when price liberalization dealt a heavy blow to newspapers that had developed their independent streak during perestroika.

Starting in 1995, writes Kachkayeva, 'organizers and businessmen, who provide for broadcasting under half-authorized economic conditions, took to the front stage. The enormous investments which they poured into broadcasting were obtained through barters and deals with the government elite'.[18] Hence, the very freedom that the fall of the Communist Party endowed upon the Russian press was a double-edged sword, and following a few years of free-market competition, the stage was set for a dubious liaison with the government that would compromise the very foundations of that free press.

The Yeltsin campaign

This environment offers a good clue as to why the emerging media barons of the mid-1990s were so eager to support Yeltsin's campaign for re-election at any cost – including the reputation of their respective media outlets.

At that point in Russia, the Communist Party and its leader, Gennady Zyuganov, still posed a viable threat to private capital – at least in the presidential elections. Unlike previous or subsequent elections in Russia, the 1996 campaign was unique in that few could predict the outcome with any real certainty. Zyuganov had as much a chance at the presidential seat as the incumbent Yeltsin did, and supporters of the Yeltsin clan simply feared that they would lose their assets were Zyuganov to come to power.

To that end, the media empires of Gusinsky and Berezovsky, who up until that point had been competitors, joined forces to launch a campaign that was to essentially 'scare' the masses into voting for Yeltsin. The alternative that was successfully presented by the leading news television channels involved a veritable return to a totalitarian past were Zyuganov elected, with property confiscation, revolution and instability. Zyuganov was effectively deprived of access to the airwaves. At NTV, for instance, which a year earlier had flaunted its independence with an oppositionist stance in the first military campaign in Chechnya, the channel's director was appointed to forge a 'positive' presidential image.

In the case of the 1996 presidential election, the massive media consolidation was no mass trend, but a carefully planned campaign. Indeed, President Yeltsin's campaign staff had a lot to worry about at the end of 1995: the communists had won a majority at the parliamentary elections, the print media – as well as NTV – were in the middle of an all-out campaign *against* Yeltsin for alleged failures in the Chechnya military campaign, and the presidential ratings were catastrophically low. According to a January 1996 poll by the All-Russian Public Opinion Research Center, only 5.4 per cent of respondents were prepared to vote for Yeltsin (twice as many – 11.3 per cent – for Zyuganov). All this, according to Ivan Zassoursky, created a ripe atmosphere for media barons to reinvent their outlets and turn them into a consolidated propaganda apparatus aimed at Yeltsin's victory – even if it meant covering for voter fraud and falsifications.

Zassoursky describes the sudden media campaign as an ultimate exercise in media theatrics, a fundamental moment when the Russian media obtained the technology for producing (and reproducing) virtual reality.[19] While this know-how had been developing in the West for decades, in Russia it was implemented practically within a single campaign season. But given the general oppositionist climate mentioned above, what was it exactly that so successfully rallied an unruly media to the cause of re-electing a hopelessly unpopular president?

One of the lesser-known, but very important cornerstones of the beginning of the campaign was a document produced by the recently-created Foundation for Effective Politics, a think-tank that has worked on political strategies for the Russian government. Aptly titled *The President in 1996: Scenarios and Technologies of Victory*, it served as a blueprint for reorganizing media priorities in ways that were previously unheard of, being anathema to a top-down, centralized, *instrumental* media system that was forged in the Soviet Union. What the report offered as an alternative was another instrumental model, albeit a more effective one:

> The media are important only to the extent that they present the content, ideology, and newsworthy events for mass chatter – in other words, for the real political discussions in mass society that in Russia never cease for a minute. Political initiatives and situations can be translated to the masses ... to the extent that they are dramatized – i.e., to the extent that they have transformed into an interesting and accessible plot (anecdote, scenario, myth – all these are varieties of sociopolitical dramaturgy). The media are necessary in this campaign to forge a direct channel between the 'Russian capital' and the 'Russian country'.[20]

The document served, in other words, as a blueprint for reorganizing Russia's leading news media into a reality show. As such, it was a success. The question still remains, however: was it enough to rally both ORT and NTV to the causes of re-electing a hard-drinking president?

Anna Kachkayeva suggests a more natural motive for the campaign:

> The pro-Yeltsin front turned out to be a success not just in terms of keeping the elite in the government, but brought its ideological warriors considerable economic results. Following the elections, Gusinsky's NTV gained [broadcasting rights] on the entire Channel 4 frequency, while Berezovsky and Mikhail Lesin got posts in the Security Council and the Presidential administration, respectively.[21]

The fact that both channels' loyalty to the government was so short-lived also gives weight to the media barons' financial, rather than editorial, interest in supporting Yeltsin at that particular period in time.

If Gusinsky's NTV supported Yeltsin for the presidential campaign, the channel's support for the state appears to veer off in the second half of the 1990s, but in a way that would ultimately lead to its ruin. Over the years, NTV had hundreds of millions of dollars in loans pouring in from state-controlled banks like Vneshekonombank, Vneshtorgbank and Sberbank. NTV also ran up a $1 billion tab with the state-owned Gazprom, which was an ally of Gusinsky in 1996, when it first bought shares in the television network. Of course it would be wrong to view this money as a direct 'kickback' for Gusinsky's 1996 support of the Yeltsin team, but in retrospect it does seem to reflect a mindset that tied financing with political or media support. In his book, *Inside Putin's Russia,* Andrew Jack, a journalist who spoke to Gusinsky on a number of occasions, cites a businessman, apparently one of several, who was threatened with bad press if he refused a request for a loan. More importantly, Jack cites some of the key players in those events who admit the extent to which their support of Yeltsin compromised their media holdings: 'It was a mistake to get involved in the Yeltsin campaign', NTV's chief anchor Yevgeny Kiselyov reportedly said later on, 'but we were not ignoring the other candidates. We were trying to keep a certain balance'. More revealingly, Gusinsky, in a 2001 conversation with Jack, himself linked NTV's fall with the presidential campaign: "We made a mistake. Not because we supported Yeltsin ... but because we didn't have the right to decide who would be president. It is the right of the people to choose the president. But we were learning. That period has passed. And today we are paying for 1996'.[22]

If in the previous section we saw how the government reined in an 'unruly' press, the origins of that very press show how the process of consolidation between the government and private media capital was not an obligatory clampdown. It involved media capital that seemed more than willing to compromise its objectivity in order to forge a more lucrative relationship with the state. But another aspect of this relationship was that the electronic media had never been fully weaned from the state in the first place, and if private media capital had ever set out to accomplish that objective, by the end of the Yeltsin campaign, it had failed. If a lot of questions remain to be answered as to why the media suddenly rallied to support Yeltsin in 1996, the reasons for subsequent media wars and anti-government muckraking flow directly from the way that the electronic media compromised themselves in that year.

The Svyazinvest scandal and other information wars

If the Yeltsin campaign illustrates how the state apparatus could influence media capital to its own gains – and how media capital was a willing player – the media wars that followed in the late 1990s showed a playing field that was not always so levelled. The clout mustered by the oligarchs, as they were now dubbed, put the financially struggling government at a disadvantage when it came to a conflict of interest between media capital and state interest.

The conflict sparked by the privatization of the Svyazinvest telecommunications monopoly showed just how far media oligarchs could go in wielding their media to virtually run Yeltsin's government. In 1997, clashes between Berezovsky and Gusinsky on the one side and the emerging oligarch Vladimir Potanin on the other over the latter's privatization of Svyazinvest grew so bitter as to lead to a series of resignations of pro-reform ministers in Yeltsin's government. To understand the origins of this conflict, it is helpful to clarify some of the mechanisms of privatization during the mid-1990s that essentially created the wealth of key players like Vladimir Potanin and Vladimir Gusinsky.

By 1995, Yeltsin's government was struggling in a financial Catch-22. Privatization income in August 1995 covered only 6 per cent of the yearly budget.[23] Backlogged pensions and salaries for doctors, teachers and other civil servants were some of the more common grievances that helped Yeltsin's ratings plummet over the years. Democracy or no, Yeltsin's government was desperate for cash and was pressed to rely on more privatization. But by that time, privatization had already earned itself a catastrophically poor reputation, riddled as it was with corruption and favouritism. By 1995, a relatively oppositionist State Duma had put a ban on the privatization of 'strategically important' objects like oil plants.

It was Vladimir Potanin, then head of Oneximbank, who first proposed the idea of a loan-for-shares programme that would allow the government to sidetrack the Duma ban by giving it access to cash by virtually mortgaging off its industrial assets. The shares in the industrial assets were to be given to the highest bidder, but good connections in the government were still just as crucial. A total of 12 such auctions were held: Vladimir Potanin scored the biggest deal, giving the government $170 million for a 38 per cent share in Norilsk Nickel, and $130 million for a 51 per cent share in the oil company Sidanko. Similarly, Mikhail Khodorkovsky's Menatep Bank gave the government $159 million for a 45 per cent share of the Yukos oil company.

Deals like this, although forged with the help of already considerable Kremlin connections, only fortified the lender-debtor relations that developed between the state and some oligarchs. Anatoly Chubais, a first vice-premier between 1994 and 1996 and a reformer who probably suffered most from Berezovsky and Gusinsky's media campaigns, called the $170 million garnered from the Norilsk deal a financial breaking point in the era. The contemporary historian, Irina Karatsuba, quoted Chubais as saying, 'With the money we got from auctioning off Norilsk Nickel we immediately patched up a huge number of budget holes. First and foremost, the salaries'.[24]

But if Potanin could count on loyalty from the Yeltsin government, so could Berezovsky and Gusinsky, who, using their media empires, provided the president with a second term in the first place. They had every reason to count on Svyazinvest as a lucrative reward for their efforts. They also felt that a telecommunications asset would be an important part of their media empires. The holding company included controlling shares in 76 regional telephone enterprises, five city telephone companies, four telegraph centres and three international communications operators. According to Ivan Zassoursky, for them,

> access to the telecommunications sector was tantamount to admission to the twenty-first century, since it would not just allow them immediately to stake out strong positions in the rapidly developing markets for local telephone and mobile communications, internet access, and so on, but also eventually to integrate their telecommunications channels with the content supplied by their print media holding companies.[25]

It is suggested that were it not for Potanin's valuable connections in the government apparatus, and his stint as first vice-premier after the elections, the telecommunications company would have most likely gone to Berezovsky and Gusinsky.

However, official figures point to an auction in which Potanin, together with George Soros, offered the best price – $2 billion as opposed to the $1.4 billion offered by Berezovsky, Gusinsky and their partners. Rumours that Potanin and co. never actually ended up paying that price could not be verified. Berezovsky and Gusinsky felt snubbed: a major stake in a valuable telecom monopoly went to the highest bidder instead of the oligarch that 'deserved' it. Hoping that the deal could be reversed, Berezovsky and Gusinsky rallied once more in yet another muckraking campaign, this time against the pro-democratic 'young reformers' in Yeltsin's government who were behind the unfairly 'transparent' auction.

The ramifications this campaign had for Russia's fledgling democracy were noted by some of the more liberal critics. According to Karatsuba,

> Television stations controlled by the snubbed "oligarchs" organized a lashing for then chairmen of the State Property Committee Alfred Kokh. The recently appointed "young reformers," like Anatoly Chubais and Boris Nemstov, whom Yeltsin had publicly proclaimed

as his successors, came to the defense of the [Svyazinvest] deal. And so the "young reformers" became the main target of the media magnates. Anatoly Chubais and his colleagues were accused of accepting a bribe in the form of payments for a book that had never been written. The book, however was successfully published in 1999. But in 1997, as a result of the scandal orchestrated by oligarch-owned media revolving around the "author case," the "authors" were discredited and sacked from the government. Thus, Yeltsin's last attempt to activate reforms and renew the government failed.[26]

According to Yassen Zassoursky, meanwhile, the muckraking information wars heralded a subsequent return to government control of the media that was to begin following President Vladimir Putin's election in 2000.[27] Besides Svyazinvest, we have seen the role Berezovsky's ORT itself played in backing Putin ahead of his election. It was this campaign that would prove pivotal in eventually bringing down both NTV and ORT, and, most importantly, in explaining the later demarcation of the government model that would take hold of television and newspapers in the new decade.

Vitaly Tretyakov, who in 1999 was the influential editor-in-chief of the legendary (albeit, Berezovsky-controlled) *Nezavisimaya Gazeta* (literally, independent newspaper), identifies NTV and ORT – and Gusinsky and Berezovsky – not so much as media empires but as political parties. In that light, it makes sense to view their demise not necessarily as an outright attack on press freedom, nor as financial takeovers, but as political campaigns in their own right. Tretyakov describes the magnitude of the influence wielded by the chief anchors at NTV and ORT – Yevgeny Kiselyov and Sergei Dorenko, respectively – in their media campaigns against and for Putin:

> How much did Sergei Dorenko's programme on ORT raise Putin's rating? We can argue that it was either 5 per cent or 10 per cent. But it's clear that it was by a lot more than a single vote – by a lot more than the single vote of Sergei Dorenko. To what extent did these programmes lower the ratings of Primakov and Luzhkov? We can argue about the exact numbers, but not about the general answer to the question. The same question, formulated backwards, is fair regarding Yevgeny Kiselyov on NTV [whose programme attacked Putin and supported Primakov and Luzhkov]. Were these programs a part of a carefully planned and coordinated battle between two political camps that were vying for power in Russia in the fall of 1999 and the winter of 2000? Absolutely. Moreover, the owner of one channel (NTV) and the individual who controlled the other channel (ORT) were informally members of the respective campaign staff of the competing camps.[28]

It is telling, then, that both ORT and NTV met the same fate at approximately the same time despite the fact that while NTV had been virulently campaigning against Putin, ORT was consistently – at least starting in 1999 – loyal to Yeltsin and his appointed successor. To recap, then: NTV was critical of the Yeltsin administration through 1995 while Berezovsky's ORT was relatively loyal; NTV and ORT joined forces to uphold Yeltsin in the 1996 presidential campaign; NTV and ORT likewise joined forces in 1997 in an attempt to discredit the Yeltsin administration over the Svyazinvest deal; NTV and ORT were once again pitted against each other in 1999–2000 during the parliamentary and presidential elections, with ORT staking on Yeltsin and Putin and NTV staking on the Primakov-Luzhkov opposition.

Why, then, did ORT too come under fire? While ORT did indeed turn critical of Putin over his handling of the *Kursk* submarine disaster, Tretyakov also identifies another development that played a role in the campaign against ORT. In the summer of 2000, Berezovsky launched a political movement called 'Civilization'. This, together with his stance on *Kursk*, meant that Berezovsky was intending to launch a quasi-party, with the intention of using Russia's most powerful television network as a propaganda tool.[29]

Thus, we may very well interpret Putin's handling of the electronic media as a form of revenge when he finally came to power. The key issue is that this kind of behaviour – politics and special interests dictating what ends up being broadcast on television – was not unique to the president. The way the media empires were forged relied first on personal relations – including rewards and revenge – making independent commercial growth impossible. If Yeltsin never used his power to clamp down on the media directly, then the on-off ties between him and powerful media magnates – and the determining role those ties had in what went on the air – created a situation where that sort of abuse of power was inevitable. According to Tretyakov, the government was not so much using its power to suppress free speech, but engaging in a political campaign using the same methods as its opponents. This might not make for good media policy in the long run, but judging by the way the media playing field had developed through the 1990s, it was all but inevitable.

Ownership in the printed press

Russia's print media also found itself caught in the crossfire of warring media capital. Just a few years after winning independence from the Communist Party, the print media were being snatched up by influential media barons who used their media in the service of political campaigns.

The fate of Russia's newspapers throughout the 1990s can serve as an echo of the dynamic power plays that revolved around the nation's television stations. Today, like television, newspapers have increasingly come under the control of various media holdings acting as conglomerates in their purchase of media assets. Often they are either state-owned, like Gazprom's Gazprom Media, or loyal to the Kremlin, like Vladimir

Potanin's Prof-Media. The chief difference is that the printed press has less potential to influence and manipulate the masses than does television and, perhaps for this reason, benefits from relatively more editorial independence. Hence, with an increasingly diverse print market, Russia's print media offers a far wider scope of views than can be found on national television.

Russia's leading newspapers went from enjoying unbridled freedom to becoming semi-independent media assets of the state. However, the print media were affected to a greater extent by the economic upheavals of the early 1990s, when rising prices nearly paralysed the newspapers that had been freed by Gorbachev's reforms, and the new publications that had just sprung up. The price liberalization implemented after the collapse of the USSR dealt a serious blow to newspapers, which functioned in a controlled economy. The liberalization policies had sought to help stabilize food shortages and prices, but instead led to inflation that wiped out the population's savings. Faced with rising costs for paper, printing and distribution services, newspapers were also quickly losing readership, particularly in former Soviet states that had become independent nations. Meanwhile, the reformist government did nothing to regulate the existing monopoly on the press distribution network, which continued to dictate prices. This combination of factors was disastrous for newspapers, and government aid was not forthcoming at first. State subsidies were handed out to publications that were closest to the regime, but little was being done to curb the fatal effects that liberalization was having on newspaper media.

These conditions launched a domino effect that would take newspapers on a journey through precarious independence, oligarch control and, finally, to various extents, state-controlled 'stability' towards the later half of the first decade of the twenty-first century. We can trace this journey with examples of ownership in two influential newspapers that played a decisive role in determining the new print media playing field in the 1990s: *Nezavisimaya Gazeta* and *Izvestia*. These examples will show how the formation of media ownership systems following the breakup of the Soviet Union affected the most vulnerable sector of the media – print. While serving as an important – and oftentimes exclusive – forum for opposing and independent viewpoints, newspapers, unlike other media, are often hit hardest by economic factors like decreasing readership, high printing costs, an unstable and shady advertising market and general infrastructure issues that compound these problems. In the mid-1990s, these factors made newspapers easy prey to politicized capital. By the time Soviet media entered a new era in 1990, *Izvestia* was already a well-established central daily, but the success and failure of *Nezavisimaya Gazeta* reflected the fate of a new and independent press in post-Soviet Russia that was up against the odds of harsh market conditions.

As new concepts of competition on the information market began to emerge during the post-Soviet period, the number of all-national newspapers grew more than eightfold: from 43 in 1990 to 405 in 2003. Magazines and regional newspapers showed more modest growth:

22 per cent and 61 per cent respectively. But these increases in the number of publications were not accompanied by a rise in readership, except in the regional press. Meanwhile, the circulation of all-national newspapers and the share of periodic journals in the general press circulation plummeted.[30]

According to Y. Zassoursky, total circulation was 100 million in 1992, but by 1997 it was just 7 million.[31] However, he identifies another important factor that toughened competition for the printed press in the new media system that sprung up in the early 1990s. While legislation, as we have pointed out, essentially freed the press from government control in 1990, it failed to establish such concepts as ownership and what powers an owner had over his media. While Russian media law includes such concepts as founder and publisher, there is no *owner*. *Izvestia* turned out to be an apt illustration of this particular problem.

Another major difficulty for the printed press was its relatively limited access to advertising, which, coupled with infrastructure, circulation and readership issues, further served to marginalize the print media. While income from advertising has grown considerably since 2000, it remains, predictably, just a fraction of television advertising. The gross budget for television advertising was $1.7 billion in 2004 (nearly a twofold increase from 2002), and was just $250 million for newspapers (up from $165 million in 2002). By 2008, the gap had widened. In four years, television's advertising market had grown 224 per cent to $3.8 billion, while the newspaper advertising market had grown just 160 per cent to $416 million.[32] These factors pushed newspapers – whether well-established like *Izvestia*, or newly-created like *Nezavisimaya Gazeta* – under the wing of big business. Among the most powerful companies to enter the new media playing field were Vladimir Potanin's Prof-Media, which today controls some 90 newspapers, and which the World Newspaper Association has called the largest media company in Russia working in the print media sector, and Gazprom Media, one of Europe's largest media holdings, 86 per cent of which is controlled by the state-owned gas giant Gazprom.[33]

Nezavisimaya Gazeta

Nezavisimaya Gazeta in many ways epitomized the spirit of the free press of the early 1990s and its crusade to finally form a 'fourth estate'. This made it particularly vulnerable to big business as it struggled to forge itself as an independent outlet. I. Zassoursky describes the paper as a 'weathercock that points in the direction the country is headed'.[34] Its founder and editor, Vitaly Tretyakov, stubbornly insisted on independence until this became financially impossible towards the end of the 1990s – he was arguably the last of the idealists to 'sell out' to politicized capital. Given the impossibility of sustaining a publication under the economic conditions described above, it would hardly be accurate to speak of a sell-out with all its negative connotations, however. We shall see why.

While based editorially in part on *Le Monde* and Britain's *The Independent*, the financial formation of *Nezavisimaya Gazeta* was truly a forerunner in post-Soviet history. The first issue came out on 21 December 1990, with an initial run of three times a week. Buoyed by positive print factors – the cost of paper and rent were still low at that time, while the demand for the printed word, in the last days of glasnost, was still remarkably high – to finance the new publication, Tretyakov found 83 'shareholders' among the intelligentsia, each of whom contributed 1000 rubles towards the paper. Some of them remain shareholders to this day, long after the paper was bought and sold by Berezovsky, but these holders have no formal or financial status as such.

After the price liberalization of the early 1990s raised printing costs and lowered the income of the paper's readership, *Nezavisimaya Gazeta* – which occupied one of the most saturated sectors of the nation's media market – began to lose circulation. Unlike well-established papers such as *Komsomolskaya Pravda* and *Izvestia*, *Nezavisimaya Gazeta* did not initially get a helping hand from the government. It was offered subsidies later on, but Tretyakov, who was already actively criticizing the Yeltsin administration, refused. Financial difficulties led to a break within the journalistic collective – a team of journalists went on to form the short-lived *Segodnya* newspaper in 1993. In the meantime, the newspaper subsisted on donations from a multitude of individuals with 'politicized capital'. In the politically-charged atmosphere that prevailed between the parliamentary standoff of 1993 and the presidential election of 1996, media offered attractive political and financial investment opportunities for businesses.

Finally, by autumn 1995, when the newspaper was catastrophically close to having to shut itself down, it was taken over by Boris Berezovsky, who, in the words of Tretyakov, became the paper's chief sponsor and de facto owner: 'I simultaneously acted as a person who 1) formed professional standards for employees of *Nezavisimaya Gazeta*, 2) *directly or indirectly translated corporate standards of the owner for the journalists* [emphasis added], 3) acted as a journalist who had to choose between accepting and not accepting these standards'.[35]

Tretyakov, without a lot of excuse-making and self-justification, does a good job of describing the precarious position that journalists found themselves in, as de facto employees of powerful, government-connected businessmen like Berezovsky. As we can guess, the balanced relationship described by Tretyakov did not last long. In spring 2000 Tretyakov wrote in his paper that all oligopolies – including that of Berezovsky – should be destroyed. He called this a 'challenge' that Berezovsky was forced to reply to. Later that year, Berezovsky hinted at plans to sell *Nezavisimaya Gazeta*, something that Tretyakov interpreted as a personal warning. By spring 2001, the rift between owner and editor over their ideological attitudes towards the Putin administration grew critical – Tretyakov supported Putin, while Berezovsky had already broken with the new president. Finally Berezovsky decided to 'remove' Tretyakov from 'all the posts [he] occupied at the paper', including that of editor-in-chief. In exchange Tretyakov was offered a position of chairman on the board of directors, a lump compensation sum of $300,000, a monthly salary of $10,000 and other 'perks'. Tretyakov, who admits that he was well-enough off financially to have the option to choose, declined the offer because he did not want to take part in destroying his brainchild.

While I. Zassoursky calls *Nezavisimaya Gazeta* a failed experiment that reflected what might have developed in post-Soviet Russia's media system,[36] it was the longest-lived.

Izvestia

The history of this newspaper probably illustrates the most successful example of how a traditional, Soviet-era publication survived and transformed into a serious, all-national paper that was neither a tabloid nor a politicized attempt to cultivate a fourth estate. Nevertheless, the course it traversed reflects how papers with an established past faced both advantages and disadvantages in terms of their relationship with the government. The paper had been coming out since March 1917, serving as an official organ of the Soviet government. After 1990, what started as a cooperative owned by a 'journalist collective' was plagued by the same problems the national press suffered, including lack of a clear-cut relationship between publisher, editor-in-chief and journalists. Papers were accustomed to high incomes from subscription which went directly to the party, labour union or communist youth league which controlled it, but this abruptly ended in 1991. According to Y. Zassoursky, for long-running publications like *Izvestia* the 'shock-treatment' of the early 1990s was literal indeed.[37] By this time, *Izvestia* was positioning itself as an analytical publication with more than 80 years of history, and a readership that identified it as the 'first paper', of the country much as ORT was the 'first button'. As a liberal, independent publication, it catered to an educated class with a high level of political awareness.

But the very independence of long-running publications like *Izvestia* and even the tabloid *Komsomolskaya Pravda* was challenged almost immediately after the fall of the Communist Party. During the economic crisis in 1992, the situation had grown so dire that several long-running, mass circulation papers failed to come out for several days. That February, President Boris Yeltsin signed a decree subsidizing the costs of some of the more high-circulation papers and fixing the price of paper. This also allowed for the privatization of distribution networks.

Not only did *Izvestia* accept this help from the government, but it also published an article that very month supporting the government's decision and arguing that such subsidies would not undermine the paper's independence, pointing out that help in paying printing costs was not going to keep the paper from criticizing the government.

Still, dependence on cash from a cash-strapped government that was indeed tolerant of criticism from the press was not enough for financial independence. By 1996, two companies, Lukoil and Vladimir Potanin's ksimbank, gained control of a majority of the paper's stock. This led a rift among the journalists, with one team, led by former *Izvestia* itor Igor Golembiovsky, forming the *Noviye Izvestia* daily in 1997.

During the Putin years, Potanin was an oligarch not only favoured by the government, but purportedly maintaining close ties with the administration. Even so, the greatest editorial controversy at the paper in recent years occurred in 2004, when *Izvestia* published explicit photographs on its front page of children being rescued from the Beslan school that was attacked by terrorists in September of that year. In the scandal that followed, the then editor Raf Shakirov resigned from his post, claiming pressure from the Kremlin. According to various sources, however, Shakirov was asked by Potanin to leave. While some argued that the case was politically motivated, others pointed out that the *Izvestia* scandal could also have been sparked by a debate over whether it was in good taste to publish such explicit photos.

Nevertheless, in June 2005, the newspaper was swallowed up by the Gazprom Media holding, which was consolidating its control over a number of press and electronic outlets. In terms of the history of the paper's independence, the circle was complete: despite moderate criticism of the government, the paper took a visibly more loyalist stance following the purchase. Gradually, it began reinventing itself as a 'serious' paper with a 'tabloid' twist.

Ownership vs. independence

By the end of President Vladimir Putin's second term in 2008, not only was much of the nation's television directly or indirectly controlled by the state (either through state-owned companies or by companies whose owners were loyal to the government), but a trend towards similar conglomeration was becoming increasingly visible in the printed press. By 2005, *Izvestia* was under the ownership of Gazprom Media. In 2006 Boris Berezovsky sold his stake in the liberal business daily *Kommersant* to Badri Patarkatsishvili, who immediately went on to sell the paper to Alisher Usmanov, the general director of Gazprominvestholding (a Gazprom subsidiary) and a man reputed to have close ties with the Kremlin.

Much of Russian television was indeed under the ownership of the state: the government directly controlled Channel 1 (formerly ORT), formally through a small number of state-controlled holding companies; the All-Russian State Television and Radio Broadcasting Company (VGTRK) now controlled not just Channel 2 (RTR), but also a culture channel on the fifth button, and a sports channel on the sixth. Gazprom, meanwhile, through its holding company Gazprom Media, controlled NTV, and had a considerable stake in the entertainment channel TNT. Where entertainment channels like STS (controlled by Alpha-Bank) and TNT are concerned, it would be difficult to speak of the extent of government influence or censorship – channels like this have long adhered to a policy of no politics and very little news, and focused their efforts on sitcoms and films. They could hardly be accused of appeasing the government, however – heavy entertainment content instead of news was simply more commercially viable. One exception is REN-TV, controlled by the Severstal steel company and the Surgutneftegaz oil company. While focusing more heavily on entertainment, it is perhaps the only popular network to broadcast in-depth coverage of the opposition and to take a slant that is critical of the government.

How does this speak of independence on television and in newspapers? In the new, post-Soviet economy, does ownership entail full control, and does full control entail censorship? In other words, just because most of the truly influential media in Russia are owned by companies close to the state, does this mean that media is free in Russia only to the extent that it is independent from government-associated capital?

As we have explained in this chapter, the print and electronic media entered the post-Soviet era with a great degree of financial independence. The 1990s proved, meanwhile, that under market conditions in a country unaccustomed to them, this type of financial independence was unsustainable. There was hardly a clear-cut Kremlin policy to 'rein in' the free press, although experts identify that the media playing field was indeed turning towards a more government controlled model by 2000. But the forces behind that transformation were as much economic as they were political.

In the case of television, the result is indeed striking: the news programmes that are aired focus heavily on the president; on the state-controlled channels there is little, if any, balanced coverage of controversial issues like the Khodorkovsky trial. This does not mean that national problems are not raised on television – social issues like corruption, hazing in the army, the demographic crisis and poverty are widely talked about, and programmes covering these problems are a major venue for criticism.

In the case of Gazprom, whose NTV channel only rarely ventures to criticize the government, its other media seem to have a lot more luxuries. Gazprom Media controls, for instance, perhaps one of the most outspoken liberal vestiges of the early 1990s – the Ekho Moskvy radio station, one of the most critical outlets remaining. Vladimir Potanin's Prof-Media publishes *Komsomolskaya Pravda*, a mass-circulation tabloid that, unlike serious, 'quality' papers that are categorized as 'all-national', is widely available in the provinces. The tabloid has a good reputation with the Kremlin (Putin visited its newsroom on its birthday), but permits criticism of the government.

And so, two decades after perestroika, the Russian media is still not independent – indeed, it is less independent than it was in 1991. We have seen how the economic and political conditions of the very democracy that the media helped foment actually hindered that independence. Under unstable market conditions, media freedom itself inevitably comes under threat. But control by the government and politicized capital are not the only factors that threaten media freedom in Russia today. We will examine in the next chapter what media freedom means in Russia, and what continues to threaten it.

3   FREEDOM IN THE RUSSIAN PRESS

- The origins of Russian censorship
- The dangers of reporting in post-Soviet Russia
- Mechanisms of control in the age of the free market
- Towards a free press: the meaning of freedom

The current state of media independence bodes grim prospects for media freedom in Russia. With the country's decades-long reputation as a place ridden with censorship, where civil and journalistic liberties are downtrodden, and where freedom of the press is non-existent at worst and suppressed at best – as it is currently – it would be meaningful to examine just what exactly media freedom – and lack thereof – means in Russia.

The Committee to Protect Journalists calls Russia the 'third deadliest country in the world for journalists'.[1] According to Freedom House, Russia's press has been 'not free' since 2004. Reporters without Borders currently ranks it 148th according to a 2003 world press freedom ranking, where the watchdog organization called it a place where

> a truly independent press exists … but Russia's poor ranking is justified by the censorship of anything to do with the war in Chechnya, several murders and the recent abduction of the Agence France-Presse correspondent in Ingushetia. Russia continues to be one of the world's deadliest countries for journalists.[2]

The situation has become worse. In May 2007 the US State Department labelled Russia among the seven worst offenders in terms of press freedom: others were Afghanistan, Venezuela, Pakistan, Egypt, Lebanon and the Philippines.

When assessing the state of press freedom in Russia, however, there is a tendency by the press, watchdog groups and government officials to lump together more complex problems like censorship, security and persecution under the issue of 'press freedom'. Another problem that is under-examined is how lack of financial independence – an issue that has far more global implications beyond Russia – affects media freedom.

In this chapter, we will examine what media freedom means in Russia by looking into various separate problems that affect it. The security of journalists is one problem; another concerns financial relationships between journalists and media owners, while yet another involves the self-identification of the journalist himself.

We must also differentiate between the different kinds of pressure that are put on journalists and on the press precisely because when we speak of lack of journalistic freedom we tend to imply that the government is trying to control information. But looking at a country like Russia at the beginning of the twenty-first century, it is clear that a multitude of forces are behind this pressure – social, criminal, stylistic, financial and, of course, political.

Political pressure on the media can be manifold. The most drastic examples are libel and other lawsuits targeting newspapers and television channels and, rarely, direct pressure on the journalist – threats, persecution, assault or even murder. Yet by far, many of the problems journalists encounter – including violence – have criminal or financial origins rather than directly political ones.

Finally, in order to appreciate the uniqueness of Russia's current press freedoms, we must understand what kinds of censorship Russia has experienced historically.

The origins of Russian censorship

A key aspect in press freedom or lack thereof is the differentiation between preliminary censorship, posterior censorship and self-censorship. In the first case, information is suppressed once it is created and before it is distributed. Posterior censorship means that the government confiscates questionable publications once they have been published and even distributed, or punishes the journalist or publisher after the fact. When speaking of lack of media freedom in Russia, these crucial distinctions are seldom made. In reality, it is hard to underestimate how groundbreaking Gorbachev's reforms really were: in 1990, for the first time in Russian history, a presidential decree did away with preliminary censorship. In practice, relative to other developed western nations, post-Soviet Russia has suffered limited preliminary censorship – when we speak of lack of media freedom in Russia, this usually involves a complex blend of posterior censorship and self-censorship. And however dire the current situation may be, we must keep in mind that there was only one time when the Russian press was any freer than it is today, and that was during the post-perestroika years, up until 1993.

The press as an organ of the czar

The origins of government censorship in Russia go back centuries, to an era when the country itself was just taking shape. One of the first documents limiting freedom of the press involved Church manuscripts. G.V. Zhirkov identifies 1551 as the year the first official censoring document was adopted in Russia. This is the Stoglav compilation, consisting of 'one-hundred chapters' or decrees that dictated Church affairs and established rules for book printing and manuscript editing.

The 'chapters' also included regulations for teaching establishments and printing presses. For instance, the chapter 'On book scribes' gave Church authorities the power to confiscate uncorrected manuscripts. Ironically, it would be these regulations that would lead to the creation of the first printing press in Moscow.[3]

The seventeenth century was marked by unprecedented religious repressions following the schism between followers of Patriarch Nikon and the Old Believers, who were persecuted. During that period, the Orthodox Church also cracked down on folk literature. A 1682 decree forbade the distribution of any literature on religious themes that had been penned by anyone except Church authorities, making writing on the walls a punishable offence. All printing presses were required to have special permission from the Moscow patriarch before they could publish.

The decree illustrates to what extent the Orthodox Church controlled everything that was printed in Russia – so much so that that even the government began making attempts to throw off the yoke of Church censorship. In 1678, under Czar Alexei, the first printing press that was not controlled by the Church was established, but the manager of the press, Sylvester Medvedev, was later tortured and executed as a bandit.

In terms of press freedom, the government would only win its independence from the Church under Peter the Great, who ended the Church's monopoly as censor only to establish an equally controlling and intolerant role for the government. Peter's successful efforts to gain independence from the Church sparked a 'media campaign' of sorts on the part of Church officials, which led to a severe retaliation by the new czar. By 1701, Peter issued a decree that forbade clerics to 'wield pen and ink'.[4] In 1708, the czar issued a decree establishing the first form of military censorship.

More importantly, however, Peter usurped the Church's monopoly on the printing presses, once and for all establishing the government's direct role in printing and publishing. Government control impacted not just printing, but grammar as well. By 1708 spoken Russian was such a far cry from the official Old Church Slavonic that Peter introduced a layman's alphabet. Several secular printing presses were established by the 1720s. By 1723 the country's institutions began using domestically produced paper. In 1701 the number of books published in Russia was 8 – 23 years later the number had grown to 149.[5] The fact that Peter became the founder of Russia's first newspaper, *Vedomosti*, in 1702, points to the deeply subordinate, top-down origins of Russian journalism itself.

In this sense, Peter's 'pro-western' reforms – particularly ones aiming to separate Church and state – lay firm foundations for a dynasty of strong preliminary censorship by the government. Peter's direct involvement in publishing meant that he personally edited secular manuscripts, a practice that continued, to various extents, through the reign of Joseph Stalin.

With a traditionally subordinate press, it was hard for writers working under the system – especially those who did not travel – to imagine a press that could function in any other way. We must keep in mind that the government's monopoly on censorship was not arbitrarily usurped from above – instead we are dealing with a press that was functionally created and sustained by the government from the start. This centuries-long tradition sheds some light on what made it so difficult for new media outlets to establish their financial independence during the 1990s.

Even European influences on Catherine the Great only reinforced this tendency. In 1769 the empress launched the magazine *Vsyakaya Vsyachina* (*This and That*), which was intended to directly mould public opinion. It did so – not just by dictating journalism ethics, but by sparking a whole slew of privately-launched imitations. It did, however, set its own standard for journalism ethics, namely one that would inspire journalists to praise the Russian government and society. G.V. Zhirkov calls the magazine the first attempt by the state to control information by means of an official press organ.[6]

Catherine issued a number of decrees that established systematic censorship by the government by means of the police. An important decree from 1777, for instance, set limits on the kind of books that could be printed in Russia in foreign languages. The decree of 1783, meanwhile, established the right to create private printing presses, but strengthened the role of the police as censors. A special directorate was established to monitor everything that was being printed, confiscated and eradicated anything that had violations in it and, most importantly, sent the violator to the courts. In this sense, Catherine both stimulated the emergence of private journalism and at the same time set enduring mechanisms of control. In 1796, fearing the influence of the French Revolution, Catherine issued one of her most famous decrees, formally establishing preliminary censorship by stipulating that all manuscripts issued by any printing press must first undergo screening by a censorship organ in one of the nation's capitals.

Thus, the organizational structure of Russia's censorship apparatus was complete by 1800. We should look at the establishment of this structure not only as a means of repression, but as a reflection of the way society functioned and saw itself. In many ways, Catherine's decrees only institutionalized what was already common law. In this context, the words of poet Alexander Pushkin, who was at one point exiled from the court of Czar Nicholas I for his writings, are revealing:

> Of course, if spoken word was not an attribute common to all mankind, but only to a millionth part of it, then the government would have to limit by law the rights of speaking people. But being literate is not a natural ability given by God to all mankind, like speech or vision. And, among the literate, not all possess the opportunity or the ability to write books or magazine articles ... Print is not accessible to everyone.[7]

Over the next century, Russian literature and journalism would be subjected to a pendulum of various degrees of liberal reform and reaction.

The reformer Czar Alexander I began his reign by eradicating the harsh policies of his father, Pavel I. In early 1801 he decreed that the 'sciences and the arts' be freed from police surveillance. Private printing presses were allowed once again, with each being obligated only to notify the authorities upon being established. Preliminary censorship carried out by government organs was abolished, and each institution was responsible for 'censoring' its printing presses itself.

This did not mean, however, that preliminary censorship was abolished. By laying censoring duties on its universities during the educational reforms that Alexander I pushed through in 1802, the state did not ease the censorship – it merely restructured the bureaucracy of the censorship apparatus. In this case, the Educational Directorate pushed for a legislative document that would regulate censorship as well as the powers, responsibilities and rights of censors. In one incident, one of the members of the body, Count N.N. Novosiltsev, proposed adopting a set of regulations based on a relatively liberal Danish law that stipulated for a series of fines and penal measures for publications that libelled against the state. His initiative was overturned by the Directorate, which argued against a document that did not stipulate any preliminary censorship at all. In the end, the body decided to continue with the type of preliminary censorship that was already being adopted by educational institutions, which Zhirkov calls 'more customary for Russian society'.[8] In the final censorship statute signed by Alexander I in 1804, censoring powers and duties were accorded to a committee of professors and university magistrates, headed by the Ministry of Public Enlightenment. Nothing could be published, distributed or sold without going through this censorship apparatus.

If Alexander's reign was characterized by initially liberal leanings that in the end utterly failed to materialize, the reign of the century's most repressive czar, Nicholas I, began with his suppression of the Decembrist Uprising of 1825. His later policies, particularly the creation of the notorious Third Section, or the secret police, in many ways came as measures undertaken in the wake of the investigation into the revolt itself. Because of the powers given to the secret police, the policies also led to the most repressive censorship apparatus Russia had ever known, while Nicholas, in the best of Russian tradition since Peter the Great, assumed the role of chief censor during an era celebrated later as Russia's 'golden age' of literature.

In 1828, Nicholas introduced a new censorship statute, which was much longer and more elaborate than the one adopted by his predecessor in 1804. Apart from detailing strict control of all the agencies involved, the document differed from the previous one in that it established the censor as a separate professional entity, a profession 'so important that it cannot be joined with any other'.[9] Zhirkov calls the statute progressive for its times, but notes that the various amendments and clauses that it acquired, as well as the fact that more and more agencies and institutions were given censoring powers, all introduced potential for abuse of power. Every ministry had its own censorship department, with only poetry left to the jurisdiction of the censorship committees proper. More significantly, Count Alexander Benkendorf, the notorious chief of Nicholas' secret police, began getting increasingly involved in dictating censorship policy. By 1845 Bekendorf had introduced a series of restrictive measures: state employees who contributed any sort of literary materials to newspapers and magazines could not do so without prior approval of their supervisors, and ministers were given censoring powers over everything printed that pertained to their particular ministry.

This latter circumstance was particularly insidious and remained widespread in the Soviet Union, if not in letter then certainly in practice. The fact that ministers acted as censors for centuries continues to impact journalism today, when reporters find it next to impossible to obtain information from a state agency. Following the end of the Soviet Union, several documented cases pointed to how unaware many bureaucrats were about the fact that they no longer had any leverage over what was printed about their agencies.

What would have the most impact on the letters of the era were the personal efforts Nicholas I took in censoring literature and journalism. In 1826, the emperor granted Alexander Pushkin a dubious favour by becoming the poet's personal censor. Pushkin's famous ode to Peter the Great, *The Bronze Horseman*, is personally edited by Benkendorf. Despite Pushkin's later comments in support of general censorship, he notes this in his diary with a degree of irony.

All this together leads to what has been called the 'censorship terror' between 1848 and 1855, sparked by the emperor's strong reaction to the revolutions sweeping Europe. It is an episode that was compared with the Putin administration's reaction to 'colour revolutions' across the former Soviet bloc in 2003–5.

Censorship in transformation

One of the more significant episodes in the history of Russian censorship was the struggle for press freedom between 1905 and 1907. Several factors made the reforms that followed some of the most extensive in Russia's history: the empire was rapidly industrializing, leading to the creation of a media system that included more effective printing means, radio and photography. Meanwhile, the regional press had developed at a rapid pace but, unlike publications in the capitals, Moscow and St Petersburg, regional papers underwent strict preliminary censorship by governors and bureaucrats. Finally, the Bloody Sunday of 1905, when peaceful demonstrators in St Petersburg were shot at by imperial guards, rallied journalists and editors to demand an overhaul of Russia's ageing censorship legislation.

In December 1904 a decree had already cancelled a number of the more restrictive regulations of this legislation and, more importantly, called for an assembly to pen a new press statute. The Kobeko Committee, named after public library director Dmitri Kobeko, who chaired the assembly, was established in January 1905. While the assembly did not succeed in issuing a new censorship statute, it served as a reflection of the processes that were taking place in the nation's press. Acting against a backdrop of increasing dissent among the press, it prompted the czar to complain to his interior minister of newspapers that had got completely out of hand. According to G.V. Zhirkov, despite a series of compromises on the part of the state, representatives of the press and publishing institutions rallied together in a collective attempt to print newspapers and magazines without censorship, helping each other in their struggle for free speech.[10]

These efforts led to a short-lived outburst of near-total press freedom. It was sparked by the state-issued Manifest of 17 October 1905 which 'grant[ed] the population irrevocable freedoms based on the inviolability of the individual, the freedom of conscience, the freedom of speech, assembly, and union'. So vast were the freedoms unfolding in the Manifest that the Chief Directorate for Press Affairs reacted by issuing a dubious memo stating that whatever the Manifest stipulated, all previous regulations regarding the censorship apparatus were still in force. This implemented a contradictory state of nominal freedom of speech, without eliminating the existing restrictions.

The burgeoning press, nevertheless, chose to interpret the Manifest to its own benefit, leading to a brief period when periodicals were printed without preliminary permission. This did not last long, however. On 24 November 1905 the czar issued the *Temporary Regulations*, a document that nominally abolished preliminary censorship for city periodicals while maintaining it for the regions. While the courts were now charged with determining responsibility for violations instead of censors, most other more autocratic regulations from the 1890 decree on censorship remained in place. Moreover, the bout of unbridled publication that month sparked a government clampdown in late November, leading to the closure of 370 publications and the arrest of 607 editors.

In the end, what started as a feeble attempt to reform and renew a repressive censorship apparatus first led to chaos and then to further repressive measures. Initiating the reforms, the government feared an avalanche that would do away with the entire institution of censorship. As a result, old repressive measures were simply replaced with new ones.

Developments such as these shed light not only on the roots of Russia's failure to build a free press, but underscore how the mechanisms of repression have remained very much the same. One of the central problems that rallied journalists to fight for press freedoms during the first Russian Revolution of 1905 was the catastrophic difference in the working conditions for regional journalists. Not only was the contemporary censorship apparatus outdated, it also did not provide for the fact that since its adoption Russia had witnessed a burgeoning regional press. If journalists and editors in Moscow and St Petersburg enjoyed practically no preliminary censorship, those in the provinces were censored by governors and bureaucrats at their own discretion. This meant that when journalists in the capital were censored, it was more often than not by a 'professional censor', while the actions of regional officials were too often dictated by nothing more than their personal tastes. Unfortunately, this reflects to some extent the current state of affairs in Russia, where regional officials will sue newspapers for what they perceive is an attack on the Party directive (the Party, in this case, being United Russia) without such a 'directive' actually existing on a centralized level.

Under these dubious conditions, with some successful efforts at emancipation on the one hand and restrictive legal measures on the other, the Russian media witnessed one of its most successful periods. The awareness of the need for a free press, together with the growing capital that came as a result of Russia's rapid, if belated, industrialization, provided both the impetus and the means for newspapers to flourish in ways they had never done before. But the role of big business in newspapers – particularly, in Russia's case, with its tendency to lean on the side of the state – in many ways foreshadowed many of the failures that would characterize the 1990s.

One of the crucial aspects of the processes that undermined Russian media freedom in the early twentieth century was that the surge of capital came too late and too fast. As Zhirkov notes, private capital emerged as a driver in the development of an information sphere. Its dynamic influence, however, meant that it began taking on the trappings of the state in 'penetrating and controlling' the journalistic sphere.[11]

This led to an unprecedented surge in private newspapers in the true sense of the word, including bulletins, tabloids and advertisements. Much like they would in the post-Soviet era, businessmen begin buying up newspapers that were unprofitable. Capital became involved in political parties and their periodicals, just as it did in the 1990s, in an effort to control and take advantage of it. Other entrepreneurs began to use newspapers for the first time as part of profitable holdings. Zhirkov cites the example of L. and E. Metzel and Co., which benefited from an affiliation of the Azov-Donskoy commercial bank. By 1914, the holding boasted an income of over 10 million rubles and was notorious for dictating both editorial and advertisement policy at the newspapers it controlled.

There are many aspects linking the financial situation of the early twentieth century with the one that emerged following the breakup of the Soviet Union. Zhirkov mentions how the surge of advertisements sought to undermine the ethics and independence of journalists, citing several contemporaries who bemoaned the negative role advertisers had on the newfound freedoms of the press. On the one hand, advertisers were no longer individual entrepreneurs but powerful commercial, industrial and financial organizations. Their size and might now meant that newspapers got at least 35–40 per cent of their income from advertising alone. This 'commercialization' was aptly bemoaned by a contemporary in 1904: 'The perversion of the press inevitably came to be from the fact that under the pretext of a struggle for spiritual values, due to its notices, it transformed into industrial and financial speculation'.[12]

There was another, even more fundamental tie that bound the press with the government: seeking to reward journalists for their loyalty, the Interior Ministry undertook the task of subsidizing the press, underlining the traditional role that law enforcement in Russia played as censor. By 1916, the ministry had a secret fund for these means that grossed up to 1.7 million rubles.[13]

Essentially, Russia was undergoing natural capitalistic processes that the media in the West had experienced more gradually in the past. With the surge of advertising and capital came the desire of advertisers and media moguls to take advantage of the press they controlled. The war and the Revolution, meanwhile, left them no time to gradually reconcile press freedom with financial sustainability. Instead, the Revolution ultimately and completely subverted the press to its own ends. What had once been a state of various degrees of autonomy turned into a permanent state of war censorship. We should not equate Soviet-style censorship – which, after all, officially did not exist – with ideological Bolshevism. As we can tell from the civil war period between 1917 and 1920, there were essentially two Russias for all purposes, including that of the press. Each side – the Bolsheviks and the White Guard – used their information apparatus brutally.

How seriously the White forces took their censorship task is illustrated by a decree issued by White Guard General F. Pul, 'in complete accordance with civilian authorities':

> Any individual in Arkhangelsk and nearby regions caught distribut-ing false news (capable of sparking fear or dissent among civilians or troops friendly to the allies) will be punished, in light of the siege, to the full extent of the law – in other words, with the death penalty.[14]

In November 1918 in Siberia, during the brief military dictatorship of Admiral Alexander Kolchak, chief of the White Guard, the information department of the chief of staff headquarters issued a decree that it was implementing preliminary censorship over all Russian territory (de facto, this decree was effective only in the Siberian territories that Kolchak controlled). The reactionary coup in November sparked a whole slew of newspapers bewailing the extent to which periodicals across the country were censored – papers literally came out with white, blank pages, others with holes right in the middle of the text.

The establishment of the Soviet censorship apparatus

While Bolshevik propaganda demonized the czar's secret police for its censoring function, the first thing the Bolsheviks did when they came to power was monopolize the press. The Soviet censorship apparatus that would be established in the coming years consisted of two nodes of control: the Communist Party, which dictated, through various agitprop departments, the general 'line' that all printed production had to take, and the Glavlit, an executive institution which de facto carried out the role of censor.

Much like towards the end of the twentieth century, at issue was a problem that was not as much ideological as it was financial. The war dealt a severe blow to the nation's paper industry. With major producers (Poland and Finland) gaining independence, by 1920 Russia produced just 6 per cent of the paper that it had used prior to the war. It was this problem that prompted Vladimir Lenin to launch a series of laws that would in effect monopolize the media. The first such decree, in November 1917, introduced a state monopoly on advertising. By next year the Petrograd Military-Revolutionary Committee shut down a whole series of newspapers, including *Birzhevye Vedomosti*, only to confiscate their printing presses. This led, gradually, to Bolshevik control of printing presses across the country and to the ultimate seizure of the telegraph agency in Petrograd, the radio telegraph and all radio stations in the capital. Government institutions charged with controlling these outlets were subsequently established. By 1920 the deteriorating state of the nation's paper industry led to the 'militarization' of another 16 major printing presses in Moscow, Petrograd and Nizhny Novgorod.

Much as in the days of glasnost and perestroika, this came against a backdrop of press freedom rhetoric. The year 1917 saw two revolutions. The February coup put the moderate provisional government in power, eventually headed by Prime Minister Alexander Kerensky. In October, the Bolsheviks took the majority in a coup led by Lenin. Between the revolutions, the press was in turmoil. In March 1917 the provisional government liquidated the Chief Committee for Press Affairs, the head-quarters of the imperialist censorship apparatus. This launched a legislative overhaul that officially declared freedom of expression and the press for the people's majority. Implementing the declaration was another matter, however.

As early as February 1917, a St Petersburg university professor recalled what he witnessed at an assembly of literary men who formed a new official revolutionary press committee:

> Who charged them with representing the press? I asked myself. Here they are, self-styled censors, clamouring for power in order to suppress anything that in their view is undesirable, preparing to strangle freedom of press and expression. Monarchist newspapers have already been banned and their printing presses confiscated. The socialists have agreed with this as an inevitable necessity. But how can this necessity be reconciled with freedom of the press, which they earlier so vehemently supported? As soon as the ambitions of the radicals are satisfied, they become more despotic than the reactionaries.[15]

Indeed, if the provisional government battled to shut down Bolshevik periodicals, then the Bolsheviks, once they came to power in October, did the same with 'counter-revolutionary' periodicals. Despite legislative press freedom, the Decree on the Press, issued immediately once the Bolsheviks came to power, was used to shut down some 470 oppositionist periodicals within six months.

And so despite a de jure state of free press, the latest abolition of censorship, coupled with the decree, led to another period of a press dictated by arbitrariness until the Soviet government began forging a censorship apparatus anew. One of the first attempts at such an apparatus was State Publishing (Gosizdat) which dictated all publishing activity between 1919 and 1921.

The decree on the creation of the Glavlit – the Central Directorate for Affairs of Literature and Publishing – in 1922 lay the cornerstone of the Soviet censorship establishment. Throughout the decade, Glavlit, framed by a series of discussions on the necessity of censorship and freedom of speech by such notables as the people's commissar for enlightenment, Alexander Lunacharky, would gradually establish itself as the central apparatus of censorship. The decade would see the Communist Party appropriating the function of chief censor, instrumentalizing Glavlit – and through it the press – solely for the means of spreading propaganda of the main party line.

We can draw many parallels between Soviet Russia of the 1920s and post-Soviet Russia of the 1990s and early 2000s. The Bolshevik Revolution – much like the breakup of the Soviet Union – created vacuums that would be filled with economic chaos. The years of NEP – the early Soviet experiment with liberal economic policy – spawned a whole raft of new, private periodicals, much like perestroika would 70 years later. It also spawned many dissenting voices. In this fermenting intellectual and economic environment, Lunacharsky, as chief censor, displayed a dubious attitude towards censorship. Unlike the atmosphere of doublethink that would reign in decades to come, the NEP years allowed for open discussion, and it was in this climate that Lunacharsky, as the head of Glavlit, would weigh censorship as both a gift that would protect against counter-revolutionary uprising and a 'necessary evil' at the same time. This dubious climate – with a burgeoning de facto free press on the one hand and the beginnings of official discussions on the necessity of censorship on the other – also reflects the kind of atmosphere Russia would witness during the late 1990s, when the abuse of oligarch-controlled media would lead to increased government control.

We can also draw another parallel, and this concerns the dangers of being a journalist in a quasi-democratic regime that is in a perpetual state of upheaval. We see that the term 'administrative pressure', so ubiquitous in Putin's Russia, was no novelty in 1923: 'The persecution of the workers of our press continues ... Comrade Iyevlev – a correspondent for a local newspaper – was slain by murderers. "Administrative pressure" on correspondents has become almost a normal phenomenon'.[16] Unexpected economic freedom, together with the 'administrative' arbitrariness that has been a feature of Russian life for centuries, in this case began to lay the groundwork for a Soviet law on media.

One of the cornerstones of Soviet censorship, however, was the fact that unlike censors before them, the Soviets faced the ideological conundrums of censorship head-on, and in many ways succeeded at least in presenting a compelling case for it. Vladimir Lenin, one of Russia's more underestimated censors, wrote at the time:

> Freedom of the press in Soviet Russia, surrounded by enemies around the world, is freedom of political organization for the bourgeoisie ... This is an undeniable fact. The bourgeoisie the world over is many times stronger than we are. To give it such a weapon as freedom of political organization (freedom of the press, since the press is the centre and the basis of political organization) means to facilitate the work of our enemy, to help the class enemy. But we don't want to end in suicide, and that is why we will not do it.[17]

We can easily discern how Lenin's logic can be successfully applied to the realities of the twenty-first century and the war on terrorism, a war that has been used to justify censorship in both Russia and the West. Lenin, of course, was not privy to the technological and informational nuances that made twenty-first century terrorism so pervasive and successful (the mesmerizing effect of live television and the internet), but he did understand, without any underestimation, the effectiveness of information as a political tool. Indeed, it was this logic that was applied when Russian legislators debated amending the law on the media following a spate of deadly terrorist attacks in 2002 and 2004.

After years of debate throughout the 1920s, official censorship in Russia was reinstated if not in word then in deed, and the Glavlit was established 'for all kinds of political, ideological, military and economic control of works intended for the press or distribution, manuscripts, photographs, pictures, etc.; and also of radio broadcasts, public lectures and exhibits'.[18] More importantly still, with Glavlit the Soviet government created a set of limits for 'free' speech, mechanisms of control that the real censors at Glavlit could incorporate for a number of uses. These were: 1) agitation against the Soviet government; 2) revealing state secrets; 3) inciting public unrest by disseminating false information; 4) inciting nationalist or religious fanaticism; and 5) disseminating material of a pornographic character. What is noteworthy is that these limitations are officially in place in today's media laws, although worded differently. The real mechanism of control here was the broad scope in which these limitations could be interpreted.

The other node of the Soviet censorship apparatus was the Central Committee of the Communist Party itself. A series of decrees empowered the Central Committee as an ideological overseer that 'coordinated' publishing activity across the country. In another sense, of course, the Central Committee controlled Glavlit by issuing directives for Glavlit, as the executive node, to carry out. The relative autonomy of Glavlit, however, spawned several instances of power struggles and ideological clashes.

Zhirkov points out an important nuance in this state of affairs that would characterize censorship in the Soviet Union: officially, there is no censorship, but there is control.[19] This would lay the basis for the doublethink that pervaded Soviet press politics between the reign of

Joseph Stalin and the appointment of Mikhail Gorbachev. Indeed, in 1927 Stalin would eloquently wave away allegations of lack of press freedoms in Russia:

> What kind of press freedom are you talking about? Press freedom for what class? For the bourgeoisie? We don't have it and we never will while there is the dictatorship of the proletariat. If you're talking about the proletariat, then I must say that you will not find another state in the world where such wide and multifaceted press freedom exists for the proletariat as the USSR.[20]

The Soviet censorship apparatus, characterized by the role of the Central Committee and, hence, by the powers of the general secretary of the Central Committee, would allow for various gradations of control: from Stalin's role as ultimate censor (to the point of composing history books himself) to the thaw under Nikita Khrushchev. To a large extent, this apparatus allowed for the taste of each general secretary to dictate the extent to which dissenting views could be represented in the media, as well as to mould the style of the printed press, the airbrushed picture magazines and, of course, the pre-edited nature of television.

What is important to keep in mind, however, is the extent to which this apparatus reflected a centuries-long legacy of mechanisms of control, and served as an inevitable blueprint for forging a new mechanism of state control over the media when such a necessity became apparent a decade after the breakup of the Soviet Union. Russian history follows a cyclical pattern and tends to repeat itself, something that is particularly evident in its press.

The dangers of reporting in post-Soviet Russia

Attacks on journalists under Yeltsin and Putin

The October 2006 murder of crusading journalist Anna Politkovskaya signalled a turning point in worldwide awareness of the grim state of Russia's press. As a reporter for *Novaya Gazeta*, her provocative, controversial coverage of the war in Chechnya, and particularly the dire human rights abuses committed by federal forces there, led both investigators and observers to seek out a Chechen link. Others pointed out that Chechnya's powerful president, Ramzan Kadyrov, could have been behind the murder – Politkovskaya had been investigating embezzlement of federal budget funds under Kadyrov.

Whatever the various theories surrounding the murder, in the international arena they crystallized into a simplistic picture fed to the western press: Politkovskaya was a virulent critic of the Putin regime, she was shot to death, therefore Putin must have played a role in her murder. To an extent, of course, we can and should blame the presidential administration for its failure to provide safe working conditions for the nation's journalists, as for its failure to solve dozens of cases of attacks on journalists. But by automatically laying the blame on the then president, we fail to understand the deeper and more significant origins of why it is so unsafe to work as a journalist in Russia.

Following Politkovskaya's murder, papers and news agencies around the world began to grow particularly vigilant to clusters of journalist deaths. After the suspicious suicide of *Kommersant* reporter Ivan Safronov in March 2007, London's *The Independent* published a recount of the 20 journalists killed since Putin came to power, echoing similar recounts in other papers of the supposedly worsening climate since 2000.[21] This paints a skewed picture of how dire the climate actually is, making it seem that prior to Putin's administration being a journalist was much safer. Nothing could be further from the truth.

According to a 2007 estimate by the Committee to Protect Journalists, 44 journalists have been killed in Russia since 1993. What is illustrative is that between 1993 and 1999, inclusively, 31 journalists where killed while on duty, while only 15 were killed on duty between 2000 and 2007. Granted, these years included the first Chechen military campaign and part of the second, both of which claimed the lives of a large number of Russian and foreign journalists. Four out of the six killed in Russia in 1996 were killed in Chechnya. In 1999, all three journalists died in Chechnya.

Another problem is attributing these attacks directly to the government. According to Andrew Jack, alcohol, money disputes and other issues unrelated to what the journalists wrote were behind many crimes, while the struggling state of media organizations often resulted in journalists getting caught in the corporate crossfire.[22] Indeed, one of the murkier aspects of the problem is determining whether the journalist 'on duty' was killed in connection with his work, or was the victim of random crime. Harder still is determining what actually constitutes the 'connection'. For instance, Yuri Soltis, a crime reporter for the Interfax news agency, was found beaten to death at a train station on the outskirts of Moscow. The link between his death and his work is testimonies from colleagues to the Committee to Protect Journalists (CPJ), according to which he was murdered in connection with his crime investigations. Among the list of journalists killed on duty according to CPJ in 1993 was Vladimir Drobyshev, who died of a heart attack while covering the siege of the Ostakino Television Centre, when pro-Yeltsin forces stormed the tower. One murky case is the February 2006 death of Ilya Zimin, an NTV reporter who made documentaries for the channel. He was found in his apartment, reportedly clubbed to death. While his murder was condemned by UNESCO, Russian media later reported that the prime suspect in his killing was a Moldovan immigrant whom Zimin met in a bar. In one version of events, Zimin took the young Moldovan to his apartment, where he made sexual passes at him.

In cases where it is fairly obvious that a journalist is attacked over what he wrote, what stands out is not the government's involvement, but its inaction. In November 2008, Mikhail Beketov, editor of the *Khimkin-*

skaya Pravda, a weekly district paper published in Moscow's Khimki suburb, was brutally attacked and beaten with steel rods and hospitalized with severe head injuries. Beketov had criticized local authorities for their deforestation plans, and had received death threats prior to the attack. Indeed, he continued receiving death threats even while doctors at Khimki's local hospital were amputating his leg, leading law enforcement to transfer him to a central hospital for his own safety.

While the case highlights how criminalized business overlaps with corrupt local authorities, it also shows the relative powerlessness of the central authorities. One official who came to Beketov's defence was Oleg Mitvol, the outspoken deputy head of the Federal Inspection Service for Natural Resources, a man who had faced his own share of smear campaigns, lawsuits and attacks simply because his position frequently forced him to interfere in the business and real estate interests of certain local authorities. This time, Mitvol asked President Dmitri Medvedev, who launched an anti-corruption campaign soon after being sworn in, in May 2008, to take the Beketov case under his personal control.

Undermining freedom through violence

The ambiguities of the circumstances under which so many journalists are killed make it difficult to view their deaths as an outright attack on free speech. Were their murderers deliberately trying to silence them, or did the journalists fall victim to factors of instability, crime and upheaval? The CPJ notes that seven of the eight journalists killed in 1993 died during the attack on parliament and the siege of Ostankino – while killed in their line of duty, they were literally caught in the crossfire. While this should not diminish the importance of their deaths to issues of security for journalists in Russia, we should be careful if we decide to qualify their deaths as an outright attack on free speech.

Another problem when lumping together journalist deaths is their relation to the government, if any. Because Anna Politkovskaya was a vocal critic of the Kremlin, it was too often assumed that the Kremlin played a part in her death. But no less significant was the murder of *Forbes* editor Paul Klebnikov in July 2004. Gunned down in Moscow by several unidentified assailants, Klebnikov had penned numerous controversial articles and several books, but he was not a critic of the Kremlin. Instead, he was more famous for his allegations against the oligarch Boris Berezovsky in a book titled *Godfather of the Kremlin: Boris Berezovsky and the Looting of Russia*. Previously, Klebnikov had alleged that Berezovsky was connected to Chechen organized crime groups. His murder, however, had followed the 2003 publication of yet another controversial book – *Conversations With a Barbarian*, based on a series of interviews with Chechen separatist leader Khozh Akhmed Nukhayev. Because of the accusatory nature of the book, and because it investigated the role of organized crime in Chechnya, investigators and observers linked Klebnikov's murder to his work on that book.

Far too many journalist deaths have gone unsolved in Russia, and Klebnikov's, unfortunately, is no exception. Russian authorities have repeatedly been accused (and perhaps rightly so) by the world community, by media watchdogs and by Klebnikov's family for failing to punish those responsible. But we can hardly say that Klebnikov's case is still open only because he was a journalist, in a country where far too many murders have gone unsolved. Klebnikov's trial reflects nationwide problems with the justice and law enforcement system. In May 2006, following a four-month trial, the Moscow City Court acquitted two prime suspects in the murder, Kazbek Dukuzov and Musa Vakhayev. According to the CPJ, 'authorities failed to guarantee the safety or impartiality of jurors after the proceedings'.[23]

The question inevitably arises: was that failure deliberate? If, in the case of Kremlin critics, such a failure might at least sound logical, it does not in the case of Paul Klebnikov. Another important factor that is usually not covered for lack of space is that the Klebnikov trial was one of the first to use a jury, a newly-introduced and much debated practice in Russia, where it has been criticized precisely for the propensity of jurors to acquit the suspects on trial. The failure of law enforcement to protect jurors and witnesses is indeed a serious problem for justice in Russia, but one that does not necessarily pertain to a government clampdown on free speech.

While it can be questioned that the murders described above were deliberate attacks on free speech, there is no doubt that they undermine free speech by creating an atmosphere of fear for reporters. They all point to the fact that there is an undeniable degree of danger in being a journalist in today's Russia, a danger that is much greater than in other developed countries. However, there is also an equally large degree of danger in being an entrepreneur or businessman in Russia, and for much of the same reasons.

Oleg Panfilov, director of the Centre for Journalism in Extreme Situations (CJES), a Moscow-based watchdog that monitors cases of harassment and attacks against journalism, concedes that safety for journalists in Russia is a separate issue from freedom of speech per se:

'Russia is not Colombia,' Panfilov said. 'They won't kill a journalist here for what they write.' Discounting the idea that exposure of official corruption can lead to death, Panfilov comments that 'the authorities don't read the newspapers about corruption. *The Moscow Times* wrote something alleging Putin's corruption once, and *The Moscow Times* is still open. No one was killed, and everything is fine.'[24]

While crime and unchecked corruption undermine media freedoms much as they undermine most anything else, there are still mechanisms by which the state can and does put pressure on the press. These important mechanisms should be examined separately.

Mechanisms of control in the age of the fr market

The state as censor in contemporary Russia

While Gorbachev de facto abolished censorship in 1990, legal mechanisms limiting freedom of speech continue to exist – and new ones continue to be introduced. While we can say, based on the above sources, that attacks against journalists have actually decreased under Putin, we can also say that instances where journalists and editors have been persecuted have *increased* since 2000.

In the previous chapter, we looked at how the failure of independent financial sustainability brought television channels and newspapers under the ownership of the government or state-affiliated corporations. We should be careful, however, to separate this factor from state-sanctioned censorship. Much as corporations influence the content of their media outlets across the world, so does the government, as owner of media outlets, dictate, to an extent, the content of the media outlets it owns. According to Oleg Panfilov in his report at a UNESCO-sponsored debate in London in May 2007, the president and government dominated news reports on state-owned channels, taking up some 93 per cent of airspace. The remaining 7 per cent was dedicated to sports and the weather. This situation does not reflect, however, the existing legal leverage that the government still has over the media.

If we speak of a government 'crackdown' on media freedom in Russia, we must note the legal instances when restrictive measures were actually adopted, and look at how the legal framework allows this to happen. To this end, it would be meaningful to examine excerpts from Russia's current media law.

To begin with, there is officially no censorship in Russia, as stipulated by Article 3:

> No provision shall be made for the censorship of mass information, that is, the demand made by officials, state organs, organizations, institutions or public associations that the editor's office of a mass medium shall get in advance agreement on a message and materials (except for the cases when the official is an auditor or interviewee) and also for the suppression of the dissemination of messages and materials and separate parts thereof. No provision shall be made for the creation and financing of organizations, institutions, organs or offices whose functions include the censorship of mass information.[25]

What this essentially means, as we have pointed out earlier in this chapter, is that there is no *preliminary* censorship: 'no provision shall be made ... for demands that ... shall get *in advance* agreement ... and also for the suppression of the dissemination'. But where posterior censorship – in other words, pressure on a publication after the fact, which can serve as source of intimidation for journalists – is concerned, legal prosecution is actually quite possible.

Article 4 states that:

> No provision shall be made for the use of mass media for purposes of committing criminally indictable deeds, divulging information making up a state secret or any other law-protective secret, the performance of extremist activities, and also for the spreading of broadcasts propagandizing pornography or the cult of violence and cruelty.[26]

In particular, 'extremist activities' comprises a wide scope of information that could be used to legally shut down a paper. But recent changes have further broadened the scope. In the latest instance, in summer 2006 President Vladimir Putin signed a bill into law that broadened the definition of extremism to include 'public slander directed towards officials fulfilling state duties of the Russian Federation'. Prior to this, Russia already reflected the situation described earlier in the first years of the twentieth century, when provincial bureaucrats persecuted local journalists and editors practically on a whim. In recent years, cases of arbitrary libel trials against journalists and editors have grown increasingly common; the latest law, observers have said, would only perpetuate this kind of arbitrary persecution.

Indeed, the new law followed numerous cases where it could have been invoked. One was that of Vladimir Rakhmankov, editor of the Kursiv website. In May 2006, following a presidential address which urged Russians to have more babies, Rakhmankov posted a satiric article titled 'Putin as Russia's Phallic Symbol'. The article joked that a sudden wave of fertility at the local zoo could be directly attributed to Putin taking on the role of the nation's fertility symbol. Local prosecutors immediately launched a criminal case, but based it on an already existing law in the penal code – insulting a representative of authority. Meanwhile, there were no reports that the presidential administration had complained or had even heard of the insulting article.

Police searched the editorial offices and Rakhmankov's apartment, confiscating several computers. Without any sort of court order, days later the site was shut down, with the URL showing a message from the provider that the site had been closed because of a failure to pay the fees. Rakhmankov, who had faced a fine and possibly a year-long sentence of hard labour, was fined in October.

But if Rakhmankov's satire was indeed directed at nothing less than the president, other editors had been persecuted for printing what could be termed insults to taste. In February 2007, in the wake of the worldwide controversy over the publication by a Danish newspaper of cartoons satirizing the Prophet Muhammad, the *Gorodskiye Vesti*, a Volgograd-based newspaper, published a harmless cartoon depicting Jesus, Muhammad and Buddha expressing their dismay over the violence committed in the name of religion. How the federal agency, Rosokhrankultura, inter-preted the cartoon as an insult to religious feelings remains a mystery, but the Federal Service for the Oversight of Mass Communications and the Protection of Cultural Heritage immediately launched a crackdown on the paper, effectively closing it by the end of the month. The same agency would also issue a warning to the widely-read Gazeta.ru online newspaper for reprinting the Danish cartoons that March. But other papers who had reprinted cartoons, especially smaller papers that operated in the regions, had to face much more than a warning. Pravda.ru, for instance, was closed down for a day and forced to remove the cartoons.

These cases represent some of the more outright examples of government-sanctioned posterior censorship. Others, particularly in the provinces, reflect more the chaotic state of corruption in local government. In June 2005, for instance, Nikolai Goshko, a Smolensk-based journalist, was handed down a one-year suspended sentence for libel. He was convicted of falsely accusing the regional administration of murdering the president of a local radio station, Sergei Novikov. But because Goshko had already been given a five-year suspended sentence for fraud in 1996, he was sent to a penal colony. Interestingly enough, Goshko had been involved in another trial in 2004. This time, he had to apologize for insulting a member of the currently outlawed National Bolshevik Party in one of his articles.

A higher-profile example was the persecution of *Permsky Obozrevatel*, an independent business weekly based in the city of Perm. The paper had been subjected to harassment since 2005 – distributors and printing presses had been refusing to work with it. In August 2006, some 20 Federal Security Service agents wearing camouflage uniforms raided the offices and confiscated computers and electronic equipment, as well as accounting records, claiming the paper was under investigation for divulging state secrets. After another raid, the paper's editor, Vladimir Korolev, was detained for disclosing similar secrets.

The case of *Forbes* magazine illustrates the leverage of government-connected business and the lack of independence in the court system. In December 2006, the Russian edition of *Forbes* magazine ran an article about Elena Baturina, head of the powerful Inteco company and the wife of Moscow Mayor Yuri Luzhkov. In the article, Forbes quoted Baturina as saying, 'As any investor, I am guaranteed protection'. But on its cover, the headline ran, 'Baturina: I am guaranteed protection'. Inteco sued *Forbes* on two grounds: defamation of the company in the article, and libel, for allegations made by editor Maxim Kashulinsky that Baturina had tried to stop the magazine from printing the article. Indeed, the Germany-based publisher Axel Springer Russia had tried to halt publica-tion of the article, but *Forbes*' US office insisted the Russian edition go ahead with the piece. In the winter of 2008, following a ruling in favour of Baturina, a Moscow court ruled once again that *Forbes* was guilty of defamation, and fined the magazine and the two authors of the article thousands of dollars each.

Very often, the consequences of a corrupt judicial system are confused with deliberate, centralized attempts to tamp down the press. Journalists do go to jail in Russia, but not as a direct result of the central government's efforts to silence them. Rather, business interests use their leverage with corrupt law enforcement and court officials to literally frame inconvenient reporters, or convict them on fabricated claims. Such is the case of Aigul Makhmutova, a 24-year-old editor of a Moscow district paper who went to jail for publishing evidence that a developer was taking over a playground against city regulations. Makhmutova's case is a perfect example of journalist partisanship (it was taken up by the state-launched, quasi-opposition 'Just Russia' party), but it also highlights just how difficult and dangerous grassroots reporting really is. According to the now-defunct *Moskovsky Korrespondent* newspaper (a publication owned by Moscow business tycoon Alexander Lebedev, who is a member of the Just Russia party), Makhmutova was framed by the very police whose corruption she was investigating. Her case, however, began as a much more mundane journalistic assignment.

At 22, Makhmutova was a correspondent for *Sudba Kuzminok*, a district newspaper that covered the southeastern Kuzminki region of Moscow. In 2006, she began covering protests against the building of a parking garage in a dense residential area, which would inevitably replace a playground with cars. Reporting for her articles, Makhmutova learned that the developer's rights to build on that land were not properly documented. Finally, she was able to get confirmation from City Hall authorities that the businessman was acting illegally. With her help – and the documents she was able to obtain from city officials – residents were able to hold off the construction, at least temporarily. But for Makhmutova, the repercussions of her reporting were more serious. In December 2006, she was under investigation for extortion. According to prosecutors, employees of the kiosk that she kept at a local outdoor market had allegedly threatened competing kiosks with arson and other violence. Makhmutova was detained by police, only to arrive at a local hospital the next day with documented head wounds and other trauma that doctors, according to *Moskovsky Komsomolets*, attributed to a case of the flu. In other words, she was reportedly beaten at a police precinct. A court found her guilty of attempting to extort the equivalent of about $200 and sentenced her to three years in prison.

While some of the details of her case could have been exaggerated by *Moskovsky Korrespondent* for political reasons, if we are to talk of journalistic security, then hers is perhaps the most typical example of the mechanisms by which journalists are harassed and otherwise kept from doing their duty. What is characteristic is that there was no top-down effort to silence Makhmutova; instead the influence of corrupt law enforcement and its leverage over district prosecutors and courts turned out to be so pervasive that a top-down effort on the part of City Hall to investigate was not worth its while. The journalist, after all, is not the only victim of corruption, nor, even, the most important, in the mind of officials at least.

The power of self-censorship

To a larger extent than the cases noted above, one of the stronger mechanisms of control in a Russia that has purportedly no preliminary censorship is self-censorship. Given the tradition of both forced and willing government deference – arising in part because the whole media system was traditionally a mere organ sustained and regulated by the government – it is no surprise that many journalists are either too mindful of a reaction from their bosses or the authorities, or themselves feel a necessity to follow a certain party directive.

Dmitri Bykov, a writer, journalist and TV anchor of the *Vremechko Show* (the title is a diminutive of Vremya – time – and, hence, a pun on the Soviet-era news programme) – an interactive programme covering social injustices and battles with communal authorities sent in by viewers – has said that he has never experienced government pressure: 'But I've always experienced very strong pressure from my bosses, who would always try to run in front of the government train. People are overly cautious without any basis in being so'.[27]

This reveals a deeply-embedded Soviet legacy. The typical Soviet newsroom had a professional censor on staff, but it was actually the editor (appointed by top government officials) who decided how far a story could go. In my own experience, self-censorship is compounded by the fact that the unspoken 'party directive' is never really spelled out – editorial policy in politics is vague in a country where no censorship officially exists, but the chance of an obliquely-worded reprimand after the fact remains. Editors sometimes urge reporters to 'sense' what is expected 'from above', pointing out that it is impossible to lay out any clear instruction on how to cover this or that story. The true policy is frequently shrouded in mystery so that it is impossible to predict how authorities will react to any particular article: a case in point is how *The New Times* reporter Natalia Morar was barred from Russia in the autumn of 2007 on order of the FSB after penning an article on corruption in the presidential administration and in the parliamentary election campaign. Similar articles in the otherwise loyal tabloids go unpunished, but Morar, a citizen of Moldova and a long-time Russian resident, was barred entry at the airport. On order of the FSB, her visa was revoked, and no explanation was given other than that she was a person who 'presented a threat to the Russian Federation'.

Towards a free press: the meaning of freedom

What is often overlooked when criticizing Russia's lack of media freedoms is the crisis of identification within Russian journalism. For a country that knew no press freedoms until 1990, emancipation from the government or the Communist Party was not enough. We have seen how the media's financial interdependence with the government from the start undermined its freedom. Many of the problems that plague journalists today arise not from censorship or lack of security, but from failures of purpose, identification and credibility.

At the roots of this failure lies a treatment of independence not as a means but as an end. After obtaining independence from the state in 1990, Russian journalists struggled to instrumentalize that independence, but these efforts were derailed by the media itself becoming an instrument in the hands of politicized capital. The struggle remained in an infantile stage – it became clear that independence in itself was not enough, that other motives were necessary, but these had not yet been articulated.[28]

Indeed, with a centuries-old legacy of the media as an organ of the state, it would be next to impossible to forge a new identity of the media as an independent entity, particularly in the information age, when a variety of new 'bosses' besides the government can influence editorial policy. As media scholar Elena Androunas pointed out in 1993, when there was still hope of a free and independent press in post-Soviet Russia,

> It appears that journalists, on the whole, do not see this problem. They confuse freedom from control by the communist nomenklatura with freedom itself. In the majority of cases, however, everything finishes up with a change of bosses: from the old boss of whom everyone is tired, to a new boss who seems liberal and understanding.[29]

Androunas' criticism of contemporary Russian journalists only reflects the historic, systematic status quo in Russia. But the failure to reconcile freedom with journalistic purpose, to forge a new journalistic ethic, also lies in Russian journalism's struggle towards a fourth estate, the journalist's traditional vision of himself as an 'engineer of human souls'. With their mission to convey the 'truth', Russian journalists have often neglected their task of informing the reader.

This failure also makes journalists far more vulnerable to state control. Lacking the resources to dig deeper beyond official reports, journalists often end up simply rewriting the government's version of events. I have written in the past of lack of a true reporting culture in Russia,[30] but these problems cannot be blamed on journalists alone. Journalists, including myself, are faced with the next to impossible task of asking questions as opposed to simply reprinting an official press release. As a result, constraints of time and especially resources make the latter far more ubiquitous, crowding out real reporting.

Failure to inform, when coupled with rampant corruption, has consistently undermined the journalist's credibility before the people. But it is also corruption – to a greater extent than a heavy-handed government clampdown – that has dealt the most severe blow to journalists' security. Writes Ivan Zassoursky:

> The phenomenon of corruption in journalism deserves separate treatment. In Russian publications, corruption is encountered in the most diverse forms, starting with a provincial review written to

order for a thousand dollars, and extending to reports of new discounts for cellular phone operators paid for through advertising departments. 'Black PR', or in the slang of Russian journalists, 'jeans', is a serious problem for any editorial office.

Nevertheless, articles written to order represent perhaps the least harmful type of bias in journalism. For anyone who dreamt of a free press, one of the unpleasant discoveries of the late 1990s was that journalists rarely formed and defended their own positions, but preferred to solidarize with the position of the owner of the publication. A characteristic of Soviet psychology was identification with the interests of the collective, the institution, the production unit, the enterprise, the party, the country, and so forth – that is, the very spirit of corporatism. Overall, the privileged position of journalists in the publications of the large politicized holding companies did a good deal to mould this feature of the Soviet, or to be more precise, corporatist mentality.[31]

Apart from undermining security, these conditions often made it impossible for the journalists themselves to identify adequately with their own profession. In other words, one of the biggest problems posed by corrupt journalistic practices was that the journalists themselves stopped believing in any possibility of a journalistic ethic. Western reporters like Andrew Jack, of *The Financial Times*, picked up on this cynicism from the start:

> Such was the cynical, mercantile atmosphere of the period that any critical article or broadcast was perceived as having been paid for. The reality was not always so simple. There was so much 'dirt' in circulation that it was perfectly possible for a good journalist to unearth true but scandalous materials in all honesty and objectivity.[32]

Vestiges of the atmosphere that Jack describes in the 1990s became so ingrained that even today allegations of journalistic corruption are still the most common and easiest means to put pressure on journalists. So frequent is their use, however, that the value of this currency has devalued – it is used in attempts to discredit journalists seeking information by both government officials and *other* journalists. Today, rare is the journalist who has never been accused of printing or broadcasting paid-for material. In my own experience, the varied sources of these allegations are illustrative.

Perhaps more sinister and obtrusive are times when these claims come from the authorities themselves in response to requests for information. While reporting for a piece on orphaned infants for *The Moscow News* in 2007, I had repeatedly attempted to obtain information from the Ministry of Health. Two weeks before scheduling to print the article, I had filed a formal request for comment by fax and was promised a response within days. Instead, a press officer contacted me nearly a month later (we had decided to postpone printing the article as we lacked commentary from the Ministry) and promised to look into the matter only once I had sent them the draft of my article. After reading the draft, the head of the press service contacted me by phone and said that she refused to comment on the issue because it was clear that my article was *zakaznaya* (paid for) and one-sided. When I pointed out that it was one-sided precisely because the Ministry of Health was refusing to comment, she agreed to a compromise: I could print my side of the story provided that I also printed their written commentary, uncut and unedited, side by side. Of course, the Ministry of Health press service could not force me *not* to print the article nor to cut the commentary they had sent us once we received it, and my editor and I indeed decided to print their comments, uncut, next to my piece. All too often, however, countless journalists, including myself, who have sought official sides of troublesome issues are rebuffed with 'How much money are you getting for this article?'

The problem of corruption in journalism is therefore not tied directly to a journalist's freedom in the sense that it does not endanger him personally. But this attitude – both the prevalence of paid-for materials and the suspicion that so much is paid for when it actually is not – undermines the credibility of what the journalist writes, especially for the masses. If in Soviet times it was mostly the dissidents who distrusted the press and learned to read between the lines, in today's Russia, journalists in general suffer from a poor reputation and the value of what is printed can be questioned arbitrarily.

While this situation does not directly endanger the freedom of the journalist, it does endanger and harm the freedom of the nation's press as a whole. When journalism as a profession is not trusted, the effect that investigative reporting can have on society is diminished precisely in its social function: it becomes little more than a condiment to celebrity tabloids. As one of the most independent newspapers in Russia – *Nezavisimaya Gazeta* – wrote in 1997, years before the Putin administration 'clamped down' on the media,

> The mass media have effectively lost their role as intermediaries between society and authorities and as catalysts of social change, while their ability to serve as a means for dialogue between social groups has been weakened significantly. Russian society has often come to perceive the media as a continuation of politics by the 'dirty means' of *kompromat*, as a tool for the squaring of accounts in the struggle between the powerful of the world, people who are indifferent to the everyday needs and cares of ordinary readers. An atmosphere has arisen in the mass media that does not reflect public interests at all, but only private interests, that are divorced from the real feelings, moods and preferences of the overwhelming majority of the country's population.[33]

Is there hope that the government can and will act on its promises to make the Russian press free? History has shown that state-led efforts to free the press are counterproductive, by definition. A free press is one that is established from the bottom up, not from the top down. That is why statements by President Dmitri Medvedev are promising but little else. In his first parliamentary address in November 2008, Medvedev repeatedly mentioned the need for the media to have more access to government officials, as well as the necessity of developing digital television to bolster the freedom and independence of Russia's press. Ironically, these statements were made just days before the Prosecutor's Office warned journalists in every medium about making careless statements regarding the financial crisis that had picked up momentum in Russia by that time.

This irony should not be taken as an example of a benign czar surrounded by corrupt, repressive officials. In fact, the signals coming out of the presidential administration and the Prosecutor's Office are part of the same phenomenon: a media subordinate to a paternalistic government. There is little doubt that Medvedev, a relatively young lawyer with a particular fondness for the internet, is sincere in his statements about the role of journalists in improving transparency in the government. But in order for journalists to actually gain more freedom, independence and leverage, the effort to 'free' them, as history has shown, must happen on all levels simultaneously, starting from the journalist himself. However liberal Medvedev may appear to be, this is hardly a task for one man, albeit one with an iPhone.

4 THE RUSSIAN NEWSPAPER, THEN AND NOW

- The origins of the Russian newspaper
- The failure of ideology: the origins of objective reporting and the case for *Kommersant*
- Propaganda as commodity: *Izvestia* – a source of information or a political pamphlet?
- The Russian tabloids: yellow journalism at its worst or the neglected fourth estate?
- *The Moscow News*

In December 2007, the management of *Moskovskie Novosti* announced that shareholders of United Media, a holding that snapped up the struggling paper in 2005, had decided to stop publishing it from 1 January 2008. *Moskovskie Novosti* is the Russian edition of the legendary 78-year-old English-language *The Moscow News*, and a newspaper in its own right with a 27-year legacy that had played a pivotal role during perestroika in helping tear down Soviet rule. 'We have respect for sociopolitical publications, but we don't see enough commercial benefit in continuing to develop *Moskovskie Novosti* under its current format,' general manager Daniil Kupsin then said in a press release.

The announcement – which had followed months of bickering between United Media management and the paper's editor, Vitaly Tretyakov – caused an uproar in media circles as the Union of Journalists rushed to the defence of the beleaguered weekly, calling the closure of such an important newspaper nothing short of a crime.

The outpouring of concern for the paper did nothing to save it, although United Media management had suggested plans to resurrect *Moskovskie Novosti* as a tabloid. All of this served to raise an important question about the state of Russian newspapers today: should they be profitable, or should they be meaningful? And why, indeed, can't they be both?

As the oldest medium and as a venue for the journalistic profession, the newspaper in Russia has illustrated with its history to what extent media and power have been irrevocably bound – and what happens when those bonds are broken, as they were in 1990. To understand the contradictions plaguing Russian newspapers today, we must delve into their historic origins where we can see that, to an extent, the same contradictions were present from the start.

The origins of the Russian newspaper

One of the prevalent dichotomies in the tradition of Russian journalism has been that of 'quality' newspapers versus 'mass-circulation' newspapers, intended 'for the masses'. As it exists today, this dichotomy plays into some of the inherent contradictions within a post-Soviet media that had first dubbed itself 'the fourth estate' and then increasingly succumbed to state control after failures to secure commercial independence.

Today, any true commercial independence of any newspaper is questionable. But as the dichotomy plays out, from the perspective of the elites, at least, it appears that newspapers that are identified as 'quality' tend to either verge on an oppositionist slant or at least allow for abundant criticism (*Nezavisimaya Gazeta*, *Novaya Gazeta* and, until recently, *Kommersant*), while mass circulation newspapers, identified as 'tabloids' tend to adhere towards a loyalist position (*Moskovsky Komsomolets* and the unabashed Kremlin favourite, *Komsomolskaya Pravda*). The leading 'serious' nationwide newspaper, *Izvestia*, waddles in between, increasingly on the receiving end of accusations of sensationalism and pandering to the government.

This is not always the case, however, since both *Moskovsky Komsomolets* and *Komsomolskaya Pravda* can be quite critical. Much more important is the social divide. Quality newspapers can be seen as writing for the 'elites' (something that *Kommersant* even boasts of) while mass circulation newspapers 'pander' to the malleable, uneducated and frequently disenfranchised masses. In that, they reflect a deeper division within Russian society that was manifested in Russian journalism as early as the nineteenth century: the *tolsty*, or 'thick' journal versus the 'boulevard' daily. The former focused on ideas and literary criticism, while the latter 'pandered' to the newly-literate masses with news on celebrities and crime. The problem was that, for reasons of censorship, neither succeeded in fostering a viable venue for political news or investigative journalism.

Official, literary and commercial print in imperial Russia

Journalism and mass media got off to a relatively late start in Russia, and when it did so was under the full auspices of the government, in this case, Emperor Peter the Great. Officially, *Vedomosti* (*The News*) is considered to be the first newspaper in Russia's history. Its first issue was published in December 1702.

The question of what constitutes the first newspaper, and what factors – be it a periodical nature, a mass audience or mass production – make it a mass medium is open to debate. In that sense, Russia has had several 'firsts'. The republic of Novgorod had its *letopisi*, a recount of events written on birch bark, as early as the eleventh century. The predecessor of

Vedomosti was *Kuranty*, which began to be released in 1621. Unlike the newsletters freely distributed among members of Europe's merchant class since Guttenberg invented the printing press in 1447, however, *Kuranty* was hand-written – hardly a 'mass medium' in the strict sense of the word. More importantly, the *Kuranty* manuscripts did not have a mass audience – this 'newsletter' was distributed as a closed memo among key government and Church officials, and contained political, military and economic news that was frequently taken from existing European newspapers. Indeed, its very distribution was shrouded in secrecy.

The first *printed* newspaper in Russia was *Vedomosti*. What is significant is that Russia's first newspaper was launched by the decree of Emperor Peter the Great on 16 December 1702, allowing us to credit Russia's emperor with founding the nation's journalism. The first issue did not survive to the present day, but the front page *lede* of the edition dated 2 January 1703 is, surprisingly, not too different from the front page of one of today's newspapers:

In Moscow at this time 400 copper cannons and howitzers and mortars have been cast. The cannons with cannonballs weighing 24 pounds, 52 pounds, and 12 pounds, and howitzer bombs of a pound and half a pound, mortars with nine-pound, two-pound and smaller bombs.[1]

Presented without a headline, this is the first surviving *lede*. Published two years after Russia's defeat at Narva in its war with Sweden, its painstaking documentation of weapons reflects a nation staked on rebuilding itself and showing its defensive potential.

The page goes on with other news from around Russia and the world. Correspondents from Persia write of an elephant sent to Russia as a gift. Another piece touts the discovery of oil in what is now Tatarstan: 'From Kazan they write, on the river Soka much oil has been found and copper ore, and from that ore much copper has been cast, and from that copper there is to be much profit for the State of Moscow'.

The first issues of *Vedomosti* usually comprised just 4 standard A4-sized pages, bound together as a little book. Sometimes it came out as an 8-pager, rarely with 16 pages. At times it was published as a single sheet that was supposed to be glued to walls and polls as a newssheet.

However modern-looking, *Vedomosti* was the first print medium in Russia at a time when Europeans had enjoyed at least a century of printed newspapers. Germany had manuscript newssheets as early as the late fifteenth century. By 1556, the Republic of Venice was publishing its notorious *Notizie Scritte*, whence the name 'gazette' was literally coined: the *Notizie* cost a small coin, called a 'gazetta'. By 1605, Germany was publishing one of the world's first modern newspapers, *Relation*, while France had its *Gazette* in 1631, already bent on reporting on the latest British royal scandal.

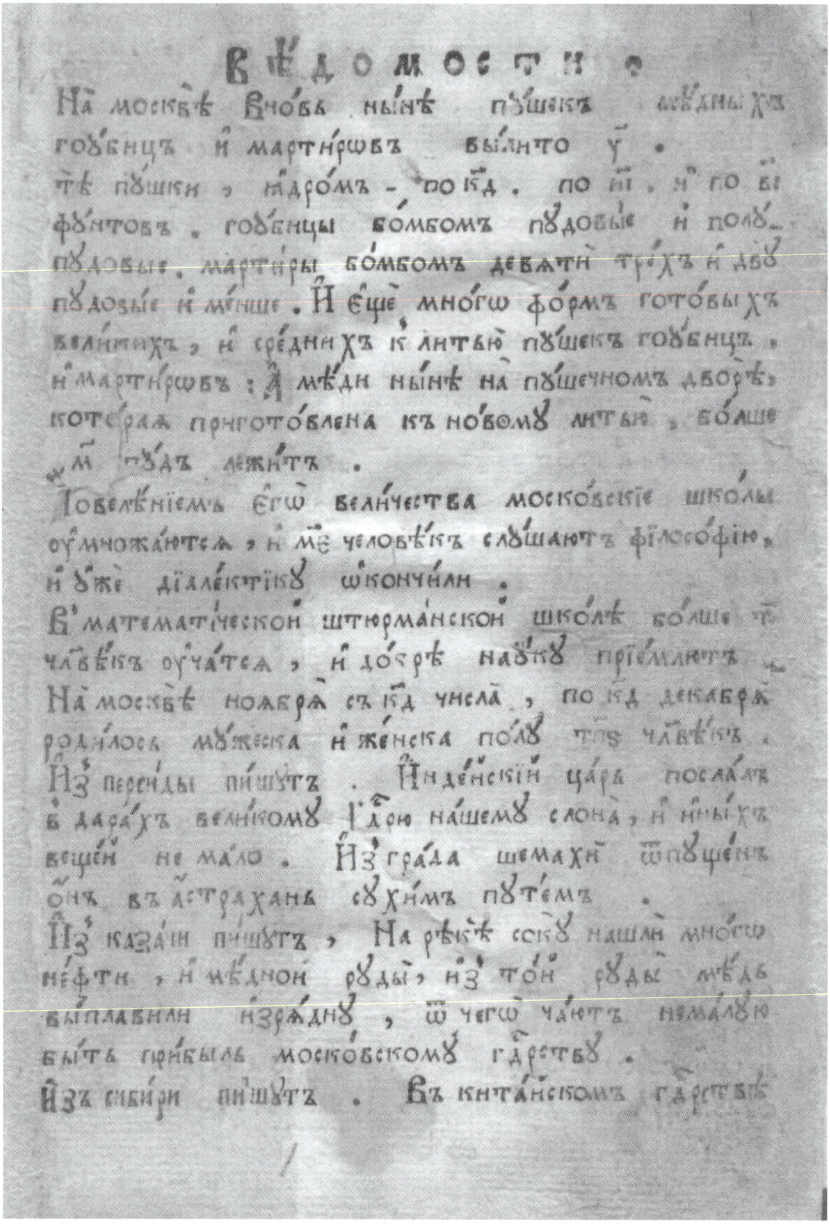

Вѣдомости.
На москвѣ вновь нынѣ пушекъ медныхъ
гоубицъ и мартировъ вылито у҃.
тѣ пушки ядромъ по к҃д. по и҃і. и по в҃і
фунтовъ. гоубицы бомбомъ пудовые и полу-
пудовые. мартиры бомбомъ девяти трехъ и дву
пудовые и менше. И еще много формъ готовыхъ
великихъ и среднихъ к литью пушекъ гоубицъ.
и мартировъ: А мѣди нынѣ на пушечномъ дворѣ,
которая приготовлена къ новому литью, болше
҂м҃ пудъ лежитъ.
Повелѣнием его величества московские школы
оумножаются, и м҃е человѣкъ слушаютъ философию,
и уже диалектику окончали.
В математической штюрманской школѣ болше т҃
человѣкъ оучатся, и добрѣ науку приемлютъ.
На москвѣ ноября съ к҃д числа, по к҃д декабря
родилось мужеска и женска полу т҃пѕ человѣкъ.
Из персиды пишутъ. Индейский царь послалъ
в дарахъ великому гдрю нашему слона, и иныхъ
вещей не мало. Изъ града шемахи отпущенъ
онъ въ астрахань сухимъ путемъ.
Изъ казани пишутъ, на рѣкѣ соку нашли много
нефти, и медной руды, изъ той руды медь
выплавили изрядну, отъ чего чаютъ немалую
быть прибыли московскому государству.
Изъ сибири пишутъ. Въ китайскомъ государствѣ

Figure 4.1 A page from *Vedomosti* from 2 January 1703

Why the lag in Russia? The simplistic explanation that the government would not 'allow' it should be discarded: all European papers in the

seventeenth century were subject to heavy censorship. They were, however, frequently published by private persons, even if local issues would
only begin to be covered by the end of the seventeenth century. In Russia,
meanwhile, there was no private initiative to launch a printed mass
medium until over two centuries after the invention of the printing press.
According to newspaper historian M. Kozlova, Russian journalism was
established 'from the top', and, as an element of state policy, was destined
for propaganda. Kozlova, meanwhile, attributes lack of private initiative
to a feudal society structure that did not have a need for a regular
exchange of information, apart from trade correspondents. As for the
academic community, it 'felt no need to publish its own magazine'.[2]

Because the origins of the first mass-produced paper in Russia were
fundamentally different from those in Europe, so was its purpose. This
inevitably impacted – and would continue to impact for centuries – its
content. While the differences between the *Vedomosti* of 1702 and, for
instance, the state-run *Rossiyskaya Gazeta* of today are quite obvious, we
can also glean a number of striking similarities, if not in news presentation, then certainly in the choice of news. Russian literary historian Boris
Yesin notes that 'despite the fact that it predominantly consisted of
information, the ideological level of the first Russian newspaper was quite
striking'.[3] This, he writes, is a direct result of the chief difference between
the first Russian paper and newspapers in other European countries:
Vedomosti was in no way a commercial publication. It was, in other
words, destined for propaganda precisely because it was not commercial.

To appreciate the inevitable bias of the government-run *Vedomosti*, we
must view it in the historical context of the day. Words like 'propaganda'
and 'censorship' ring with reactionary connotations, but in the case of
Peter the Great, they can be misleading. The despotism of the emperor
was directed at bringing about Eurocentric, modernizing reforms, and it
has since been a tragic feature of Russian history that radical reforms
were brought about by oppressive, undemocratic measures. By launching
a newspaper, Peter was inevitably aiming to bridge the gap between what
he saw as a backward nation without any civil society and modern
Europe. As we explore the future struggles of contemporary newspapers
to forge a lasting civil society in Russia it would help to remember this
precedent: Russian journalism, as well as many budding attempts at a
civil society, was all too frequently forged from the top down. In other
words, the government was usually the one initiating such reforms, thus
establishing a firm monopoly both on journalism and civil society.

The reasons for the government's monopoly on the development of the
printed press are debatable. We can arguably single out the relatively low
literacy rate, although these numbers are notoriously hard to gather. By
some estimates, in the late 1600s in Russia, the literacy rate among adult
city dwellers did not exceed 13 per cent, while among peasants it was just
2 to 4 per cent.[4] By comparison, in England the illiteracy rate for men in
the 1640s was 65 per cent – meaning that some 35 per cent of men were
literate.[5] But whether illiteracy in Russia was a cause or effect of the lack
of printed periodicals is up to debate. Indeed, we can attribute the

increase in literacy among Russians during the eighteenth century to the spread of periodicals. But it was not until the second half of the nineteenth century and the mass education campaigns of Emperor Alexander II that we would see any true surge of literacy rates among Russians. Given this history, it is all the more ironic that throughout the twentieth century, thanks to obligatory education instated by the Bolsheviks, Russia had one of the highest literacy rates in the world.

As to the fact that by the end of the seventeenth century Russia had no printed periodicals and a minuscule literacy rate, one can also argue that various economic and geographical factors made Russian society backward in its core and ready neither for a free, private newspaper nor for any semblance of civil society. But this is no trivial historic problem, and it would not do it justice to discuss it in the context of the history of journalism.

What we can see, however, is that the precedent of this top-down management of the nation's civil society had ramifications for the journalistic endeavours launched by private individuals in the later decades of the eighteenth century. Historians note that as of 1755 Russia had seen a number of short-lived journals and only two newspapers, both of which were official and predominantly focused on the emperor, the court and the government. The newspapers were *Vedomosti* and *Moskovskie Vedomosti*, the other government-run publication, launched in 1755 on the initiative of Mikhail Lomonosov, the founder of Russia's first university. Russia would see its first privately run, albeit short-lived, periodical as late as 1759.

That year, the poet and playwright Alexander Sumarokov launched *Trudolyubivaya Pchela* (*The Hardworking Bee*) as a private entrepreneur publishing a periodical with a 1200 circulation and no initiative or funds from the government. Its title was intended to reflect its multifaceted content, where readers could gather all the information they might need. But it was shut down only months later because of its critical stance on the corruption under the government of Empress Elizabeth.[6]

We can, however, single out *The Hardworking Bee* as the first privately-run periodical in Russia, and like the two official newspapers of the day, it would set the stage for the types of periodicals that Russian journalism would have. At this stage, any news was the domain of officially-run newspapers. As a private periodical, *The Hardworking Bee* took advantage of the only format that would allow for any sort of criticism – that of a literary publication. It is important to note that until the invention of the telegraph the concept of news as an aspect of mass media was infinitely vaguer than the one we adhere to today. In Russia, up until the appearance of *Vedomosti* as a mass-produced source of information, this was even more so. That somewhat explains the fact that *The Hardworking Bee* was not so much focused on information as it was on criticism – and the only plausible venue for criticism among the intellectuals of the age was the literary one. Of course, another factor was the low literacy rate, which meant that those who published or wrote periodicals were inevitably men of letters, perhaps even more so than in

Europe. The more notorious periodicals of the day – satirical journals like *Drug Chestnykh Liudei* (*Friend of Honest People*), published by the writer and playwright Dmitri Fonvizin, and Ivan Krylov's *Obozrevatel* (*The Viewer*) were all literary journals with a biting, satirical slant. Their creators, as primarily literary figures, used literary criticism as a pretext for social commentary. News and information exchange in the stricter sense did not allow for that kind of freedom of thought at the time in Russia.

By the end of the eighteenth century, there was a curious state of affairs in Russia. In terms of mass-produced sources of information, there were only two newspapers, and both of them were state run. There were dozens of printed periodicals, but these were published by and for a very narrow circle of literary figures. In effect, this meant that beyond *Vedomosti* and *Moskovskiye Vedomosti*, periodical literature in Russia was but an appendage – albeit a very significant and often driving one – to the world of literature in the sense that it was accessible to only an educated few, an elite brought up and educated in a certain way.

It was the poet and writer Nikolai Karamzin who effectively introduced political news as a genre in his famous magazine, *Vestnik Yevropy*, (*Herald of Europe*) which began publication in 1802. A political conservative, Karamzin was publishing his *Vestnik* during the Napoleonic wars; hence the heavy emphasis on politics and international affairs. But his audience remained limited to the aristocracy.

The first more or less popular magazine would appear only in the late 1820s – this was *Moskovsky Telegraf*, published by Nikolai Polevoi, who, as Yesin notes, understood that the new, educated reader was interested as much in politics, trade and housekeeping as he was in literature. Polevoi, therefore, was prepared to reach out to readers by catering to their 'low tastes' without giving up his role as an educator.

Russia's first privately-owned daily newspaper was the *Severnaya Pchela* (*Northern Bee*), which started coming out on a daily basis in 1838. As such, it was stringently loyal and patriotic, strictly adhering to the ideological triumvirate of Nicholas I's reign: autocracy, orthodoxy and nationality. And while daily newspapers (usually with the word *vedomosti* in their names) were published by various state agencies in the early nineteenth century, the *Northern Bee* was the first private, daily paper with a relatively high circulation – even before becoming a daily, by the end of the 1820s it was selling 2500 copies, which was considerable for its time.[7] Before becoming a daily in 1838, it published the poetry of Alexander Pushkin, Ivan Krylov and Alexander Griboyedov. Nevertheless, its sections – 'New books', 'Letters', 'All sorts of things', 'Mores' and a section on the theatre identified it more as a literary publication rather than a source of news.[8] Interestingly, the *Northern Bee* had earned a reputation as an organ of Nicholas I's secret police. The chief of the Third Section, Count Alexander Benkendorf, self-admittedly used the *Bee*'s publisher, Faddei Bulgarin, who frequently wrote in the paper, to disseminate and comment on political news to the liking of the regime.

All things considered, the fact that Russians would see little resembling investigative journalism until well after the establishment of Soviet rule – and perhaps not until perestroika – is easily explained when one considers the level of preliminary censorship involved in the country's journalism. With the establishment of the censorship apparatus in letter and spirit by the beginning of the nineteenth century (prior to that control came more directly from the emperor), a vast network of state-run agencies would issue permission to publish any sort of information on anything relegated by the state. It is no wonder, then, that by the middle of the nineteenth century the journalistic scene resembled a closed literary club where the best pens of the age discussed each other's ideas. In a tightly censored environment, there was hardly space for information exchange. Instead, there was a vigorous exchange of didactic thinking.

An essay by the writer Nikolai Chernyshevsky – most famous for his novel *What is to be Done?* and later lauded by the Bolsheviks for his progressive ideas – offers a typical and illustrative example of what could be expected from the more notable periodicals of the day:

> Among new periodical publications that were supposed to appear at the beginning of this year, three were awaited with special anticipation: *Russkaya Rech, Vek*, and *Vremya. Vek* and *Russkaya Rech* are weekly newspapers …
>
> But concerning *Vremya* we can already say that this publication deserves the attention of the public. The thick book of the magazine, which comes out once a month, offers so much material that one issue is enough to determine its direction … *Vremya* holds as its chief virtue to be its independence from the literary clique, which gives it space to directly and pointedly speak its opinion on other periodical publications and their writers which other magazines might fear to speak of. It cannot go unstated that all of the old magazines with a good reputation have indeed established close relations with this or that writer. Thus, the new magazine is not mistaken to ascribe to itself this advantage.[9]

It seems, then, that one of the defining moments of Russian journalism as late as the mid-nineteenth century is the literary figure. Therefore, the history of Russian journalism is really a history of literary journals, while mass circulation newspapers could easily be set aside in a separate category. Indeed, by the mid-1800s the literary-social monthly journal came to be defined as the 'leading' publication of the press system of the day.

Among leading journals were the democratic *Sovremennik* (*The Contemporary*), edited by Nikolai Nekrasov, and the revolutionary *Russkoye Slovo* (*Russian Word*), which, since 1860, was edited by Grigory Blagosvetlov. The writer Fyodor Dostoyevsky edited *Vremya* (*The Times*), where he published several of his works as well as a number of critical essays. The irony, however, is that while political views that were discussed in such journals indeed directly impacted the political developments of the day – notably the liberal reforms of Emperor Alexander II – those journals' 'high social standing' meant that they continued to cater exclusively to the elite. By the end of the nineteenth century, meanwhile, literacy rates, estimated to be about 40 per cent, provided for a social strata that expanded far beyond the elite. Nevertheless, the commercial daily newspapers and penny gazettes that burgeoned as Russia was making its first industrial leaps get only passing mention in most Russian journalism textbooks. Their short-lived legacy – and the occasional contempt they elicited from the purveyors of the agenda-setting 'thick journals' – would foreshadow the troubles that commercial newspapers would grapple with in the 1990s. Their ultimate shortcomings were both an underlying cause and simultaneously a result of lack of civil society and any democratic basis in Russian culture.

Two developments, closely related, would make commercial press possible in Russia, decades after underlying conditions in the USA, England and France would provide for a gradual, grassroots sprouting of commercially-sustained dailies. The first development was the Great Reforms instituted by Emperor Alexander II, most notably his statute on easing censorship in 1865. The second involved developments in lifting restrictions on advertising in private periodicals.

If the *Northern Bee* was the first private daily newspaper – notwithstanding its status as a de facto organ of Nicholas I's regime – then it was Andrei Krayevsky who laid the foundations for the commercial press with his first independent commercial daily, *Golos* (*Voice*) in 1863. Of course, despite the relatively liberal times, this was only possible after Krayevsky got special permission from the government to publish. Foreshadowing Vitaly Tretyakov, who launched his legendary *Nezavisimaya Gazeta* in the early 1990s, Krayevsky laid out the first quasi-objectivist mission that Russian journalists had ever known:

> What a responsibility lies on the newspaper, charged with acquainting the public with contemporary social questions, and working with that public to solve them. The obligation of a newspaper is to speak honestly, to serve truth and action, and not people, parties, or reigning theories.[10]

In places like the USA, where lack of censorship, a solid commercial base and somewhat higher literacy rates were already embedded in the local journalistic tradition, this sort of debut came about more naturally. However, in Russia, where the press had hitherto been the domain of the government on the one hand and a politicized intelligentsia on the other, Krayevsky's approach was hardly welcomed by his peers. Primarily, this was because Krayevsky opted to inform rather than to criticize. This went against the culture that the intelligentsia had fostered (and which continues to hold strong even today) – a defining characteristic of this 'elite club' was, first and foremost, one's opposition to the state. American scholar Louise McReynolds highlights Krayevsky's unwillingness to criticize the government as the chief source of annoyance with the intelligentsia:

By stressing information over opinion, Kraevskii [*sic*] hoped readers of differing sentiments would read his paper. This intent contributed to the intelligentsia's impression of him as 'unprincipled' because in his bid for circulation he was relinquishing his responsibility, as they saw it, to take a stance against the government. As his man in Italy, reporting on Garibaldi's fight for unification, ruefully noted: 'If my responsibility as a correspondent permitted me to venture into my personal predictions about the future, I would be able to tell you something about the ministry here. But only information about what is happening here is required of me.'[11]

Despite a changing attitude during the 1990s, even among newspapers that prided themselves on their objectivity and independence, this pervasive credo of the Russian intelligentsia – bolstered by the cause of dissidence during the Soviet period – prevailed. From the perspective of Russia's fourth estate, it can be argued that the commercially independent newspaper was bound to fail even in post-Soviet Russia – either by failing to sustain itself commercially, or by failing to 'take a stance against the government'. Indeed, McReynolds writes that not only were commercial newspapers looked down upon during their own time, they were often ignored by historians who were more interested in 'the liberals' dejection':

> Those who recorded the events of the 1880s by and large distorted the past by omitting the growth of the mass-circulation daily because they themselves, the learned elite, fought and lost a battle for influence among a critically important segment of Russian readers. Writing in exile after 1917, for example, pre-revolutionary historian Venedikt Miakotin entitled his section on post-assassination journalism 'The Impotence of the Press'. The historian pitied the disconsolate intelligentsia, not the vast majority of newspaper readers.[12]

The tragic assassination of Alexander II in 1880 put an obvious end to his reforms, so the 'dejection' of the intellectual elite that McReynolds talks of comes as no surprise. But Russia's journalism history does indeed overlook the era of sensationalism in commercial newspapers that Alexander's reforms appeared to herald. And with sensationalism, the reporter was born.

One of the notorious local tabloids of the day was *Moskovsky Listok* (*Moscow Sheet*), run by Nikolai Pastukhov. Using the arrival of actress Sarah Bernhardt as a news launch-pad, Pastukhov began publishing a newspaper that, in McReynolds' words, was 'intended for those most likely to purchase candies wrapped in her portrait'. If political reforms helped foster an industry for commercial newspapers, then celebrity sensationalism coupled with the buying power of an emerging middle class fuelled Russian newspaper reporting.

Pastukhov, as publisher, epitomized the 'scoop' reporter for his own paper. But he also contributed local news to Russia's leading politicized newspapers, *Moskovskie Vedomosti* and *Russkie Vedomosti*. It was one step away from sensationalist fare to using his reporting for political commentary. In his newspaper, Pastukhov covered everything from the problem of highwaymen to the failures of local politicians to provide citizenry with clean water and street lights.

By the 1890s, the status of the commercial daily was well established as the number of publications surged. Coinciding with increasing buying power in a burgeoning middle class, the professional reporting that began appearing in Russian periodicals was shaped to a large extent by the increasing needs of this middle class. News was becoming a commodity that consumers were willing to pay for, thus fashioning the periodical landscape as much as allowing it to fashion them as a class. In much the same way, perestroika would see the appearance of newspapers that would also reintroduce the treatment of news as a commodity.

To an extent, the commercial newspaper towards the end of the nineteenth century in Russia came to reflect much of the same processes that were occurring in western journalism. But in Russia even reporting was taking on its own, inherently Russian flavour, exhibiting saplings of a unique journalistic tradition. 'A significant portion of the reporters' story consists of how they tried to harmonize the potentially contradictory notions of commercialism and public service', writes McReynolds. She goes on:

> Russians, like their Western counterparts, hoped to circumvent possible conflict by organizing their occupation on a professional basis. Russia's reporters drew from the legacy of the importance of the writer to society that they had inherited from the intelligentsia. If on the one hand newspaper journalists wanted the respect and occupational controls associated with professionalization, on the other they wanted the prestige enjoyed by the generations of intellectuals whom many reporters revered.[13]

Private capital and the commoditization of news on the one hand, and the traditional partisanship of periodicals on the other, helped form a print media sphere that, during the first two decades of the twentieth century, began to resemble a relatively balanced newspaper market. A slew of national newspapers were both commercial and partisan in the European sense of the word. The most widely-read newspaper at the time was *Russkoye Slovo* (*Russian Word*), launched in 1895 as an official, pro-state publication that was at one point supported by the royal family (It should not be confused with the 1860's journal of the same name).[14] In a testament to the commercialization of periodicals at the time, the news-paper was purchased in 1897 by the famous publisher, Ivan Sytin, who turned the paper around, transforming it into a profitable, liberal national newspaper. In the course of its lifetime, the paper gradually slanted towards the left, repeatedly drawing the attention of censors.

This period also saw the emergence and growth of a precursor to a modern-day business daily, the *Birzhevye Vedomosti* (*Market News*).

Founded in 1861, it gained renown only in 1880, once it was bought by Stanislav Propper, a publisher and an Austrian national. It got off to a tough start, but after 1893, when Prime Minister Sergei Witte gave Propper special permission to publish the paper (with an eye on government interests such as battling the wine monopoly), circulation shot up to 8000 copies. Its niche as a business paper, however, did not make it any more 'objective' or non-partisan than any other paper. From the start, Propper exhibited a liberal slant. Then, in 1905, the paper changed its name to *Svobodny Narod* (*Free People*) and began coming out as a 'political and literary newspaper'.[15]

The two revolutions of 1917 that finally propelled the Bolsheviks to power would result in the closure of most of the country's non-party newspapers, even those that supported the new regime. Besides *Russkoye Slovo* and *Birzhevye Vedomosti*, these were moderate commercial papers like *Vremya*, *Utro Rossii* and *Den* – all were shut down with little regard to their political views.

The communist years: what soviet rule contributed and took away from Russian journalism

It would be much too simple to brush away the 70 years of communist rule as a dictatorial wasteland where the newspaper was concerned. The traditional view of Russian media from the West – both current and historic – paints a picture of an authoritarian state stifling independent voices, but as we have already seen through a brief history of the Russian press, this was clearly not the case: not because independent voices were not stifled, but because the 'independent' voices themselves were too often initially a product of the state.

Likewise, it could be said that the establishment of communist rule in 1917, the Civil War and the Red Terror put an end to the 'saplings' of commercial, independent journalism that McReynolds described, replacing them with the didactic declamation that was characteristic of a media subverted for use as a propaganda machine. To an extent this is true, but it is certainly not the whole picture of a much more nuanced, and often contradictory system.

First of all, we should examine what exactly subverted Russian media for use as a propaganda machine. Fortunately, we need not go far – the idea of the media as a social engineer (not far from Stalin's subsequent idea of the writer as an 'engineer of the soul') lies with Vladimir Lenin, in his 1905 article, 'Party organization and party literature':

> Today literature, even that published 'legally', can be nine-tenths party literature. It must become party literature. In contradistinction to bourgeois customs, to the profit-making, commercialized bourgeois press, to bourgeois literary careerism and individualism, 'aris-

tocratic anarchism' and drive for profit, the socialist proletariat *put forward the principle of *party literature*, must develop this principle and put it into practice as fully and completely as possible.

What is this principle of party literature? It is not simply that, for the socialist proletariat, literature cannot be a means of enriching individuals or groups: it cannot, in fact, be an individual undertaking, independent of the common cause of the proletariat. Down with non-partisan writers! Down with literary supermen! Literature must become *part* of the common cause of the proletariat, 'a cog and a screw' of one single great Social-Democratic mechanism set in motion by the entire politically-conscious vanguard of the entire working class. Literature must become a component of organized, planned and integrated Social-Democratic Party work.

Newspapers must become the organs of the various party organizations, and their writers must by all means become members of these organizations. Publishing and distributing centres, bookshops and reading-rooms, libraries and similar establishments – must all be under party control. The organized socialist proletariat must keep an eye on all this work, supervise it in its entirety, and, from beginning to end, without any exception, infuse into it the life-stream of the living proletarian cause, thereby cutting the ground from under the old, semi-Oblomov, semi-shopkeeper Russian principle: the writer does the writing, the reader does the reading.[16]

These excerpts lay the foundations of Soviet media policy, indeed they define the way that the Party would view newspapers and television for the next 85 years. But it would be wise to note the inherent paradoxes in Lenin's prescription. 'Down with non-partisan writers!' sits next to 'Down with literary supermen!' The 'literary supermen' that Lenin refers to were in fact possible, as we have seen, in the thick journals that concerned themselves with essays and ideas. For one thing, we have seen how didacticism was a feature of journalism, particularly in the thick literary journals of the intelligentsia – usually the very 'independent voices' that were 'stifled'. As venues for polemic, their star writers were anything if not 'partisan' – though not exactly in the sense that Lenin had in mind. Most importantly, however, these excerpts show that while Lenin sought to break from Russia's 'bourgeois' tradition, he was in fact perpetuating some of its more fundamental elements – and one of these, indeed, was the literary superman. As we shall see later, Soviet journalism was full of them.

Another important aspect is that Soviet didacticism had exceptions that served as a continuum in the development of Russian news. To understand this, we need to realize that the Soviet propaganda machine had other objectives besides proclaiming communism and serving as the mouthpiece of the proletariat. Much like in other times, one important objective of Russian state-run media was modernization.

To that end, we should not completely dismiss the influence that international news agencies had on Russian and Soviet news presentation. In their efforts to modernize professionally, Russian journalists would often look to the West, and the early Soviet period was no exception. Scholars note, although from various perspectives, that foreign news agencies did much to impact Russian news presentation both before and after the Revolution.

The years of the New Economic Policy (NEP, 1921–8), when Lenin's government decided to introduce some elements of free market to keep the economy from collapsing, served as a notable exception. A semi-free media allowed some elements of objective reporting as journalists grappled with a new identity both as reporters and social engineers. In 1922, for instance, private newspapers made up to 20 per cent of circulation. It was a time when editors sought new standards of professionalism on the one hand while adhering to their mission as teachers or, to put it less politely, demagogues. Finnish media scholar Jukka Pietlainen points to these western influences in his study on regional newspapers: 'The Soviet editors knew that their newspapers were boring, but they were not supposed to resort to "sensationalism". Therefore, they took their example from Western models of the mass press like Lord Northcliffe's *The Daily Mail*'.[17] The solution was wedding western standards of communication – albeit in terms of 'bourgeois ideology' – with 'correct' explanations provided by Soviet journalists. To the Soviet journalist-demagogue, facts were important, but they needed a lot of explaining.

These various, often contradictory elements would lead to the typical newspaper style of the 1930s, the one we conjure up when we think of Soviet journalism. Thus, it was not just Lenin's 'social engineer' that informed the style that would define Soviet and post-Soviet journalism – it was a whole slew of factors, from attempts to imitate western-style objective reporting, to elements of sensationalism, to the didactic polemic that characterized the thick journals of the first half of the nineteenth century.

Before it crystallized into the easily-recognizable style that we know today, Russo-Soviet journalism spawned something different. The combination of a literary tradition with the need to report on the Civil War and educate the masses ironically gave rise to a style that we would recognize today as very similar to 'new journalism', or the sometimes fictionalized account of a reporter immersed in his environment. The genre was the *ocherk*. Literally, the word translates into 'sketch', and connotes a kind of writing that falls somewhere in between the essay and the feature article, aiming to show detail and summarize some aspect of life while offering commentary that would draw the reader deeper into the essence of the situation.

Here, L.M. Reisner writes in *Izvestia* in 1918 of the horrors of war and the fate of Red Army soldiers who fought in Tatarstan:

The night bells beating the time on board the torpedo boat are surprisingly similar to the clock on the Petropavlovsk Fortress. But, instead of the Neva ... the ringing spreads over the vast banks and the clear waters of the Kama River, and little islands of forgotten villages ... The wives and children of the dead do not run for the border, do not write memoirs of their burnt-down ancient estate with its Rembrandts and libraries ... No one will ever know, no one will ever sound out over all of sensitive Europe about the thousands of soldiers shot dead on the high Kama bank, buried by the current in the sludge of the river.[18]

The mix of descriptive narrative and exhortation, while quintessentially both Soviet and Russian, was a far cry from the declamations that would appear in the same newspaper – taken from the TASS wire service – just 12 years later:

> PARIS, 3 December (TASS) – In wake of the trial of counter-revolutionary saboteurs in all of France an impetuous wave of solidarity has risen among French proletarians with the workers of the Soviet Union. In Paris an assembly of 3,000 shovelmen, members of a labour union, has sent a greeting to Soviet workers.[19]

Examples from early Soviet journalism would already foreshadow what would be a feature of the best and the worst. The first thaw of the late 1950s and early 1960s would see some of the best-acclaimed Soviet journalism. *Izvestia*, under the editorship of Alexei Adjubei (1959–64), would witness a flowering that would propel the newspaper's readership nationwide. Part of its success as an alternative to *Pravda* came from the fact that it was controlled by the Central Executive Committee of the Supreme Soviet, or the Soviet government, as opposed to the Communist Party, which de facto controlled the country. *Pravda*, meanwhile, was the mouthpiece of the Communist Party. At the heart of *Izvestia*'s flowering, however, was not so much news reporting as understood in the West, but an enhancement of the *ocherk* genre. Adjubei was not only an ambitious journalist, he was also the son-in-law of General Secretary Nikita Khrushchev. In the arcane system of Soviet nepotism, this position granted Adjubei a certain amount of editorial immunity. But this relative freedom to print more than was allowed in *Pravda* did not mean critical exposés and inconvenient news stories. Much as criticism seeped into some of the more independent journals of the nineteenth century, the key to quality Soviet journalism was not the *what*, but the *how*. Soviet readers were being conditioned to read between the lines not because they tried to gather – in the manner of western Sovietologists looking at Politburo photographs – 'the truth' in between the lines of official reports; they were reading between the lines of literary prose. Indeed, unlike western-style investigative reporting, the *ocherk* genre was deeply individual, making writers something more than columnists and less than novelists. Such was the case, for instance, with the legendary writer Anatoly Agranovsky.

The recollections of Alexander Nikitin, an *Izvestia* correspondent during the 1970s, are telling: 'From a "respectable organ", successfully replacing toilet paper, [Adjubei] created the best newspaper in the country and harvested a whole *nest of talents* [italics added]. It could happen that you walk into the subway and everyone has a copy of *Izvestia*, and everyone has it turned to an *ocherk* by Tolya Agranovsky'.[20]

There were other exceptions to the Soviet journalism establishment. Soviet newspapers knew no investigative journalism, but cases when 'letters to the editor' complaining of abuses by local party officials or factory directors would launch local investigations by authorities were not that rare. They were, however, frequently used as propaganda, to showcase the grassroots power that local workers otherwise did not have.

Another important phenomenon in this era was *Literaturnaya Gazeta*. During the nineteenth century, as we have seen, the literary genre served as a venue for political discourse. *Literaturnaya Gazeta,* which was launched in 1830 and then remade in 1929, served this function perfectly during the Soviet years. Because it purportedly dealt with literature and not news or politics, censors were less keen to go over its materials with a fine-tooth comb. As a result, it once again came to serve as source of polemic for the intelligentsia, a place were discussions went largely unhindered (as long as they did not directly criticize the government).

In many ways, these 300 years of journalism could not give rise to any other media system than the one that post-Soviet Russians are grappling with today. The contradictions inherent in today's newspapers were all there – from the 'official' organ of 1703, through the nineteenth-century literary journals, to the politicized pamphlets of the revolutionary era, to the 'mouthpieces' of the communist years. The tensions in highbrow vs. lowbrow, in the literary vs. the didactic, in the state-owned vs. the independent, and the state-funded vs. the commercial, played out to different extents throughout Russian history, forming the same contradictions that Russian newspapers know today. It would not do justice to generalize on such a great number of contradictions, but it would be wise to keep these aspects in mind as we explore the Russian newspaper in modern times.

The failure of ideology: the origins of objective reporting and the case for *Kommersant*

When we think of what pushed Russian newspapers to transform during the early 1990s, we tend to focus on glasnost, the *openness* proclaimed by Soviet leader Mikhail Gorbachev during the mid-1980s. But there were many other factors that helped recreate the format and style of news and reporting in the nation's printed press. One important development was the influence that news agencies had on reporting style. In her study on the impact of news agencies, T.I. Frolova singles out Interfax as being responsible for first introducing the 'just the fact' approach to news presentation in Russia. Before that, it was common practice that 'facts were replaced with assessments'. Interfax, meanwhile, widely began using the format already adopted by western news agencies, and this style gradually came to be used by Russian newspapers as well.[21]

It is hard to estimate the impact that the hard style of news had on Russia's printed press, which was already undergoing a fundamental transformation in the early 1990s. But the implications of that style on journalistic genre and ethics are still uncertain today, when hard news reporting – undergoing an apparent crisis in newspapers worldwide – has reached a dead-end of sorts in Russia.

If Interfax introduced wire-style news presentation to Russian news agencies, then it was the *Kommersant* newspaper that was responsible for embedding it in post-Soviet Russia's journalism culture. In effect, the newspaper was trying to revive a journalistic tradition that had begun to form in the nineteenth century, when commercial newspapers began moving towards the commoditization of news and adopting elements of objectivism. Its efforts, rooted as they were in the commercial power of a buying class, were cut short by the Bolshevik Revolution and the re-establishment of a primarily didactic role for the journalist, which in itself harkened back to the intelligentsia's vision of the writer. The only problem for *Kommersant* and others like it was that they were writing for a middle class that was only beginning to form. McReynolds notes that it is the readership and its changing needs that create a demand for more fact-based journalism and less commentary; in the early 1990s the strata that could create that demand was as yet slim.[22]

If the informational needs that McReynolds speaks of did exist in a nineteenth-century Russia where consumerism was gaining impetus, for Soviet information consumers in 1989 the situation was complicated by a need not so much to consume news as a commodity, but to uncover and undo the wrongs of the Soviet regime. Once again, even during glasnost and perestroika, the function of the journalist was a didactic one. Because the shift to a consumer society in Russia during the 1990s and 2000s was a far more drastic one, there was hardly a way to resume the development of the Russian reporter from where it had been interrupted in the early twentieth century. In any case, as Svetlana Juskevitz elaborates in her dissertation study of the Russian journalist, the reporter's role changed repeatedly in rapid succession during the 1990s:

> There are studies revealing causality between a change of the social character of a contemporary journalist and the reforming social-economic structure of society. According to its classification the journalists of perestroika are 'knights of glasnost', the journalists of the period of shock therapy are 'spitboys' (*pljuiboi*) who equated information with misinformation, the journalists of the second half of the 1990s are ordered journalists (*zakaznoi*) servicing the ruling elite and financial oligarchs ... Kuzin ... prognosticates an increasing number of journalists with market character, those who identify themselves as a seller and a commodity simultaneously. According to Svitich ... the perceptions of professional roles transformed from propagandist and educator (*vospitatel*) in the 1970s toward informer

and conversationalist at the beginning of the 1990s. The study done later, 1993–1995, identified a change in the perception of the roles from mouthpiece of public opinion, commentator and generator of ideas toward critic, informer, agitator with a tendency toward being an organiser, propagandist, entertainer ... [23]

Now a leading, 'quality', 'serious' business daily, *Kommersant* has its origins in the Soviet era, although the paper features a cheeky 'official' history: 'Published since 1909. Between 1917 and 1990 was not published due to circumstances beyond the control of the editors'. This line alludes to a real business newspaper of the same name, but the actual similarities end there. However, it served a very important purpose: by politely distancing itself from the entire Soviet era and everything that was associated with it, *Kommersant*, which means 'businessman' in Russian, hoped to stake out a new identity for its typical reader: the educated, savvy businessman who had no time for Soviet-style demagoguery but was willing to pay for 'just the facts'.

The newspaper owes its existence to Vladimir Yakovlev, who in 1988 was a correspondent for the *Ogonek* magazine. In June of that year he registered the first news cooperative in the Soviet Union, called 'Fakt'. According to *Kommersant*'s official history, the paper really starts there. In December 1989, Fakt began publishing *Kommersant* on a weekly basis, many months before Gorbachev's new law on the media would give individuals the power and freedom to found newspapers. *Kommersant* identifies itself as the first private business periodical in the country and by the end of 1992, it was coming out on a daily basis:

> In order to understand what kind of revolution *Kommersant* accomplished, one should recall that journalism in the USSR was very different – from the headlines to the way the information was presented. In those times, every intern, even when writing about a fire at a poultry plant, strove to demonstrate the talent of a columnist. That was why news articles so often started off with a lyrical digression, with historical or philosophical allusions.[24]

Kommersant's presentation style, in the leap of a few years, attained what western newspapers took over a century to accomplish – stripping the facts, at least in a number of newspapers, of commentary and moralizing. But because of that fast pace, it is questionable how lasting that journalistic style would be for a medium struggling financially, politically and socially. In hindsight, nearly 20 years after creating the innovative periodical, Yakovlev himself would question whether 'just the facts' was indeed enough for Russian journalism:

> Periods of fast change, such as the one that went on in Russia during the last 10–15 years, create a hunger for information. In a certain sense this is heaven for journalists, because the reader needs simple, filling informational food, which doesn't take a lot of artistry to prepare. When society stabilizes, as it is doing now, there

is no more hunger for information, but rather an appetite. This means that one needs to learn new ways of preparing the food. We need reporting, stories, presentation ... In a larger sense, we need new models. And creating them is a very interesting challenge professionally.[25]

Propaganda as commodity: *Izvestia* – a source of information or a political pamphlet?

With its circulation of over 150,000, the *Izvestia* daily is one of the oldest-running and most popular nationwide newspapers that Russia currently has. Purchased in 2006 by the state-owned Gazprom Media holding from Prof-Media, a holding that belongs to the Kremlin-connected oligarch, Vladimir Potanin, it has lately been criticized for turning yellow due to its treatment of political issues and its increasing penchant for sensationalism. Nevertheless, it remains identified as one of Russia's 'quality' newspapers with a serious, in-depth weekend culture section. As such, it appears to straddle the divide between mass circulation papers and serious periodicals.

Aside from its more recent history, the path that *Izvestia* took is in many ways representative of other Russian periodicals, whether independent or official, 'serious' or 'tabloid'. Getting its start in 1917, prior to the Bolshevik Revolution, it was published as an organ of the Central Committee of the Worker's Council (Soviet). After the Revolution, it became the official organ of the Central Executive Committee of the Soviet Union (in effect the government paper, as opposed to *Pravda*, the Communist Party's paper), moving from Leningrad to Moscow along with the rest of the new government. Enjoying sporadic periods of wide readership and acclaim after World War II, it was, for an official organ, one of the more 'interesting' publications. The newspaper was privatized by the newsroom staff in 1992, when it formed an open joint stock company.

Together with other leading 'serious' or quality newspapers like *Kommersant*, *Izvestia* offers an indicative picture of what today's print journalism in Russia is all about in terms of style and content. To that end, excerpts that illustrate its news presentation are a good way of examining the unique journalistic ethic that Russian journalists still adhere to – despite the more recent appearance of the western, objectivist portrayal of the hard facts diluted with carefully balanced commentary and analysis (a style adopted, to some degree, by the *Kommersant* daily). *Izvestia* depicts a venue where news can be both commoditized and didactic at the same time.

Excerpts from the following story portray a journalist not as an impartial transmitter of information – a style adopted by most western news agencies and newspapers – but as an inevitable commentator and even judge of the event. At the same time, a sensationalist twist caters to an ordinary consumer of news.

Stepfather killed paedophile, saving child

For Alexander Kuznetsov, the New Year will hardly be a happy family holiday. On the night when everyone was drinking champagne and setting off fireworks, Kuznetsov, a former boxer, beat a man to death.

Alexander recalls the events reluctantly. 'I'm certain that I will be convicted,' he told *Izvestia* yesterday. But anyone who learns the details of this heart-rending story is unlikely to judge him. Because Kuznetsov killed a paedophile, frantic from rage and sorrow. He came upon the monster just as he was molesting [Alexander's] son ... Now he is being accused of 'inflicting grave bodily harm leading to the death of the victim.' The victim, it should be clarified, is scum that tried to rape a child.[26]

Featured at the bottom of the front page and widely covered by other tabloids, the story's presentation contrasted starkly with the western objectivist style, primarily because it virtually abandons the presumption of innocence until proven guilty in court. The paedophile described in the article was a 21-year-old Uzbek national identified under the last name of Hairillayev. There is no testimony from the child who survived the attack, nor statements from law enforcement officials. The reporter essentially took Kuznetsov's comments as fact, drawing conclusions that the described paedophile was a 'monster' and 'scum'.

On the one hand, it is understandable that the reporter chose to 'call things by their rightful names' and not hide his own emotional or moral outrage from the readers, taking on, in many ways, an alternatively honest journalistic approach. On the other hand, establishing straight out that the victim was indeed a paedophile and a monster who deserved to die without first proving in a court of law that he was indeed guilty of rape could lead to questions regarding the writer's objectivity in covering other stories. Indeed, by November 2008, when Kuznetsov was sentenced to two and half years in a penal colony, it was clear that this former boxer was no model citizen. Throughout the 1990s, Kuznetsov had been handed down at least four suspended sentences on convictions of battery.

The fact that *Izvestia* ran this story on the front page of its Moscow edition (under its cover story featuring new uniforms for the army) plays into accusations by the liberal media that the newspaper is turning into a tabloid and has descended into sensationalism and 'yellow' journalism. Such arguments can be corroborated by the fact that it hired several editors and staff writers from the *Komsomolskaya Pravda* tabloid in 2005. But it has been argued that *Izvestia* is loyal to its image of an 'elite' paper, something that will not allow it to seriously compete with *Komsomolskaya Pravda*.[27]

But the use of words like 'monster' to describe a man who has not yet been convicted of molesting a child is not really an issue of belonging in a tabloid vs. an elite newspaper. For one thing, *Komsomolskaya Pravda* ran an in-depth report on Kuznetsov that same week, and while the reporter's conclusions were indeed tendentiously sympathetic with Kuznetsov, Hairillayev was hardly called a 'monster'. Also, it is not brazen language that characterizes a tabloid.

In the USA, the Murdoch-owned *New York Post* covers local crime with a sensationalist twist, but keeps its priorities straight in terms of making sure to call confessed child abusers 'suspected killer' and to quote police sources when describing heinous crimes in news reports. Articles where any sort of judgement is passed on the suspects before a court of law has issued any ruling are penned by columnists and identified as such both in the title and in the presentation style of the article.

What does this unabashed style of news presentation in Russian newspapers tell us, if anything, about the nature of Russian journalistic ethics? Does the reporter call the unconvicted paedophile a 'monster' because they have no ethics, or because they are a bad reporter? It can be argued that neither is the case. While much of Russian reporting could benefit from a more objectivist approach, this approach is neither perfect in itself nor attainable. Moreover, given the utter lack of leverage among Russian newspapers to impact policy, polemic and exaggeration are often their only tools. Kuznetsov's case was one of several in which journalists took a stand and helped draw the attention of public officials to the issue (municipal deputies had rushed to Kuznetsov's defence and may have helped soften the verdict of the court, which otherwise might not have taken into account that Kuznetsov was acting in self-defence).

We can examine, using examples from the *Kommersant* daily and other Russian news agencies, what an objectivist, hard-news oriented presentation style achieved. But as for Russia's unique, 'involved' journalistic style, we should examine it for what it is on its own terms, exploring both the advantages and disadvantages of this approach.

When we look at the origins of Russian journalism, developing in a nation with a remarkably low literacy rate and deep social chasms between the educated class and the rest of the population, it comes as no surprise that the role and the image of the journalist was forged from the start as something between a pedagogue and a demagogue. The journalist and the newspaperman in Russia were traditionally charged with leading the population forward. As we have seen, this was stipulated as early as the nineteenth century by leading men of letters of the day when a journalist was cited as 'head of the pillar'. Vladimir Lenin called for a more involved role for the journalist in rallying the masses for revolution, while perestroika-era journalists saw themselves as a 'fourth estate'. If the role of the 'fourth pillar' has most frequently been described as a mediator between public and government, in Russia this mediator has, for various reasons, transformed into an instrument of change – whether in the hands of the government or serving other, more noble interests and movements, as was the case during perestroika.

There are specific, contemporary examples where the Russian journalist's penchant for discarding his uninvolved stance as bystander has led to the kind of impact that should be associated with a healthy civil society. At other times, however, ideological involvement of the journalist only hampered such efforts. Isolated, individual crimes such as that of Kuznetsov often point to Russia's imperfect law enforcement system, riddled with high crime levels, lack of accountability and corruption within its ranks. When journalists manage to rally society around such instances – by making the reader identify with the 'culprit's' fate but also by portraying the story in such a way that the 'culprit' stands out as the victim of an inefficient and heartless system – they can frequently achieve what other columnists and investigative reporters can't when they simply write about national issues as a whole. Frequently in Russia, such cases are first broken by bloggers and then picked up by the newspapers as an afterthought. But Kuznetsov's case was initially reported by the print tabloids and only later picked up by the blogosphere in a development that shows how Russia's print journalists are adopting new tactics from the internet.

On the other hand, the necessity to take a side – often dictated by a newspaper's editorial policy – paralyses the journalist and destroys the possibility of objective political reporting. How exactly this is done in contemporary Russian newspapers may answer some questions about their failure as mediators between the government and the people – and *Izvestia* offers another illustrative example.

In June 2007, relations between Russia and Great Britain had plummeted over an impasse in the investigation into the murder of Alexander Litvinenko, an ex-KGB agent turned Kremlin critic who died of polonium poisoning in November 2006. Great Britain accused his colleague, Andrei Lugovoi, of involvement in the plot and demanded his extradition, while Russia refused, pointing out that London also refused to extradite business and media tycoon Boris Berezovsky.

That month, *Izvestia* ran an article[28] investigating how political asylum could be bought and sold in Great Britain, following a slew of sensational statements by Lugovoi. Penned by Vladimir Perekrest, it cited Lugovoi's press conference of 31 May, in which the suspect accused Berezovsky's Civil Liberties Foundation of procuring British citizenship for Russian businessmen.

In his article, Perekrest seconded the claims, describing how the going rate for British asylum was £500,000 or more. 'The English have not denied these statements,' Perekrest wrote, 'so they must be true.' He then proceeded to investigate to what extent getting British asylum was 'realistic'. First he described how he was told by an unnamed Russian firm over the internet that 5500 rubles would launch his immigration process. The firm he described was in the basement of a run-down building, and did not actually guarantee acceptance of the applications in London. Next Perekrest cited an unnamed rights activist who elaborated on how refugees arrive in England on false passports that were made out with the help of the police. Another source was an unnamed friend who had emigrated to the UK through the Highly Skilled Migrant Programme, and described how all immigrants have to do is detail their escape from 'chekists with bloody axes' and the authorities believed them.

Without evidencing a single refugee who had successfully 'bought' asylum – apart from claiming that Litvinenko had done so – in one instance Perekrest cited lawyers who said their clients were offered asylum in Finland through 'certain middlemen'. And although Perekrest cited a number of 'correspondents' who said the scheme was realistic, he did not describe how exactly the Civil Liberties Foundation 'sold' asylum status, stating merely that it 'consulted' British authorities on the persecution of refugees.

One UK-based source that Perekrest had actually identified in the article was Claire Rimmer, the joint coordinator for Eastern Europe at the European Council on Refugees and Exiles. Because she represented a non-government association that helped refugees, it would have been likely that had any massive allegations of asylum corruption surfaced, she would have known about it. According to Rimmer, who provided her email correspondence with the Moscow journalist, Perekrest had specifically asked her whether being critical of Russia was a necessary condition to obtain asylum, as Perekrest alleged in his article. She replied that it was not. In his article, meanwhile, Perekrest omitted any mention of her denial, relying instead on one or two questionable 'unnamed' acquaintances.

Why would a journalist decide to publish allegations based on sensationalist press conferences and anonymous 'acquaintances' without even mentioning denials from competent agencies? When I asked Perekrest why he had chosen to omit this information, he explained in an email that:

> Claire ... told me about the procedure for getting political asylum, citing that a lot of the statistics were classified. Because she could not name any other political emigrants besides Berezovsky, Zakayev and [former Kremlin pool journalist Elena] Tregubova, I understood that her knowledge of this issue is limited to the information posted on the site of the Home Office, or otherwise she does not feel the need to give more detailed information. I had no intention to get dishonest answers or gather opinion instead of knowledge. Besides, no one says that Rimmer ... [is] in any way involved in 'selling' political asylum – so what's the point of asking them about it? They answered to the best of their competency. I got more detailed, 'inside' information from other sources who are more knowledgeable and who trust me.

What his answer points to is that anonymous, insider information that has not been verified is enough to base an entire article on for leading newspapers like *Izvestia*. Journalists like Perekrest can hardly be blamed for this. In a non-transparent political climate where officials are not accustomed to talking to journalists, it is indeed next to impossible to get any sort of truthful, verifiable information. Instead, reporters are forced to rely on whatever sources they can find. At times these are indeed informed insiders who occasionally leak information (obviously remaining anonymous). But very frequently they call themselves 'insiders' simply because they have talked to other 'insiders'.

A problem arises, however, when journalists extrapolate this lack of transparency to other countries, assuming, for instance, that 'in reality' the British government is equally corrupt and opaque, thus responding, in many ways, to the requirement of their government and their editors. The result, of course, is a self-perpetuating cycle of ambiguity.

Today, an ever-vigilant climate persists in many newsrooms, where managers are in near-constant fear of publishing something that can be mistaken for 'hidden advertisement' even when nothing of the sort was intended by the editor. The article is an example of all the advantages and disadvantages of combining didactics with commodity news – where sensation is wedded with propaganda. While commoditized news stories build a readership base and can condition that base to value political involvement, in Russia's journalistic climate, which is overly suspicious of anything commercial, didactic political articles can be seen as untrustworthy by default because they could have potentially been written 'to order'.

The Russian tabloids: yellow journalism at its worst or the neglected fourth estate?

Moskovsky Komsomolets is at the same time a vividly typical Russian tabloid, and deeply unique in its eclectic blend of the high and the low, the national and the local. Together with *Komsomolskaya Pravda* and *Argumenty i Fakty,* it completes the three most widely read mass circulation newspapers in Russia. Published since 1919, its Moscow circulation is 2.2 million. A weekly edition is also published in 63 Russian regions, with a total circulation of 1.7 million.

If we take the dichotomy of quality vs. mass circulation at face value, we are in for some surprises once we begin analysing mass-circulation newspapers like *Moskovsky Komsomolets.* Compared to *Kommersant, Izvestia* or *Nezavisimaya Gazeta*, it certainly has the look and feel of a tabloid, complete with punned headlines in the vein of the *New York Post*, caricatures and a bawdy obsession with the dirty laundry of celebrities. There is also a higher proportion of photographs to text.

But if we look at the texts themselves, we will find a lot more similarities, while the differences are in fact more subtle than could be expected. While *Moskovsky Komsomolets* has a particular penchant for eclectics, all Russian newspapers feature opinion and commentary on the front page alongside news and events. Increasingly a feature in Putin's Russia, political coverage that focuses on either the president, the prime minister or other central figures, is placed on pages 1 and 2. The chief difference is in presentation style and language. While 'serious' newspapers tend to strive to underline analysis and commentary, mass circulation papers highlight wider appeal by focusing on more personal nuances and presenting national problems with greater accessibility, often at the expense of linguistic style.

While it may appear that the loyalist newspapers – as much of the tabloids are – would tend to downplay government criticism, this is by no means always the case. Published just two days ahead of the presidential election, a front-page opinion piece, complete with a pun in the headline, underlined pretty much all the chief problems with the Russian elections in a straightforward manner:

If we translate from a political language to the ordinary, then the blame for western-style elections is the fact that they are turning into a show. But we are too busy and serious for shows! The problem is that any election, by definition, is a show. And the only difference between ourselves and the Americans is that their show is 'directed' by thousands and millions of people. In our spectacle everything to the last letter is choreographed in advance by a group of 'producers'. That is where the difference between our drabness and their drive comes from.

But let's not be hypocritical. Our current method of holding the elections is a part of an informal 'social contract' between the people and the government. Ordinary citizens are actually tired of the 'drive' of the 1990s. They need [stability] … But symbols can also be deeply misleading. Our current situation clearly fits that. Not only is the slogan 'stability forever' covering for a completely unstable internal system [of government]. But the conditions of this social contract between the government and the people are, essentially, deeply unfair.[29]

Further on, the article cited corruption, instability and clashes within government factions as prominent features of the current regime. Worded differently, such allegations are frequently the stuff of virulently oppositionist publications such as the weekly magazine, *Novoye Vremya* (*The New Times*). Coupling pointed criticism with accessibility, some would argue that this is a unique characteristic of *Moskovsky Komsomolets*, which, in many ways is a unique paper:

Moskovsky Komsomolets was the first in contemporary Russian journalism to offer an original formula of a daily that combines the uncombinable. Analysis sits next to epatage, intellectual writings about art are adjacent to intimate exposés from newsmakers; vivid commentary next to ideological tendentiousness; hard facts in news stories next to watered-out texts without any meaning. Its style reflects the peculiarities of the political, social and cultural environment of a metropolis.[30]

Together with *Izvestia* and *Komsomolskaya Pravda*, *Moskovsky Komsomolets* is among Russia's oldest-running periodicals. First published as a youth paper in 1919, throughout the communist years it was an official organ of the Moscow bureau of the All-Union Lenin Youth League, the youth wing of the Communist Party. During perestroika, it evolved into a lively city tabloid, with an unabashed mix of the best and the worst. In 1991, following the breakup of the Soviet Union, the crumbling of the Communist Party and the emancipation of the press from party organs, it did what most other papers did – re-registered itself as a periodical published by the journalist collective. Unlike *Komsomolskaya Pravda* and *Izvestia*, which ended up being bought and sold by businesses, *Moskovsky Komsomolets* remained a 'collective' – hence financially independent – newspaper, at least officially. Today the *Moskovsky Komsomolets* publishing house is a holding that publishes a number of magazines, including the glossy monthly *Atmosfera* and the business monthly *Delovyie Lyudi*. Apart from regional editions of *Moskovsky Komsomolets*, it also publishes the specialized hunting weekly, *Rossiyskaya Ohotnichya Gazeta*, which in itself boasts a century-long history. While unofficial, it does apparently get financial help from the Moscow government, which reportedly subsidizes its regional editions.[31]

There is no one way of answering to what extent *Moskovsky Komsomolets* can boast of independence. Prior to 1993, the paper was a typical herald of perestroika, with biting investigative journalism, in-depth exposés and a generally progressive spirit. As such, it attempted, in the words of some of its more educated readers, to break the Soviet paradigm of pandering to party bosses and instead began pandering to readers. In many ways, its transformation from a progressive, perestroika newspaper to a tabloid reflected the changing tastes of its wide readership base in a time of turmoil.

During perestroika in the late 1980s, when it was still a communist organ, the paper spearheaded efforts to delve into all the Soviet-era taboos, much like the Russian edition of *Moskovskie Novosti* did. But where *Moskovskie Novosti* tended to stick to the progressive party line – thus walking in line with Gorbachev's and Yeltsin's government – *Moskovsky Komsomolets* did this earlier, and without much prodding from the top.[32] It was the first newspaper to publish articles dealing with homosexuality and prostitution and was the first to investigate hazing in the army. According to Julia Bakhareva, who worked at the paper from 1988 to 1992 and edited the culture section, it had 'healthy' strains of yellow journalism embedded in its 'race for the news at any cost'.[33]

Its most notorious – and, ultimately, fatal – exposé dealt with corruption in the Soviet army. *Moskovsky Komsomolets* journalist Dmitri Kholodov investigated the rampant embezzlement that went on in the top ranks of the Western Group of Forces in East Germany as it was being demobilized after the collapse of the Soviet bloc. His reports were accompanied by biting editorials from Alexander Minkin, who accused then defence minister Pavel Grachev of corruption and called on prosecutors to either investigate Grachev for corruption or investigate himself, Minkin, for libel (neither took place). While Minkin continues to write for the paper to this day, Kholodov was murdered on 14 October 1994, after a bomb exploded in a suitcase that was given to him by a supposed source. He died just days before he was scheduled to testify at a parliamentary hearing on allegations of corruption in the army.

There is no question that today's bawdy *Moskovsky Komsomolets* is a far cry from the progressive, cutting-edge paper, as some of its readers describe it, circa 1990. Despite the fact that the paper is still edited by the same editor, Pavel Gusev, it seemed to undergo a fundamental transformation in 1992–3. While such transformations usually accompany a change in ownership in other publications, no such change occurred at *Moskovsky Komsomolets*. Instead, the transformation coincided with the publishing house's creation of the Okay advertisement agency. Then, Bakhareva, who was culture editor at the time, was told to cut down on much of the free-style intellectualizing in her section. Gone was the literary page and the improvisations on contemporary music, which had made the paper popular with the intelligentsia. 'We saw ourselves as enlighteners', says Bakhareva of her work prior to 1992, but under the commercial pressure that started piling up on the journalists in that year, 'we had to become lighter, more yellow'.[34]

The Moscow News

In its tumultuous, rollercoaster-ride of a history, no other newspaper has managed to combine so many fatal aspects of Russian and Soviet press under one masthead than *The Moscow News*. Launched in 1930 by the American socialist Anne-Louise Strong, as a communist-approved organ published in an intractable number of languages (most prominently English), *The Moscow News* inevitably epitomized state propaganda. Here is a news item from the front page of a 1933 edition, characteristic of the wide assortment of news items featured in the paper, and also of the paper's clunky English:

5 November 1933

YLC Subotnik November 12

The all union subotnik organized by the Youth Communist League in commemoration of its 15th anniversary will be held Nov. 12.

Work of every kind will be carried out, including cleaning up factory shops and railroad lines, loading and unloading railroad cars, sorting vegetables and carrying out work on state and collective farms. Proceeds of the drives will go to a USSR defence fund.

The youth of Moscow undertakings have answered with great enthusiasm the decision to hold the subotnik. The decision has been confirmed by the Secretariat of the Central Committee of the Party.[35]

Strong, an American journalist who had created a name for herself during her support of the 1919 worker's strike in Seattle, came to Russia in 1921 hoping to see for herself the socialist experiment at work. Her friend, the revolutionary Mikhail Borodin, suggested she launch a newspaper targeting the many English-language workers who, like Strong, had come to Moscow to experience communism.

After a brief period of relative autonomy, the *Moscow News* inevitably became a victim of censorship and repression. As a propaganda organ controlled by the All-Union Society for Foreign Culture Cooperation, the paper had to take on staff appointed by the Party. One of these was the editor, Toviy Axelrod. According to Strong's great nephew, Tracy B. Strong, in her letters and articles, Strong recalled a conflict over Axelrod's insistence to publish Stalin's speeches verbatim. When Strong tried to publish a summarized version of a speech in 1931, Axelrod reportedly told her that no one could say what the gist of Stalin's speech should be but Stalin himself. A conflict over whose name was to appear on the masthead led to a meeting between Strong, Stalin and Axelrod in 1932. Stalin reportedly insisted that Strong remain at the paper. Nevertheless, as the political climate grew more repressive, the *Moscow News* increasingly succumbed to the official line. Strong left the paper in 1936, and Mikhail Borodin, understanding that he had no choice, continued turning the paper into a propagandistic mouthpiece. It would not save him, however. The paper was halted in 1949 when Borodin was arrested in connection with an investigation into the Jewish Anti-Fascist Committee. He presumably died in Siberian camps in 1951, although some records suggest he may have been shot. Axelrod, meanwhile, failed to escape a similar fate – he was arrested in late 1937, in the height of the purges, convicted of trying to organize a counter-revolutionary terrorist attack, and shot in early 1938, according to records provided by the Memorial Society.[36] The paper resumed publication in 1956, after Nikita Khrushchev came to power.

At the time, *The Moscow News* was controlled by the Central Committee of the Communist Party, which appointed editors and assigned them instructors, or 'curators' from the propaganda department. '*Moscow News* was lucky, it was curated by Alexander Yakovlev,' recalls Yakov Lomko, who became editor of the paper in 1960. Yakovlev was none other than the man who would become known as the 'godfather of glasnost' as a member of the Politburo and adviser to Gorbachev. As Lomko described later in an interview:

> From 1956 the newspaper came out twice a week and was sometimes entirely filled with long speeches by Khrushchev. I understood that a newspaper intended for a foreign reader should not be party oriented, Soviet. Alexander Nikolayevich supported me. Essentially, [the reforms entailed] a return to the idea of 1930 – to issue a paper without ideology for sincere supporters of the USSR.[37]

Lomko was against creating a Russian-language edition, since the whole point of the paper was, in his words, to 'provide the foreign reader with objective information about our reality'. While it was indeed less ideological than *Pravda*, *The Moscow News* under Lomko was strictly conformist in the kind of 'facts' it chose to publish. Any part of 'out reality' that was even remotely negative or controversial was simply not printed. Another feature of the paper, long-time staff members say, was the star system – the number of stars indicated what country or destination a particular issue was prepared for. That way, different stories appeared in issues that were distributed in the USA than in issues destined for students of English based in Russia.

Nevertheless, just ahead of the Olympics in 1980, a Russian edition was launched. Initially it contained translated copy from the foreign newsroom, but by the mid-1980s, under the leadership of another glasnost figurehead, Yegor Yakovlev, it began publishing original content. And, as glasnost began making headway by 1986, the process came to be mirrored in the Russian edition of the newspaper. According to Yevgeny Lanfang, who worked at the paper first as a correspondent then as deputy editor from 1955 until 1989, considerable changes started taking place after Boris Yeltsin, then a member of the Central Committee, held an unusual meeting with public figures: 'We started writing about his public appearances in stores, on trolleybuses', he recalled.

Then, the paper started tackling other, far more controversial issues, like the Katyn massacre, Chernobyl mutations and dissident writer Alexander Solzhenitsyn. While editors were encouraged to continue with the exposés, the ambiguity and structural incoherence of the glasnost idea made writing freely about these topics very difficult. These practical inconsistencies are rarely considered when we think of the term glasnost itself. For one thing, despite Mikhail Gorbachev's policy of glasnost, the Central Committee still had the power to censure the press. If the paper was backed by Gorbachev's supporters in the upper echelons, it still had to deal with the pressure coming from the Central Committee. Recalls Lanfang:

> It was complete chaos and misunderstanding. Gorbachev says we have to do everything differently. But what, how ... There was internal censorship, we did not know how to write freely. We always wrote with a look towards the Central Committee. Under Yakovlev, things started to change. But censorship remained the same. The Central Committee remained the same. From the start we knew we had to write differently. But how do you write differently when there are these two forces – self-censorship on the one hand, forcing you to write so that no one understands what you are saying, and the second – the Central Committee?[38]

Moskovskie Novosti, the Russian edition of *The Moscow News*, had become, ironically, an organ of Gorbachev's glasnost policy, coming to the forefront and overshadowing its precursor, *The Moscow News*, which, in turn, largely began printing content translated from the Russian edition. The newspaper was not the only "organ" of glasnost. Vitaly Korotich, editor in chief of the *Ogonek* magazine at the height of perestroika (1986–1991), recalls just how closely progressive publications like

Ogonek and *Moskovskie Novosti* worked with the government: "We were experimental airplanes that the government decided to launch. If we flew, great, but if we started floundering, no one was going to come to our rescue." Lack of full independence meant that editors were often caught up in political power struggles, like the one that brewed between Gorbachev and Yeltsin in 1989. "Yeltsin would tell me, here are some recollections, let's print them and smear Gorbachev. And just days before that, Gorbachev had asked me the same thing about Yeltsin."[39]

Then, as Gorbachev emancipated the press in 1990, a whole new range of opportunities and responsibilities opened up for the newspaper. *The Moscow News* faced much the same challenge as other long-running periodicals – reorganize and start walking in line with the new, pro-market realities. In 1991, Yakovlev went on to chair the All-Union Television Company (VGTRK), and the newspaper was transformed into a closed joint-stock company, *Moskovskie Novosti* Publishing House, with the stock being distributed among the staff. After some manipulation, the controlling package went to the commercial director, Alexander Vainshtein, who created a holding consisting of the publishing house – which issued the Russian and English editions, MN Realty, and controlled a large building in central Moscow's Pushkin Square – and Radio Maximum. The newspaper *Moskovskie Novosti* was published by its editor, Viktor Loshak. The English edition continued coming out, largely consisting of translated content, while editions in other languages were abandoned.

The trade-off was typical for the print periodical market in the first half of the 1990s. Newspapers transformed into ZAOs (closed joint-stock companies), and then tried to subsist on whatever they could – government subsidies, sponsorship or, as was the case with *Moskovskie Novosti*, real estate. Editorial staff say the newspaper was mismanaged throughout the 1990s and was never able to recreate its former glory. Vainshtein was forced to sell a paper that was deep in the red by 2003.

In August of that year, the *Moskovskie Novosti* Publishing House was sold to Open Russia, a charity organization founded by Mikhail Khodorkovsky's Yukos oil company. Yevgeny Kiselyov, an outspoken talk-show host of NTV fame, was appointed editor-in-chief. Unofficially it was assumed that the newspaper would play a part in rallying support for the liberal opposition in the December 2003 parliamentary elections. According to deputy editor Lyudmila Telen, in exchange for financial support from Open Russia, the newspaper would offer informational support ahead of the elections. The price, according to unofficial sources, was between $1.5–3 million.

The deal, however, couldn't have come at a more inappropriate time. In October, Mikhail Khodorkovsky was unexpectedly detained when the Federal Security Service (FSB) raided his private aeroplane. The criminal investigation that ensued would later destroy Yukos and land the oligarch in a Siberian jail on fraud and tax evasion convictions.

These tensions served as a backdrop for a high-profile scandal that broke out in 2005 between the Yukos-appointed managers (including

Kiselyov) and the journalists at the paper. In an effort to revamp the still-dying publication, Kiselyov fired a number of veteran journalists, including Telen. Telen and her colleagues retaliated by launching a temporary '*Moskovskie Novosti* without Kiselyov' and accused their former boss of running the paper into the grave. The newsroom during that period was laced with various rumours about the talk-show host turned editor. The more believable one was that he repeatedly turned in his weekly column several hours late on production day. Other, less plausible rumours included allegations that Kirill Legat, the Yukos-appointed general manager, was embezzling funds and hiring girlfriends to do literally nothing for thousands of dollars a month.

It remains unclear whether personal animosity, greed or political motives (as Telen alleged) were behind the conflict, nor is it important in the long run. Whatever his methods, Kiselyov was doing what other editors had found unavoidable: either make the paper profitable or flop. If there had been an original motive for Yukos' purchase of the paper through Open Russia, it was no longer relevant: the liberal opposition had failed to gain any seats in the 2003 parliamentary elections, Putin was seen as having quashed any opposition in his following re-election, and the liberals were becoming increasingly marginalized.

If remaining a political 'organ' was no longer an option, nor was turning a 'boring, but important and necessary' print publication into a profitable media possible. In summer 2005 the paper was sold to Ukrainian businessman Vadim Rabinovich, who in turn sold it to an Israeli businessman, Arkady Gaidamak, three months later.

Gaidamak's general manager, the young, US-educated Daniil Kupsin, continued the campaign to turn the paper into a profitable, quality tabloid. For a while, it looked like he was succeeding. He hired Vitaly Tretyakov, the acclaimed journalist who had founded *Nezavisimaya Gazeta* in 1991. Despite his stance on 'independence' in the early 1990s, Tretyakov had become increasingly supportive of Kremlin policy – though it appeared that his ideological support was completely sincere. Nevertheless, it was reflected in the newspaper, which had gone from being pro-glasnost to pro-liberal reform, and now, to pro-Kremlin. At least, that was the intended script.

All this time, the English edition was confined to the shadows. Ever since the retirement of its last editor, Sergei Roy, in spring 2004, the paper was managed without an official editorial post. It consisted of two translators, and, initially, three staff editors (including myself). When Kupsin began reforming the Russian edition, the English paper's staff was expanded. Then, Kupsin proposed revamping the English paper itself into a more readable, local, and 'exciting' edition for expats.

The only problem was defining what exactly an 'expat' was. Moscow already had two popular English-language newspapers: the straight-laced, pro-western *Moscow Times* daily and the alternative *eXile* bi-weekly (a paper so scandalous that it remained a wonder how officials tolerated its frequent putdowns for so long – an audit in 2008 scared off the investor and forced editor Mark Ames to close the print edition and take the online version to a US-based domain). If the first catered to businessmen and resident employees, then the latter targeted tourists and non-conformists. So, when faced with the objective of recreating a potentially profitable paper, finding an unoccupied niche was the first step.

Kupsin put together a team of advertisement specialists and journalist veterans to forge a new image for the paper. The chief driving force, considering that management consisted of advertising agents, was making the paper attractive for advertisers, not readers. Advertisers wanted a paper that was read by people with spending power. The problem was attracting the attention of those readers – and that was a problem that was never really tackled.

In the end, faced with either selling the English weekly or closing it down entirely, Kupsin settled on the most reasonable solution. He reorganized the publishing house into a holding, United Media, which published *Moskovskie Novosti*, launched a radio station, Business FM, and followed it with a newspaper of the same name. He then sold 50 per cent of *The Moscow News* brand name to the RIA Novosti news agency. *The Moscow News* newsroom moved into RIA offices and became a newspaper under the editorship of British national Anthony Louis, a former publisher and editor of *The Moscow Tribune*. He would edit the paper for less than a year before the management, for apparently bureaucratic reasons, replaced him with Robert Bridge.

It would seem that the fate of the paper had reached full circle: launched as an English-language source of 'objective' Soviet news for foreigners, it returned to the hands of its former owner. RIA Novosti was a state-run news agency that was formerly known as Sovinformburo during World War II and APN (Print Agency 'Novosti', or 'News') during the later Soviet years. If the paper was to provide a more 'positive' and 'constructive' view on Russian processes, what better way than to do it with the help of the state-run agency that had been created in the first place for that very mission.

Back under the control of RIA Novosti, a strange atmosphere initially pervaded the newsroom. Officially there was no censorship. But editors who had stayed on with the paper learned the dubious art of self-censorship. No directive for what could go into print existed. But with practice, editors learned what kind of topics needed to be avoided lest unwanted attention was drawn.

It was in this environment – the increasing popularity of a solid, conservative, pro-Kremlin view (whether out of fear or an attempt to curry favour with the presidential administration ahead of the 2008 change of power), coupled with the impossibility of creating a profitable newspaper where no tradition of profitable and independent newspapers existed – that *Moskovskie Novosti* came to an end. *The Moscow News* had indeed come full circle now that its more outspoken, more critical Russian edition was abolished. Yet in 2009, under the new editor-in-chief, former *Moscow Times* business editor Tim Wall, the newspaper was re-launched as an 'independent' project under the financial auspices of the government. According to *RIA Novosti*, the newspaper was re-launched at the behest of Vladimir Putin himself, who visited its editorial offices in February 2009 and was reportedly pleased with what he saw. Even so, editorial independence appeared to be possible: under the new editor, journalists were encouraged to be objective, balanced and critical.[40]

No longer a mouthpiece, not yet an independent, commercial paper, *The Moscow News* echoed the state of other, albeit far more successful, newspapers across Russia: amid a worldwide waning of the newspaper business, a sudden renaissance of influential, commercially independent newspapers looked unlikely.

We can recall an even more pervasive circumstance that, if not dooming the press outright, certainly hampered its development in a climate of freedom. Lanfang recalls how censorship forced journalists to write in a way that no one could understand in order to get information across without getting into trouble, calling it 'Aesop's language'. In a word, he arguably summed up Russian journalism's most unique advantage. It was a dubious advantage, however, predestining newspapers for failure as a fourth estate. After all, this Aesop's language was not born in the Soviet Union: Russia's best pens had been using it to outwit censors for centuries. Unfortunately, it was indeed hard for talented journalists to learn to write in any other way. If capable of producing good literature, their arcane style was by definition undemocratic. And while 'necessary', it was incapable of coexisting in purely commercial conditions. Hence the divide today: with a few notable exceptions, journalism is either too elite to make a profit, or too yellow to be considered quality journalism.

5 TELEVISION AND FILM

- **Vertov, Eisenstein and the cradle of news and propaganda**
- **Soviet television: enlightenment and spectacle**
- **The televised chaos of the 1990s**
- **Television today**
- **Censorship or quality control?**

Vertov, Eisenstein and the cradle of news and propaganda

If Soviet ideology did not succeed in fully revolutionizing the newspaper genre, then its more progressive accomplishments are still felt today in cinematography. While the same cannot be said of Soviet television in general, Soviet cinema, infused in the early years with a novel cocktail of avant-garde art, journalism and propaganda, pushed the genre to new, groundbreaking heights. Such was their influence, we can arguably say that Hollywood would not be where it is today without the genius of Dziga Vertov and Sergei Eisenstein. At the same time, Vertov's newsreels can be seen as precursors to both modern television news on the one hand, and the Dogma Manifesto of filmmaker Lars von Trier on the other.

Born Denis Kaufman to a Jewish family in the Ukraine, he moved to Moscow in 1915 and soon changed his name to Dziga Vertov – literally, 'spinning top', reflecting the motion of a camera. Following the Revolution, he began work for the Moscow Cinema Committee, creating the Kino-Nedelya – Russia's first newsreel. There, together with Sergei Eisenstein, he would form a group called the Kinoks – one of many avant-garde movements that were sprouting in post-revolutionary Russia. Their philosophy, while groundbreaking for their time, reflects much of what we take for granted today when watching the news. Vertov rejected staged cinema and used the camera as a mirror of the real world. To this end, he was the first to start using montage. Thus, he created the Kino-Eye theory:

> From the viewpoint of the ordinary eye you see untruth. From the viewpoint of the cinematic eye (aided by special cinematic means, in this case, accelerated shooting) you see the truth. If it's a question of reading someone's thoughts at a distance (and often what matters to us is not to hear a person's words but to read his thoughts), then you have that opportunity right here. It has been revealed by the Kino-Eye.[1]

Today, a televised news story will show moving images unconnected by chronology or space. And while they are put together to illustrate a spoken story that consists of the who, what, when, where and how – in other words, seemingly subservient to the text – it is the image that has the most impact on the television viewer. This is a crucial element in why television is considered a far more influential medium than newspapers, particularly in Russia. A picture does not lie, especially not a moving picture.

When Vertov began making his newsreels, montage was a novel approach that facilitated self-expression rather than 'objective' reporting. In his case, however, it was his adherence to ideology that allowed him to turn montage into an instrument of recreating the objective world:

> Kino-Eye uses every possible means in montage, comparing and linking all points of the universe in any temporal order, breaking, when necessary, all the laws and conventions of film construction.
>
> Kino-Eye plunges into the seeming chaos of life to find in life itself the response to an assigned theme. To find the resultant force amongst the million phenomena related to the given theme. To edit; to wrest, though the camera, whatever is most typical, most useful, from life; to organize the film pieces wrested from life into a meaningful rhythmic visual order, a meaningful visual phrase, an essence of 'I see'.[2]

The result of this approach was indeed revolutionary: creating a product that can be viewed at once as news, documentary or, indeed, expressionist cinema. A good example of all three is the Kino-Pravda newsreel series from 1922.

The No. 6 newsreel, for instance, surpasses the contemporary television magazine in information and expressiveness without uttering a single word. A series of images interrupted by written headlines, it is the ultimate manifestation of the journalistic dogma, 'show, don't tell'. The first part, headlined 'Work on the reconstruction of the Moscow trolley system', is preceded by a hand writing the word 'Moscow' on the left, while on the right the camera sizes up a panoramic, bird's-eye view of the city. Then, following the headline, the camera captures workers laying down tracks, with a horse-pulled wagon in the background. This is followed by a moving tram, then footage of the interior with passengers inside. Indeed, the only thing missing in this 'story', which is otherwise worthy of being aired on today's evening news, is a narrative.

Vertov's newsreels were a first step in creating the documentary genre. This would manifest in his first feature film in 1929, *Man with a Movie Camera*. A vivid pastiche of daily life from Odessa to Moscow, it combined the insignificant with the uplifting. In morning shots, tramps sleeping contentedly on benches were followed by views of empty city streets. It involved several reoccurring characters, such as a Moscow woman who the camera returns to periodically as she completes her morning routine. This 'life' of the city involves such varied aspects as another woman giving birth.

If Vertov used montage essentially for reporting, then Eisenstein, his colleague and partner in introducing montage, would use it and other methods for emotional manipulation. A fervent believer in the possibilities that communism offered for artists, Eisenstein also adopted his role as a propagandist, and with acclaimed results. *Battleship Potemkin*, detailing the 1905 mutiny on the battleship of the Black Sea Fleet, used the newest cinematic technology to pit one class against another in an epic historical feature. Viewers today can easily associate the saga of the *Potemkin* with Eisenstein's most masterful and successful scene, in which a baby carriage tumbles down a stairway in Odessa with the mother watching helplessly in terror. His unique use of light, camera angle and montage served to achieve the very emotional effect that a mere description of a seconds-long scene such as this could not have.

Less innovative but perhaps even more propagandistic was *Ivan the Terrible*. Shot in 1949, it reflects the constraints that Eisenstein was forced to accept in order to use his genius to the ends of state propaganda. Having been informed by the novel techniques that Eisenstein himself had created in the past decades, the film managed to present an exemplary achievement of propaganda, accomplishing with feature film intended for entertainment what Leni Riefenstahl accomplished with documentary.

Ivan the Terrible was a far cry from documentary or historic cinematography. It was unabashedly geared towards glorifying Russian history and recreating a wholly new image of a ruler not only frequently vilified, but associated with the worst of a uniquely Russian despotism. Featuring an elaborate coronation ceremony at the beginning, it also coincided – by no accident – with Stalin's reinstatement of the Orthodox Church.

Set to the music of composer Sergei Prokofiev, this inscription, appearing immediately after the credits, sets the tone of a film created to instil that single message:

> This film is about the man who united Russia in the 16th century, the Muscovy prince who welded scattered principalities into a mighty state, the commander who enhanced the military glory of Russia in the east and in the west, the sovereign who, in order to accomplish all this, was the first to have himself crowned Czar of all Russia.

Soviet television: enlightenment and spectacle

Both cinema and television in the Soviet Union were essentially subverted by the Party as the most effective means of propaganda. The moving picture, to a far greater extent than text, instils in the viewer a certain construct that is both emotional and intellectual. If other media can take on the exclusive functions of informing, analysing and explaining, television, while capable of all of the above, also accomplishes what no other medium can with such ease: it *demonstrates*.

Unfortunately, what was appropriate for feature films and even the newsreels that were shown before them could not as effectively be utilized on television, primarily for technological reasons. But there is also another important factor in the Soviet Russian experience: if cinema benefited from party control, with the government acting as a sponsor to largely independent geniuses like Vertov and Eisenstein, then Soviet television was a purely top-down endeavour with little room for creative licence. In the West it developed under forces that were both commercial and governmental, but in Russia the diversity brought on by the commercial aspect was heavily limited from the start. Because of this, when Russian television became open to commercial forces in 1990, they wreaked havoc on the standards of quality, however contrived, that Soviet viewers had been accustomed to. But even while it was under the full control of the government, Soviet television provided acclaimed, quality programming that, in many ways, could have rivalled the work of public television stations in the West, especially when we take into account that Soviet television's 'awakening' in the late 1950s and early 1960s coincided with – and even owes its existence to – Nikita Khrushchev's thaw.

The formation of Soviet television as a propaganda tool

The official birth of Soviet television is considered to be the night of 16 December 1934, with the transmission of the first 'talking' programme. The 25-minute transmission consisted more of singing than of talking, however: an anchor introduced a short concert with the words, 'Watch and listen to our first televised concert'. This was followed by a performance by the Moscow Art Theatre star actor, Ivan Moskvin, who reportedly wondered aloud: 'Will this really be visible? Through walls? That's a miracle!'

The breakthrough was a big step for technology rather than the mass medium itself in the strict sense of the word, because most Russians did not have access to a television. In those days, a single viewer would look through a hole into the television box, much like through a telescope. Moreover, all television transmission was halted during the war, between 1941 and 1945, ruling out any televised war coverage.

Television sets would become considerably more accessible towards the second half of the 1950s, and only then would the government start seriously considering the medium as a formidable propaganda tool. By 1957, Moscow had approximately 1 million television sets, or about 4 million television viewers.[3] Moscow's hosting of the sixth annual World Festival of Youth and Students fuelled national television's development into an influential medium. On 16 May 1957, the Council of Ministers decreed that radio and television were no longer under the jurisdiction of the Ministry of Culture and created a State Committee for Radio Broadcasting and Television (Gosteleradio). At the same time, the propaganda and agitation department of the Central Committee of the Communist Party formed a special section that advised or 'curated' radio and

television. The World Festival of Youth and
in Moscow on 28 July, appeared to be one c
would fuel everything from state television to
the Olympic games, held 23 years later). One o.
to prepare young people for the festival was the t.
the upcoming event, *Vecher Veselia i Voprosov* \
Questions), launched in May. Otherwise, broadcastii.
a rather random, eclectic character. Only one availa.
transmit newsreels on Soviet life, musical and theatri\
and sports events.

That would all begin to change in 1960, when,
increasingly attentive government strategy, television would
medium that was indeed watched by millions. On 12 April 19\
of Russians watched transfixed as a five-hour broadcast docum\
Gagarin's return from space. In 1963 construction of the tallest
in Europe began: the Ostankino television tower in Moscow. The
Union would get its first news and analysis programme in Dec\
1961, when the *Estafeta Novostei* (*News and Mail*) weekly magazine
launched, comprising an analytical talk-show of sorts in which its t\
anchors, Yuri Fokin and Georgy Kuznetsov, would give their interpreta
tion of weekly events. The programme also featured reports and guests
like the anthropologist Mikhail Gerasimov, who talked about his work in
reconstructing human skulls and showed skull-based sculptures of Geng-
his Khan and Ivan the Terrible.

Kuznetsov and Fokin give special consideration to the status occupied
by role models in Soviet society and their coverage on television. If in the
past Russians had 'five-year plans' for motivation, in 1961 Nikita
Khrushchev coined the term *mayak*, or lighthouse, to signify accomplished collective farmers that should serve as examples for everyone from
plumbers to intellectuals in the Academy of Sciences. Their ubiquitous
presence came to fill not just newspapers and magazines, but hours of
television broadcasting as well.

Several factors contributed to this focus on personalities, and not all of
them had to do with ideology. When we think of Soviet television, we
tend to recall the Brezhnev years, when access to television sets and the
proliferation of channels and broadcasting made it ubiquitous in Soviet
life. One of the features of Brezhnev-era broadcasts, however, was that
they were not filmed live, something that was taken advantage of as a
control mechanism. Few recall, however, that the technological capabilities for video recording were relatively new. Prior to the mid-1960s, all
broadcasts in the Soviet Union were live, and it was no accident that they
corresponded with what some anchors have called the 'golden age' of
Soviet television. One such anchor was Vladimir Sappak, a journalist and
theatrical critic who tried to use live interviews to bring out the best in
television. His descriptions of interviewees, who were filmed in impro-
vised chats, echoes Vertov's outline of the Kino-Eye: 'In any "role", in any
circumstance, she remains herself'.[4]

uboi Ogonek (Blue Flame) was perhaps the most watched Soviet
of all time. It was launched in April 1962, and featured personalities
g to each other without a script. Years later it would feature
rities and performances, but in the beginning it focused on impro-
d speech from regular people.

By 1967, Soviet television had undergone the structural changes that
uld outlast the Soviet Union. Until then, television broadcasts were
ansmitted by the Shukhovskaya radio tower, which was built on Lenin's
rders in 1922. The opening of Ostankino in 1967 meant wider techno-
ogical possibilities. Several channels started broadcasting in colour across
the Soviet Union. Vilen Yegorov, one of the founding members of
Gosteleradio in the 1960s, recalls the birth of Central Television as it
would be known from then on:

> In 1967, just ahead of the opening of the Ostankino tower, a unique
> contest was announced. Tempting offers started appearing on televi-
> sion: 'Would you like to be a commentator? Come join us. Are you
> an engineer, teacher, economist, doctor? Wonderful. You will have
> the opportunity to tell viewers about other people in your profes-
> sion.'
>
> A large number of contestants came to the auditions. Based on
> the results of written and oral tests ... 18 people were chosen. For
> two years they studied in special courses, then they began work in
> various editorial offices of Central Television.[5]

Soviet television's focus on personalities and their successes followed a
strategy of demonstrating just how successful the government's policies
were. This was a relatively easy task for newspapermen, who used mostly
words to embellish the positive. But television anchors and correspondents often had to go out of their way to 'demonstrate' things that simply
did not exist. A case in point involved the failure of Nikita Khrushchev's
agricultural policies in the early 1960s. A poor crop nearly wiped out the
grain supply, forcing the government to purchase grain from Canada and
the USA in a notorious cover-up. In the meantime, in an incident recalled
by Georgy Kuznetsov, journalists at a Gorky television station were given
an assignment to report on positive tendencies in the corn crop. Finding
none, the crew outdid themselves and had the correspondent filmed
talking to the collective farm chairman about the corn stalks towering
over their heads. In reality, they were kneeling beneath an obviously
sub-par crop, while the cameraman was literally filming with the camera
on the ground.

A few years after Leonid Brezhnev assumed the office of general
secretary in 1964, the stagnant political atmosphere that was associated
with his rule would creep into television. But another aspect separated
television of the thaw era from Brezhnev's 'stagnation'. In 1968, Russia's
most easily recognized daily news programme, *Vremya*, was aired for the
first time. Brezhnev himself was said to like the programme very much,
but because he also liked circuses, local journalists recall how every time
Brezhnev would visit the area they would have to run a story on circuses.

The appearance of *Vremya*, however, was a pivotal moment for Russian television because prior to its launch the concept of televised news did not exist at all. But the concept of news itself was very different in 1968 from what it is today, as well as from what it was for western journalists and viewers. News certainly existed in the Soviet Union, in print periodicals and in news agencies, but the conceptual difference between facts and opinions still did not exist – nor would it appear for several decades.[6] *Vremya*, in that sense, was no different: a prominent feature of Russia's first televised news was that the facts were consumed by the anchor's interpretation, which, at that point, came directly from the Kremlin.

This lack of a difference between facts and opinions was in fact so pervasive that opinions would continue to permeate the news both in print and on television throughout the 1990s and even in the first decade of the twentieth century. Neither glasnost nor commercialized television in the 1990s were capable of completely drawing a conceptual separation.

August 1991: the first spectacle

When Mikhail Gorbachev proclaimed his policy of glasnost after coming to power, 90 per cent of airtime was dedicated to sociopolitical or cultural programmes. There were very few foreign films and no advertisements.[7] Together with Alexander Yakovlev, he began promoting his new policy – a concept which is frequently confused with 'free speech' – from the top. The difference is essential: the press was not free until 1990, and where television was concerned, given the complexity of the technological system, attaining real independence was even more difficult. This aspect is very important when we consider what independence means for today's television stations – to understand that, we must remember that just two decades before, Gorbachev's glasnost meant that Gosteleradio was ordered to run more outspoken programming. This meant, essentially, that editors were still told exactly what they were supposed to run, with the only difference being that live talk shows with westerners and more live programming in general began appearing on television screens.

That changed late at night on 19 August 1991 when, for the first time, the chairman of Gosteleradio, Leonid Kravchenko, literally did not know what to do. That day, a group of reactionary officials led by vice-president Gennady Yanayev had announced an emergency situation and formed a self-styled State Committee on the Emergency Situation (GKChP) that took power and placed Gorbachev, who just that March had assumed the new post of President of the Soviet Union, under house arrest. Viewers woke up to see a startlingly familiar picture on their television screens: instead of regular programming, they were treated to a blast from the past consisting of a drab array of ballets and musical performances. It was an ominous – and obvious – cover, a signal that something bad had happened. *Swan Lake*, after all, was the kind of programming viewers would see on their television screens each time an ageing general secretary died (and the last decade had seen a succession: first Brezhnev, then Yuri Andropov, then Konstantin Chernenko). A stark contrast to the vivid programming that Channel 1 had assumed in line with Gorbachev's recent policies, the sombre officialdom did not bode well. This much was evident even before residents looked outside their windows to see tanks on the streets.

The reactionary coup was actually a culmination of months of growing tensions, not just between the reformist Gorbachev and the Party hardliners, but between Gorbachev and the even more reform-minded Boris Yeltsin. As Gorbachev struggled to implement his democratic policies, the economy floundered and living standards plummeted, discrediting his government and dashing the hopes he had fostered in the population. Meanwhile, amid growing nationalist sentiment in other Soviet republics, Yeltsin held a referendum on creating a presidential post in the Russian Soviet Federated Socialist Republic (RSFSR). In June he won, with over half of the votes, and became Russia's first president. Inevitably, however, the progressive president of RSFSR clashed with the more moderately reformist president of the USSR, further undermining an already shaky situation in the upper echelons.

As part of the coup, GKChP shut down all newspapers except for a handful of central dailies, took full control of television, and much of radio. On the previous night, military units surrounded the Gosteleradio headquarters at Ostankino. Journalists who came to work the next morning were barred entry by troops. But that didn't keep many radio journalists from rallying around Yeltsin's White House, the office of Russia's parliament and government.

On 19 August, two televised events occurred that would play a pivotal role in the outcome of the standoff. Curiously, they both took place on the GKChP-controlled Channel 1. The first was a 5 p.m. press conference given by the members of the GKChP to address the Soviet people. Some 150 million people watched it.[8] Kravchenko's Gosteleradio decided to hold it live, and apparently, on a spur of the moment, GKChP did not object. What resulted was hardly a favour to the hardliners: while some have difficulty recalling what exactly it was that Yanayev said about Gorbachev, everyone who saw the broadcast remembers Yanayev's trembling hands. It appeared that the cameraman, meanwhile, didn't shirk from filming the vice-president at his most vulnerable. A crucial moment of the event involved not so much Yanayev himself as it did a journalist from *Nezavisimaya Gazeta*, Tatyana Malkina, who asked that day's most pointed question: 'Do you understand that last night you committed a state coup?' Instead of focusing on Yanayev, the camera panned in on Malkina's face.

The second event was a typical daily report on *Vremya*, at first glance about life in the city. Indeed, that first-glance ambiguity was responsible for getting the programme past censors at Ostankino. The first few moments showed tanks on otherwise peaceful Moscow streets. But filming ended with Yeltsin reading his own address atop a tank in front of the White House – the correspondent briefly summarized what Yeltsin had said, without commentary. It was a drastic step away from other programming on *Vremya*, which struggled to focus on an otherwise calm city. But it was also real-time news, and neither ideology nor interpretation was necessary for it to have its unintended historic effect.

The televised chaos of the 1990s

It would appear that two developments over the course of Gorbachev's rule would work towards ultimately laying the foundations of a free press in Russia: the glasnost policy and the media law of 1990. But on deeper examination, these two events were taking place in a contradictory setting, thereby also laying the foundations for the flaws that Russia's media would continue to grapple with to this day. Because television, as the medium with the most at stake in a tumultuous period, was a prime focus for Soviet leadership struggling to transform its system of propaganda, those contradictions become evident as we recall the events of the late 1980s and early 1990s.

Politicized spectacle

As we have already noted, Gorbachev's policy was a top-down endeavour. All it meant was that instead of wholly promoting the communist regime, journalists were now encouraged to report on more critical and controversial issues. No structural changes in a party-controlled media system had been made.[9] This first contradiction between the spirit of glasnost – however imposed it was on the journalists – and the structure of Party control led to the media law of August 1990. The law served as reconciliation between the spirit and the letter in that it placed registering a media outlet beyond the control of the Party. The law, however, was passed by the Party itself a full year before the CPSU coup, allowing for a number of important violations, or, at least, contradictions in spirit.

First of all, the law did not 'emancipate' the existing media. It only allowed private citizens to launch their own print or broadcast outlets. But because of costs and infrastructure, de facto television remained in the hands of the state through Gosteleradio. At certain points during his rule, Gorbachev would be forced to reassert his control of the media for hardliner elements within the CPSU. One such moment was his November 1990 appointment of Leonid Kravchenko as head of Gosteleradio. Even after the law was passed, at no time in Yeltsin's Russia did the media ever hold a 'sacred', or 'untouchable' status. Newspapers would be banned and television stations would be shut down during the coup, but this would also happen during Yeltsin's notoriously hardline stance when battling his parliament in October 1993. Many would come to see that day as the end of any true possibility for free, democratic media in Russia. However, it is arguable whether that media was truly free and democratic between 1991 and 1993 in the first place.

The important thing to remember is that even after the adoption of the media law in 1990, national television's policy of 'democratization' was nevertheless an executive order from the top. In a televised address on a show called *Direct Talk* on 9 April 1991, Kravchenko laid out his plans to 'democratize' state television:

- orientation towards civil agreement in Soviet society;
- presenting various points of view with commentary reflecting the point of view of the country's leadership;
- the creation of a new, technologically sustained Moscow-Leningrad television channel;
- an allowance of 70 per cent of entertainment programming to 30 per cent of political programming.[10]

This would prove meaningful just a few years later, when private capital had transformed television, which was struggling financially during the early 1990s, into a multi-polar mix of spectacle, reality show and ideological manipulation.

One characteristic programme that epitomized the no holds barred reporting practices that emerged after perestroika was *600 Seconds*, a news show launched in 1987 on a St Petersburg channel by the reporter, anchor and, later, parliamentarian Alexander Nevzorov. Echoing a similar trend in the print media, the show depicted, with stomach-churning naturalistic detail, all the horrors of modern life – street violence, prostitution and general decay. Nevzorov had a particularly gruesome penchant for showing anything from rotting meat in factories to dead children. In a show that blurred the lines of journalism ethics, one edition documented an uprising of a prison colony. Footage showed Nevzorov trying to interview a prisoner even as he was dying of bullet wounds.

Shows like *600 Seconds* reflected two inherent trends. On the one hand, journalists across the media spectrum were reacting to the unbridled 'freedom' that they were suddenly exposed to. If things remotely negative had been suppressed on Soviet television, they burst onto the screen with a vengeance during perestroika and particularly during the early 1990s, when life in post-Soviet Russia was bleak, hard and often violent. Against this backdrop, blatant politicization was to be expected. Nevzorov himself would go on to become a parliamentarian in 1993. In his shows, he was an outspoken opponent of the breakup of the USSR, and in the early 1990s voiced ardent support for the ultra-nationalist Vladimir Zhirinovsky.

Television channels were not alone in their general support of the Yeltsin government during 1993 and then their criticism of his war in the breakaway republic of Chechnya, but their footage was the starkest given the natural advantage of the medium, and hence the most memorable. What is noteworthy is that at their most critical, at their most oppositionist, relations between television and the government were also at their least transparent. Ivan Zassoursky admits that by 1993 the media was 'forced to accept the supreme power of the president, which bordered on dictatorship – and thus accept the fact that the very dictatorship was created through the efforts of the democratic press and television'.[11]

The NTV channel, the independent asset of Vladimir Gusinsky's Media-Most holding, which had been loyal to the president even when he used force to quell the parliamentary uprising in 1993, changed sides and spearheaded a virulently oppositionist stance in covering the first campaign in Chechnya. It was joined by the government-owned RTR television station, known as the second channel. In fact, the only channel that would remain loyal to Yeltsin during the first Chechen war was Boris Berezovsky's Ostankino on the first button, which would later be renamed ORT, and later still, Channel 1.

The first Chechen campaign was the Russian media's first exposure to military coverage. Since the war in Afghanistan in the 1980s was effectively suppressed, Russian television journalists had no experience of covering any military conflict. The same could be said for the viewers. Unaccustomed to the kind of war footage that was common in the West, Russian daytime TV viewers were suddenly accosted by visions of tents set up in the streets of Grozny filling up with bodies. Because they had not been inoculated during the war in Afghanistan, viewers were shocked to see footage of combat next to images of generals reading out 'official' statistics which differed starkly from what was displayed on the television screen.

One of the more controversial instances was the live coverage of negotiations at a hostage standoff. In June 1995, months after Yeltsin deployed troops to Chechnya, Shamil Basayev, a separatist militant leader who would go on to take responsibility for a number of bloody civilian attacks, stormed the Stavropol town of Budennovsk and took more than 1000 people hostage in a local hospital that included children and pregnant women. While Yeltsin was in Canada at a G7 meeting and his defence minister, Pavel Grachev, was allegedly on vacation, the work of securing a deal with the terrorists under the watchful eye of an NTV crew fell to Prime Minister Victor Chernomyrdin. In the end, more than 140 people would die in the raids and over 400 would be left wounded. The tragedy, however, was not frequently recalled following subsequent hostage standoffs during Putin's administration – the Nord-Ost theatre siege, and the Beslan school siege. Given the kind of chaos that live coverage could bring to a dangerous hostage event, subsequent hostage takeovers would prompt not just vivid debate on what was allowed for electronic media in such emergency events, but even specific laws limiting the power of the media to broadcast information regarding a terrorist attack.

While Yeltsin had other things on his mind in 1995 besides punitive measures against NTV journalists, the television station was nevertheless subjected to some form of pressure. NTV had aired an interview with Shamil Basayev on 20 June, right in the middle of the standoff. The Prosecutor's Office, after investigating the tape, came to the conclusion that, by airing it, NTV offered Basayev a platform to intimidate Russians, while the programme itself 'propagated a cult of violence'. Basayev had given the interview to Yelena Masyuk, an NTV correspondent who just two years later would herself be taken hostage by Chechen militants and held for 101 days until a $1 million ransom was paid. While prosecutors issued a recommendation that the Press Committee take 'measures' against NTV that were in line with the media law, the then head of the Committee, Ivan Laptev, publicly defended NTV journalists, commending them on acting professionally.[12]

When we consider that Russia's previous war with Afghanistan had hardly been covered, it is all the more reason to think that journalists were somehow making up for lost time in an effort to report on the current war. However, as noted above, Russian journalists had little experience in objective coverage in 1995. They were accustomed to a top-down ideological system, and at a time when there was no need to conform to the Party line, many, despite unarguable efforts at objective reporting, took on criticizing the government as the ultimate mission, rather than reporting the war.

In this light, it is clear that Russians were being shown combat in a general context of massive coverage of criticism and protest events. Widely covered was Nizhny Novgorod governor Boris Nemtsov's 1 million signatures urging Yeltsin to halt the military campaign. Another example of the focus on protest was a platform given to human rights activist Valeria Novodvorskaya, who, in widely broadcast footage of protest rallies, was shown calling on soldiers to desert and on Muscovites to raise money for Chechen rebels.

It is ironic, then, that the premise for the *next* major media campaign was precisely the fact that Boris Yeltsin's popularity ratings were so low at the start of 1996. Televised media had, in effect, contributed considerably to bringing down his popularity ratings with its anti-war campaign in 1995, only to have the same channels sign up to rectify the problem ahead of the presidential election in 1996. But if the anti-war campaign had essentially been a natural event, then the pro-Yeltsin campaign that followed it was also, in a replay of the best Soviet traditions, orchestrated from the top. According to Ivan Zassoursky, 'Contemporary information technologies turned out to be the very missing link that allowed them to revitalize the mass media as a propaganda apparatus of the party of power and achieve a victory in the elections, or, as certain observers recount, to create enough cover for their falsification'.[13]

Part of this dramaturgy was the carefully-crafted presidential campaign – and it's no wonder, then, that NTV president Igor Malashenko was drafted for the very purpose of recreating Yeltsin's image and orchestrating campaign propaganda. Zassoursky credits him with forging the 'virtual reality' that was created at the time to draw viewers' attention away from worrisome reports about Yeltsin's health and the many other troubles the country as a whole was experiencing. One of the more vivid examples of that virtual reality was the picture of Yeltsin dancing with singers on stage at the peak of the campaign in the summer of 1996, just weeks after disappearing unexpectedly from the limelight. In fact, it was speculated that the Russian president had suffered a heart attack in late June.

Political spectacle on Russian television reached an apotheosis in 1999, when the state-controlled RTR television channel got its hands on a dirty video that it opted to broadcast during prime time. On 17 March, the station ran a five-minute clip in which a naked man that resembled Prosecutor General Yuri Skuratov frolicked in bed with two women. This convergence of television and politics, which led to Skuratov's dismissal, illustrated a political scene in which the Kremlin itself apparently had to resort to a smear campaign to get rid of an unpopular official. Skuratov would neither confirm nor deny his guilt, and the origins of the tape, which was distributed to a number of media outlets, remain shrouded in mystery. Vladimir Putin, who was then head of the FSB, confirmed in a press conference that the man in the video was actually Skuratov.

Room for experimentation

We have examined some of the lasting footprints of the government in 1990s television, and seen the instrumental role that government capital and the political loyalties of big business played in creating the spectacle of 1990s television in Chapter 2. But it is worthwhile to point out that the very spectacle that characterized the 1990s was not all political, nor was it all pre-programmed from the top.

New opportunities in advertising and unheard of freedoms in broadcasting meant that Russian television witnessed a surge of the experimental. Daily programming was interrupted by sometimes bizarre advertising that resembled low-budget art film shorts. Lack of a sophisticated understanding of genre meant that daytime and prime time television would feature not just the soap operas and sitcoms that viewers were developing a taste for, but also unexpected, award-winning independent films that were previously censored – and not entirely for political reasons.

Long before the launch of the Russian MTV channel in 1998, TV channels would buy into the music video revolution that was also sweeping the domestic scene. Cultural figures like Artemy Troitsky would host half-hour music video shows that would feature domestic artists and then offer viewers his own critical take on the video – content that later programming directors at MTV would obviously find too highbrow.

In fact, before managers got accustomed to the constraints of ratings and profit margins, much of Russia's non-political entertainment television was a free for all that provided a valuable venue for up and coming artists, filmmakers and musicians to forge a cultural identity. It was an opportunity that they may have otherwise never had if Soviet-run television had made a smooth and sudden transition towards fully commercial broadcasting.

Much of this experimentation would be gone as television standardized towards 2000, but in the sense that it reflected the utter chaos of the 1990s and served as a valuable sound and video track to the political and social upheaval of the time it was, inevitably, part of the social and political spectacle.

Creeping censorship

The accepted consensus about the state of Russian television is that it had been free and independent following the breakup of the Soviet Union, and then fell under the sway of pervasive government censorship once the Putin administration began nationalizing television stations in 2000. We have provided a more nuanced elaboration of these processes in Chapter 2, which discussed ownership and control of television. Here it would be appropriate to look at a few examples that will demonstrate how fleeting television freedom was in Russia.

One of the most blatant instances of television censorship following the breakup of the Soviet Union occurred not during the Putin years, but in 1993. The coup that took place in September and October of that year pitted President Boris Yeltsin against parliament. At the heart of the conflict were Yeltsin's liberal reforms, which were repeatedly stalled in the communist-controlled Supreme Soviet, or parliament. Although the constitution, which had been drafted in 1978 and then amended after the fall of the Communist Party in 1991, explicitly forbade the president to dismiss the Supreme Soviet, Yeltsin issued a decree in September dissolving the legislative body because of the reforms he intended to pass.

Forces loyal to Vice-president Alexander Rutskoi and the head of the Supreme Soviet, Ruslan Khasbulatov, stormed the White House to hold an emergency session and tried to raid Ostankino tower in an attempt to get access to airtime. They were overwhelmed by Yeltsin's forces. Unlike the 1991 coup, which saw the accidental deaths of three people, at least 150 were killed during the 'constitutional' standoff in 1993. An entirely new constitution was issued in December of that year, transforming the political landscape and considerably expanding the powers of the president. A new, albeit weaker, two-chamber parliament would continue to function as a quasi-democratic institution until the next decade, when it was virtually emasculated under the increasing dominance of its majority party, United Russia, which would become headed by Vladimir Putin in 2008. While the events of 1993 were not seen in the same pivotal light as the coup of 1991, for many Russians they heralded the end of democracy in post-Soviet Russia.

More importantly, 1993 was an instance in which a liberal, pro-western president, who already enjoyed mass support in the press, used the danger posed by the communists in parliament to shut down all oppositionist newspapers and a number of important television shows – most notably, the Supreme Soviet's *Parlamentsky Chas* (*Parliamentary Hour*) on RTR, the weekly analysis *Politburo*, the talk show *Krasny kvadrat* (*Red Square*) on Channel 1 and the popular interactive news segment, *Vremechko* (which roughly means 'the diminutive of time'). In short, anything that was critical of Yeltsin was suppressed.

But if censorship in times of national calamity can be understood (if not always justified), in this case it set a crippling precedent for the fragile concepts of media freedom and independence that were taking root. We have seen how television was compromised throughout the decade by the involvement of politicized business. Together with a lack of deeply-founded values of independence, the closeness of media barons with the government did not bode well for the quality of Russia's television. There would hardly be instances of outright censorship after 1993, but the foundations had been irreparably tarnished, and television in particular would sway towards bias and government subservience.

The years after the presidential campaign of 1996 would see the demise of live analytical programming. Gone were Sergei Dorenko's Sunday night analytical news magazine, *Vremya* (*Time*), and Yevgeny Kiselyov's *Itogi* (*Summary*). These were not direct, deliberate acts of censorship. Rather, they reflected the use of pundits in political campaigning, and their discarding once they were no longer necessary for media owners.

A characteristic example of the 'creeping censorship' that began that decade and gained momentum during the Putin administration is the story of one of Russian television's leading anchors, Svetlana Sorokina. After launching her career in the late 1980s, she gained notoriety on the often scandalous *600 Seconds* news show. In 1997, she joined NTV, and was one of the outspoken journalists to leave the channel when it was taken over by Gazprom (unlike her equally outspoken colleague, Tatyana Mitkova, who chose to stay at NTV despite a penchant for risking her career to report on what was actually happening rather than what Party directive prescribed). Sorokina went on to work on several short-lived independent channels – TV-6 and TVS. In April she joined Channel 1, where she hosted a daytime talk show, *Osnovnoy Instinkt* (*Basic Instinct*). Because of Russia's 11 time zones, it is impossible to broadcast certain shows live, and daytime shows like Sorokina's *Basic Instinct* had to be taped. According to Sorokina, once her show stopped airing online, she began noticing how Channel 1 editors were making minor but significant changes before airing it. As a result, she quit.

Television today

Russian television today comprises, in the words of Y. Zassoursky, the worst of the Soviet tradition and the worst of the western tradition.[14] It is an assertion with which many educated Russians tend to agree. And yet, rather than asking ourselves why this is the case, we should ask instead what it is about Russian television that elicits such dismal assessments from the elite.

Objectively speaking, Russian television failed, like much of the print media, to transform itself into the kind of western-style fourth estate that was prescribed for it by the elites themselves. Two chief factors contributed to this failure.

The first was the failure, described in Chapter 2, of media capital to distance itself from politics. This allowed for a curious contradiction. Journalists – television journalists in particular – set out to change government policy in an attempt to carry out a legitimate watchdog function of the fourth estate. But their chief instrument of success was the fact that the media barons that owned the outlet were financially and politically close to the government.

The second factor was a unique tradition that ruled out the possibility of grassroots media organization. We have seen in this chapter that a key driver of the visual media was propaganda. To cancel and deny the propaganda function of television was possible on paper and in theory, but proved impossible in practice because no alternative system was offered to replace it. Some argue that cash and advertising replaced propaganda as the chief driving forces in television, but given the notorious murkiness of the transactions that went on as well as the fact that media barons were funded by state-owned corporations from the start, it is still hard to view pure commercialism as a viable driving force.

Essentially, this points not so much to 'bad' television, but to betrayed expectations and disappointments. The expectation that Soviet media could transform into an instrument of information, education, criticism and entertainment at the same time was at once a product of the Soviet propaganda tradition and also doomed to fail because of its inherent contradictions.

The recollections of television scholar Georgy Kuznetsov are telling in this sense:

> Once we had the slogan that print was not just a collective propagandist and collective agitator, but a collective organizer. This function was prescribed to the party press by Vladimir Lenin even before the revolution of 1905. For 70 years we dumbly applied this formula to our media, including television. When Leonid Brezhnev said in the middle of the 1970s that the Soviet man has a right to relax in front of the television set, television started including a recreation function. Then, at the height of perestroika in the 1980s Mikhail Nenashev, then chairman of Gosteleradio, modified Lenin's triad and said that television's function was to inform, convince, and console, thereby admitting that the Soviet man wasn't very happy if he was in need of consolation. Then, as we know, there was another reassessment of values, and instead of Nenashev and Brezhnev there was a new authority, Gusinsky. Arriving at our faculty, he said at once: don't bother me about educating the people, enlightenment and all that ... For me, television is a commercial enterprise, and the product is information and entertainment. That's it. And don't bother me with the other functions. Since he came to us in his four cars and with his security, we were obligated to listen to him. Apparently he'd heard somewhere of BBC's formula – inform, entertain, educate, and just threw out the last part, which he found inappropriate for our television.[15]

Gusinsky might have indeed forgotten about educating the viewers who tuned to NTV, but his chief failure was the promise to inform – in the media campaigns described above, the primary aim of the journalists was neither to educate nor to inform, but to *sway*. Soviet propaganda did not conceal that convincing was a chief function on its agenda. Post-Soviet television, and to some degree, the independent press, presented what was at times starkly biased, agenda-driven material as news and information, thereby undermining its own credibility.

To rephrase Zassoursky's assessment, we can say that Russia has neither the kind of public television station comparable to the BBC, nor are its commercial stations 100 per cent independent from the state. What kind of television are Russians watching today?

Where news programmes are concerned, the trend towards conglomerating television around state corporations has meant that state control over television has almost come full circle. According to figures revealed in December 2007 by the Center for Journalism in Extreme Situations (CJES), 91 to 93 per cent of the total news coverage (except news on culture, sports and weather), centred on the activities of President Vladimir Putin (30 to 35 per cent); the government (35 to 40 per cent) and the pro-Kremlin majority party, United Russia (20 to 22 per cent).[16]

This does not necessarily mean that government criticism does not exist on state television. While television journalists speak of an unpublished 'blacklist' of topics, prime time news programming frequently concerns inadequate local government action, failure to provide basic social services, corruption among mid-level local officials, hazing in the army, poverty and general lack of accountability. While far from direct criticism of Putin, his policies, or his administration, these issues hit far closer to home for a majority of Russians who, polls show, are far less concerned with human rights than they are with problems like inflation, crime and corruption.

There are exceptions illustrating that today's television sphere is still a far cry from Soviet hegemony and independent news reporting is widely available for those willing to find it. REN-TV, a nationwide channel that is predominantly geared towards entertainment, broadcasts in-depth, professional news programmes that rival their analogues on state-owned television. These news programmes are also strikingly independent, shedding light on a paradoxical situation surrounding the channel. Founded in 1991 as an independent holding, the REN-TV company went on to gain access to airwaves in 1997, becoming an independent channel with nationwide broadcasting. The channel was controlled jointly by RTL, a German company, the steel magnate Severstal and the oil group Surgutneftegaz. In April 2007, a controlling share of company stock went to Abros, an investment firm with close ties to the Putin administration. The transfer led media to speculate that REN-TV would share the fate of NTV.[17]

By summer 2008, it was clear that the clampdown was not happening. In September of that year news broadcasts shed candid light on the cult that was forming around Vladimir Putin, who had assumed the post of prime minister earlier that spring. Even as state-owned television went into denial regarding the financial crisis that was gaining momentum in Russia, either skirting the issue altogether or describing it as a far-away problem that the USA had brought upon itself, REN-TV addressed the economic issues head-on, with detailed coverage and expert analysis.

REN-TV's news reporters were talking about the crisis weeks before the issue was admitted by the country's top leadership. Meanwhile, the channel continued with in-depth coverage of the liberal opposition and the campaign to free former Yukos employees from prison.

Not to be underestimated is digital and cable television (DTV), which proliferated in Russia during the 1990s. New media provided the opportunity to broadcast channels virtually unregulated by the government. Cable channels such as the 24-hour business news channel RBC and Rambler TV (launched by the internet holding, Rambler) serve alternative sources of televised news, while smaller stations frequently act as venues for oppositionist political figures, experts and reporters. A widening media sphere means that DTV can be accessed via terrestrial television, cable television, the internet, satellite television and mobile phone. While state television remains pervasive, official statistics and market regulators often fail to take into account the role that DTV has come to play in Russian society. As of 2008, nearly 10 per cent of households – 4.7 million out of 49 million – had used the services of digital television in Russia.[18]

A curious situation is thus developing in Russia's media sphere that is more akin to some of the more liberal epochs of Imperial Russia than it is to the Soviet era. The fact that censorship does not officially exist means that independent news can be freely broadcast, but the number of people who statistically have access to that independent coverage is limited. In other words, those who know what to find and who choose to get their news from alternative sources in Russia should have no trouble doing so. More passive sectors of the population, however, will continue to be fed news that is shaped, to a large extent, by the Kremlin or by pro-Kremlin business interests.

The problems outlined above would appear to concern primarily news reporting, but there is a lot more to television than news – and in Russia's case, a lot can be gleaned from its entertainment sector.

Beyond the news

As of 2001, 54 per cent of broadcasting time in Russia was devoted to cinema, 20 per cent to sitcoms and soap operas, 25 per cent to feature films and 9 per cent to animation and non-feature films.[19] And given the drive to create more domestic series, there is an obvious trend towards more entertainment, not less.

While the 1990s were characterized by a wide range of foreign programming, during the following decade, fuelled by encouragement from the government, television studios embarked on churning out domestic series. One way of doing this was adopting the common practice of remaking foreign hits. This has both aided the entertainment industry and hampered it. Two of Russia's most successful series – and, arguably, among the best prime time shows – are *Ne Rodis Krasivoi* (*Don't Be Born Beautiful*), which made its debut on the film and entertainment channel STS in 2005, and *Moya Prekrasnaya Nyanya* (*My Beautiful Nanny*), which has been running on the same channel since 2004. Both are remakes, and both owe their success to the acting talent of the lead actresses. *Don't Be Born Beautiful* is a spin-off of the popular Colombian soap opera, launched in 1999, *Yo soy Betty, La Fea*, which was also adapted into an American series, *Ugly Betty*. Based on the story of an unattractive but hardworking young woman seeking a position in the cut-throat world of corporate fashion, it was easily adapted to Russian realities, which are rife with sexual discrimination and stereotypes in the office climate. This compatibility helped propel the acting career of Nelly Uvarova, a theatrical actress with the Moscow Academic Youth Theatre.

To a similar extent, compatibility and brilliant casting were behind the success of Russia's remake of *My Beautiful Nanny*. Undergoing few changes to the plot, the Russian version cast the Queens-born beautician into an outspoken woman of Ukrainian decent. Besides the fact that Anastasia Zavorotnyuk boasted a remarkable physical resemblance to Fran Drescher, the star, writer and producer of the American original, the Russian sitcom also succeeded in playing on class tensions in contemporary Russian society without altering the plot line. In other words, the scripts penned for a Colombian soap opera and an American sitcom were entirely imported.

In the case of STS, which benefited from a working tandem between Sony Pictures and the Russian Amedia company, the imports proved a success. Other imports, however, were less popular simply because the plot line didn't adapt as well to Russian realities. A case in point is the long-running US sitcom *Married with Children*, which was adapted on the REN-TV show, *Happy Together*. The original centres around a dysfunctional family in a typical, two-storey suburban home. The Russian version likewise depicts a typical 'dysfunctional' family in Yekaterinburg. To adapt to local realities, the producers housed the family in an apartment. However, like the original American set, the Russian apartment featured a staircase in the background, leading, presumably, to a second floor. Anyone who has lived in Russia knows that an apartment with a second floor is extremely rare (and expensive) in Moscow, and looks even more uncanny in the home of a lower-class Yekaterinburg family.

Such a discrepancy points to an entertainment industry that seems to depend more on luck than on talent and merit. On another level, however, in their scramble to import successful entertainment products and meet the quota for 'domestic' programming, producers appear to be perpetuating an epidemic of catering to the lowest common denominator. According to sociologist Daniil Dondurei,

> The problem is that in the last several years Russian television has been suffering from an imbalance between the movement towards the top and towards the bottom. Towards the top means addressing talent, creativity, craft, work, and confidence that does not rule out the ability to question oneself. What else is capable of thrilling viewers like, for instance, the programme *Stars on Ice* [a figure-skating contest for celebrities] ... or the series *Don't Be Born*

Beautiful? But an overwhelming majority of programmes on Russian prime time, practically on all federal channels save for the Culture channel – from *Confessions from the Heart* on NTV to the evening lineup of documentaries on the First Channel – draw downward. They share a clear penchant for demonstrating various pathologies, anomalies, and are obsessed with how dangerous our lives are. Of course, it's a lot easier to focus on titillating subjects – violence, perversion, scandals, crime – in a downward-oriented movement. Our television is already accustomed to telling us about 1,500 murders each week. And society at first got used to and then reconciled itself with this 'picture of the world', without accepting the exaggeration. Moreover, viewers are dependent on a deeply psychological addiction which can be defined as, 'I don't like it, but I watch with pleasure anyway.'[20]

In the words of Dondurei, who is a member of the Presidential Arts and Culture Council, the problems plaguing Russian television are a lot like the ones in the West: namely, the cult of sex and violence and its effects in jading society. But while in the West this conversation has been going on for decades, the short-term presence of a no-holds-barred approach to programming in Russia means that society literally hasn't had time to address these issues adequately. Going from a fully-controlled medium to a fully commercialized one practically overnight has also meant that quality control has been missing in television programming.

In the same interview, Dondurei cites a 2006 survey that identified the three most respected Russians as Andrei Malakhov, Ksenia Sobchak and Vladimir Posner. The choice of personalities is telling. Posner has been a popular television host for at least two generations, first as a defender of the Soviet regime in America, then as a political commentator in Russia. Malakhov is the host of a talk-show that, much in the style of Jerry Springer, peddles scandal and smut. Sobchak, meanwhile, is a cultural phenomenon in her own right. The daughter of St Petersburg governor Anatoly Sobchak, Ksenia has become the Paris Hilton of Russian society, a socialite who owes her success to the political status of her late father, who was briefly Vladimir Putin's boss. Regardless of her personal qualities (as a professional shopper, for instance), she both symbolizes the inevitability of the political elite's determining role in culture and its corruption as viewed by the rest of society. Lately she has been the host of Russia's most popular (and, in line with Dondurei's definition of TV addiction, most reviled) reality shows, *Dom* and *Dom-2*, where contestants live together in a house that they are building in order to pair off and win the rights to the house.

A similarly dubious situation appears to pervade post-Soviet cinema. With the transnational blockbuster success of *Night Watch*, Russian cinematography has staked much on reproducing Hollywood success – creating professional films based on a formula of collaboration with professionals. Like sports, however, cinema has taken on the vestige of a national heritage, which has meant, for all purposes, that the state has been involved, in some way or other, in very many major mainstre; films. The works of former actor and current director Nikita Mikhalkov are a good example. The last in a cultural dynasty that goes back to czarist times, he is the son of the children's writer Sergei Mikhalkov, the brother of filmmaker Andrei Konchalovsky, and, de facto, a current member of the pro-Kremlin nomenclature. It is for this reason that despite (or, perhaps, thanks to) the success of some of his for-export films, like *Burnt by the Sun* (1994), *Barber of Siberia* (1998) and *12* (a 2007 remake of the 1957 classic, *12 Angry Men,* Mikhalkov's take puts the jurors in contemporary Russia to decide the fate of a Chechen teen), is regarded with distaste by a large part of the intelligentsia for his political and cultural opportunism. With state involvement, it is also inevitable that some sort of ideology has seeped into a lot of successful mainstream films.

The increasing role of government and the Russia Today channel

In this light, it is not surprising that public figures are calling for more control in the television sphere. These calls have coincided with bolstered government control – or censorship – in the news sector, but should be viewed as somewhat separate issues. The same sociologists who decry the role of state media in determining news content will speak out for the creation of truly public television in Russia. At the heart of both issues is the lack of any responsible or accountable independent body that can create nationwide guidelines for television content. Because this function is occupied by the government, its mechanisms of control concern mainly propaganda rather than overseeing what youngsters are watching on prime time.

Rather than subsidize television and entertainment, however, the recent government has been more prone to take action to improve its own image. In the spring of 2005, Kremlin officials backed a plan to create a 24-hour English-language news channel aimed at improving western perceptions of Russia. Called Russia Today, the channel was launched in September of that year as a CNN-type information network for foreigners inside Russia and the rest of the world, spreading a 'positive' image of Russian current events. Margarita Simonyan, a television journalist, was only 25 when appointed to head the project as editor-in-chief. Significantly, the channel was founded by RIA Novosti, the state-run news agency and direct descendant of APN, and was housed together with RIA's other projects in its sprawling, central Moscow headquarters. Dismissed by the western press as a 'cheerleader' for the Kremlin,[21] the channel does nevertheless take significant strides to go beyond blatant propaganda. Other editors at Russia Today tend to be careful to avoid any sort of ideological slant, and instead present the official facts that were being overlooked by the western media.

As such, Russia Today was not averse to covering the ongoing Yukos trial. While it frequently tries to report positive news developments, correspondents and presenters in some of its departments have conflicting views on how much 'propaganda' they actually have to produce. A foreign correspondent for the business section, for instance, said that censoring pressure from above was infrequent and that she was generally free to report on her stories.

Censorship or quality control?

Unable to shake its structural connections to the government, Russian television is indeed struggling with its duties of informing and entertaining. But as we have seen, the chief problems are not so much censorship and government interference but instead involve the lack of a centralized accounting body besides that of the government, which could independently regulate educational television, which Russia lacks, as well as the quality of entertainment programming. These problems, according to Yassen Zassoursky, make Russia's television among some of the world's most backward – precisely because it was so suddenly fuelled with an influx of cash without the benefit of an independent, centralized regulating body.

6 THE ROLE OF RADIO: A COMMON EAR

> - The origins of Soviet radio
> - Levitan and the legacy of war radio
> - Music as a social statement
> - The revolution of FM radio and Russian radio today

When we think of European totalitarianism in the first half of the twentieth century, there is little that appears to symbolize its essence better than radio. The epitome of centralization in the early days, radio broadcasting meant one node and many receivers – one voice proclaiming to a herd of ears, sometimes over loudspeakers placed in the streets. It comes as a surprise, then, that radio has emerged as perhaps the most underestimated medium in terms of its influence on the population and its potential for local, grassroots organization – precisely the elements Russia has historically lacked.

If television failed to break from its top-down, propagandistic legacy of broadcasting, Russian radio, which essentially originated as part of the same totalitarian media system, has excelled in attaining a level of independence that few other media have achieved. This comes despite the fact that, having inherited a Soviet-era technological base, Russian radio also inherited some of the same troubles as print media and television. It is no stranger to political and ideological manipulation, while its journalists face the same dangers as those in print, television or the internet. Nevertheless, by the end of the 1990s, the government controlled less than 10 per cent of radio broadcast time. Easy access by commercial, municipal and public organizations has allowed radio to make remarkable strides in helping to build the foundations of grassroots communication and organization since the breakup of the Soviet Union.

A combination of two factors has allowed this symbolic medium to excel where others have failed in their duty to inform, organize and entertain: the technological capability to field calls from listeners, giving interactive potential similar to that of the internet, and its sheer scope. Indeed, the success of radio in reaching the masses surpasses even that of television. While a few households remain in Russia that do not own a television set, radio receivers are far more ubiquitous. While it is possible to spend the entire day glued to the television, it is more common to be tuned into the radio, either as background noise or for its musical content. Radio's presence in homes, cars and public places means that even in the twenty-first century, people are exposed to radio for longer periods of time than they are to any other medium.

Yassen Zassoursky, who identified radio as the most 'open' and 'accessible' medium that currently exists in Russia, also describes it as one of the most versatile. According to Zassoursky, the use of music, words and narrative coupled with its portable possibilities make it a medium with 'enormous educational potential'.[1] Radio arms the journalist with the spoken word in a way that makes it more powerful than the printed word.

The origins of Soviet radio

One voice, many ears

'All of Russia will listen to the newspaper that is being read in Moscow', Vladimir Lenin said in 1921. With its origins in the telegraph, radio broadcasting is not only the oldest electronic medium, it is also a medium whose immense popularity and influence has remained stable throughout its history. According to Ivan Zassoursky, radio can serve as a technological metaphor for the totalitarian system as a whole by working as a centralized propaganda machine with a single source broadcasting to many nodes. The irony of the medium is that its inherently totalitarian tradition and structure has also equipped it with highly effective instruments for forging a lasting rapport with the population. Today, it is all but impossible to subject that rapport to government regulation, giving radio the kind of potential for independence and influence that we typically associate with the internet.

Media historians single out another important aspect of the power of radio, particularly in the early years of Soviet rule: illiteracy. Radio was born, according to A.A. Sherel, from the specific aims that the early Soviet government set out in rebuilding its nation. Struggling with a 'destroyed economy, lack of any fast connection between the centre and the regions of the republic ... and the massive illiteracy of the two "ruling classes" – proletarians and peasants who were promised unlimited rights and responsibilities in managing the government, and, hence, unlimited opportunities in their political and cultural development', the government saw radio emerge as the perfect propaganda tool, especially since print outlets were obviously 'not capable of providing the propaganda and informational needs of the country'.[2]

If some of the central problems in Russian journalism involved its 'disconnect' from the people, then despite its immediate subversion for purposes of propaganda, radio was proving its democratic potential from the start.

The distinguishing feature that would lay the foundations for Russia's radio broadcasting system was the fact that technological capability coincided with the fundamental socioeconomic changes that the Bolshevik revolution heralded in. Technology appeared just in time to meet the propaganda needs of the new government, and so the radio system – both in its technical manifestation as well as in the purpose and style of the content it transmitted – was custom-made to answer primarily to the needs of state propaganda. Hence, one of the first wireless messages to be transmitted after the Bolsheviks took power was a 'news bulletin' of sorts to the outside world: 'The All-Russian Congress of Soviets has formed a new Soviet Government. The Government of Kerensky has been over-thrown and arrested. Kerensky himself has fled. All official institutions are in the hands of the Soviet Government'.[3]

Originally, however, radio was not so much a mass medium as it was an intermediary: the telegraph allowed for information to be disseminated from one centre to other nodes, where it was reprinted in mass circulation periodicals. The first 'radiograms' originated in St Petersburg's Winter Palace, from where, during World War I, the czar and his cabinet would send out political and ideological reports to the fronts, where they were reprinted. Between 1918 and 1921 the Russian Telegraph Agency Radio Bulletin was the chief source of content for the local press. Usually, radio stations would transmit a message in Morse code, and a receiver station would pick it up, decode it, and distribute it to the newspapers. In this sense, we should differentiate between the radio receiver as a mass medium (like television) and its telegraphic uses, which still exist today.

The first time a human voice was broadcast in Russia was in 1919 – when a radio engineer from Nizhny Novgorod was heard in Moscow and St Petersburg (renamed Petrograd during World War I). By 1922, Russia would have the most powerful radio station to date.[4]

Although Lenin's government intended to capitalize on radio technol-ogy as a propaganda tool, it would be a slight exaggeration to say that *immediate* government control was implemented at that time. If the technological and ideological conditions for broadcasting existed, *listening* to the radio was rather a different matter. People would create radio receivers locally as a massive, grassroots effort, but the government was aware that it must take action to introduce a wide network of radio receivers without hampering access to existing ones. As a result, Lenin ordered the 'radiofication' of Russia.

Instead of monopolizing on the technology, in 1923 the Central Committee issued a decree allowing virtually anyone – all state, profes-sional, Party, and public organizations – to create and use radio receivers. A second decree the following year officially allowed all Soviet citizens to own, purchase and construct radio receivers. Thus, the first decrees were arguably more permissive than any media decrees of the Soviet govern-ment. After making sure that a technological network was being created, the government started thinking about control. In 1925 the Central Committee created a Radio Commission, charged with all political and propaganda control of broadcast content.

These decrees reflected a government that saw radio as a powerful media technology, but not as a separate medium in itself. Structurally, radio programmes were still being created by newspapermen as special 'audio' editions of newspapers, even when the information they broadcast had never been printed before. The modern concept of a radio station as a fully autonomous outlet generating its own content did not yet exist, and radio broadcasting was still viewed in the early 1920s as a technologically advanced variety of the printing press.

Even though the government recognized the necessity of developing the medium, Stalin's administration tended to underestimate its capabilities as a source of propaganda, focusing instead on the importance of developing the Party press. They were thus wary of creating autonomous broadcasting stations.

From 1925, content was strictly controlled by the Central Committee's Radio Agitprop Commission, but in terms of technology the controlling body was the stock company Radioperedacha (Radio Programme). In 1928 the body would be reorganized into a special department of the Mail and Telegraph Commissariat. A separate All-Union Committee for Radiofictation and Radio Broadcasting was only created in 1933.

Content

Early Soviet radio programmes fully based their format on the only existing news medium of the day: newspapers. The first broadcasts of the Central Radiotelephone Station were recaps of news that had already been printed in the local press.

The appearance of the Radio Newspaper of the Russian Telegraph Agency in November 1924 changed that. The 45-minute news programmes were original and exclusive in the sense that they were aired *before* going to print. Besides the fact that this audio newspaper was in a sense a preliminary run – and possibly a source of breaking news for print media – the creators of the Radio Newspaper chose to adhere to a strict newspaper format. Thus, the first radio programme mimicked the newspaper. Two major foreign and national news stories dominated the broadcast. The rest comprised at least 10 telegraphed news items, 15–20 important Moscow events, 10–15 science and academic news items, and finally, short pieces on theatre, cinema, literature, sport, poetry, short fiction and even limericks.

While the government continued to view radio programmes as a byproduct of print newsrooms, the number of programmes continued to proliferate. By 1930, there were 300 radio programmes (up from just 80 in 1929) in 29 different languages, with 179 catering to factory workers and 100 to farm workers.[5] Meanwhile, by 1928, 65 radio stations broadcast over a territory of 2.94 million square kilometres, reaching several million radio listeners. Because the chief aim was to educate and thus empower a predominantly illiterate working and peasant class, early creators understood that programmes would have to cater to the informational needs of each class – in other words, to speak their language. After the launch of the first radio newspaper, this aim fuelled the creation of others – first a daily programme for the working class, then a programme for farm workers that aired three to four times a week. These attempts to reach out to segments of the population that had virtually been left out of the scope of mass media turned out to be the driving force behind the diversification of the medium. Based on national newspapers and specialized print periodicals, subsequent programmes would have names such as *Handyman and the Cooperative*, *Health and Fitness Radio Newspaper*, *Conscript*, and the like.

Other genres included live audio lectures and live concerts. In 1925, the first radio play, *An Evening with Maria Volkonskaya* would air to commemorate the hundredth anniversary of the Decembrist Uprising in St Petersburg. The play captured the afternoon tea of the wife of Decembrist Prince Sergei Volkonsky, just before she was to follow her husband into exile. Thereafter, radio plays would become a lasting feature of Soviet radio broadcasting. Technological capabilities for pre-recorded programmes appeared in the late 1920s, but they would not become widely used in radio until 1936. Prior to that, news programmes usually featured an announcer reading out a bulletin. Initial demands for announcers were straightforward: they were supposed to have clear voices and highly articulate pronunciation, as well as be able to suppress emotion while talking. Women announcers were initially barred from the profession.

Even though live broadcasts were a dominant feature well into the 1930s, many of the live reports had a staged feel, especially when they were not coming from the studio. Correspondents 'embedded' in places like the Stalingrad tractor factory and other industrial plants across the nation were instructed to engage listeners in the achievements of any workers they were reporting on. With Stalin's taste for theatre, plays were promoted not only live, but over the radio. But as an ultimately totalitarian medium, radio lauded the success of five-year plans, expeditions to the Artic and new scientific discoveries, while it kept silent about the Gulag system and about the mass hunger that resulted from collectivization policies.

Levitan and the legacy of war radio

A pivot of the totalitarian propaganda system, and hence of Soviet radio, was an underlying permanence of war (even as the government officially promoted peace). It is no wonder, then, that for many Russians the voice of radio was Yuri Levitan, the man who announced the German invasion in 1941. For 50 years Levitan, whose deep, slow, low voice caught Stalin's attention, would issue the most important state announcements broadcast over national radio. His voice would come to be associated not just with the German invasion and reports from the front during World War II, but would subsequently come to symbolize the centrality of Soviet radio in the lives of citizens. Levitan's permanence doesn't just characterize Soviet radio, but sheds light on how the immediacy of war gained a lasting presence in Soviet propaganda, particularly on the radio.

Levitan was just 19 when he became an intern for the Radio Committee, and his first tasks did not involve speaking into a microphone. An unlikely candidate in a radio culture that valued precise, emotionless articulation, Levitan impressed the jury with a booming, yet articulate voice. The night he was asked to read an article from *Pravda*, Stalin happened to hear his voice and ordered that Levitan read his next address. The next day, it took Levitan five hours to read the address – without making a single mistake. In fact, years later the announcer would admit that there was a perfectly good reason for his trademark slow speech: while he pronounced each word, he would read and prepare for the rest of the text:

> I remember the positive and proud tone on the air during the first five-year plans: 'Dnepr hydroelectric plant launched!' 'To all, to all! Chkalov's unprecedented flight over the North Pole!' On June 22 the voice of Moscow Radio sounded grave, guarded, brave. It contained grief, faith, and hope. In those days we all felt such a responsibility on our shoulders that we never knew existed.[6]

The war years would ingrain Levitan's slow, grave articulation in the ears and minds of radio listeners. On the one hand, television broadcasting was halted in 1941, on the other, wartime regulations meant that every citizen had to hand over all wireless radio receivers, leaving them with cable-radio receivers. At that time, newspapers in remote places also relied on radio for their news and especially reporting from the front lines.

For these reasons, radio during the war years became the universal medium, at times replacing access to newspapers with loudspeakers. It is no wonder, then, that Russians tuned in to Levitan's voice during those years with a particular apprehension.

On 22 June 1941, Levitan announced that Germany had invaded Russia without a declaration of war. Years later, he would recall:

> I turn on the microphone: 'Moscow speaking … ' I feel I cannot continue. A pause … I pull myself together and read on. 'A statement from the Soviet government.' And as I read, I grew more convinced that victory would come, that Hitler's crimes would not go unpunished. This was the mood that the announcement was read in.[7]

If wartime media often aided wartime propaganda, in the Soviet Union the distinction had been eliminated. At a time when television broadcasts had been halted, radio bulletins were the primary – and in places, the only – source of information for both the citizens at home and the soldiers fighting on the front. Indeed, it is noteworthy that the broadcasts intended for the front lines and for civilian use, though different, were created by the same apparatus. For this reason, Soviet war reporting – and the non-existence of the concept of accuracy – deserves separate mention: 'To understand what is happening on the front lines is very difficult', the scientist V. Vernadsky wrote in the autumn of 1941, just months after war broke out, 'Radio lies without shame, but we have no other source of information'.[8] Indeed, radio was not so much a source of information as a weapon of war. In this context, it is misleading to say that war reports were inaccurate simply because they were never intended to be accurate, or even true.

Because radio's sole purpose was serving the propaganda machine, which was considered a weapon of war, wartime news had to conform to criteria that consisted of three war slogans: 'Our work is right!', 'The enemy will be destroyed!' and 'Victory will be ours!'. As editorial policy, these slogans provided strikingly clear instructions on what could and could not be reported. Information on the superior military tactics of the Germans or their weapons was obviously forbidden, and reports on war casualties had to be presented in such a way as to not contradict the general line.

One example of radio as a war weapon was a programme broadcast for partisan fighters. With sections like, 'How to down fascist planes using any infantry weapon', 'The art of camouflage' and 'Ambushes' the programme directly addressed the potential fighters as 'people's avengers'. Programmes like this served two purposes: raising morale among the fighters themselves and exaggerating – and glorifying – their role for the population at large. So powerful was Levitan's presence as an information weapon that Hitler reportedly had a 250-mark bounty for his head.

In the end, whether intended or not, the propaganda machine was at its best in the form of radio and in wartime. Having worn the memory of war as a badge of honour, Russians today are hard pressed to part with the concept of their victory, despite some criticism of overly lavish war parades and resources spent on festivities that could have gone instead to pay the pensions of war veterans. Inevitably, the credit for elevating the Great Patriotic War to such status should go to the media and, in this case, the radio. Much of today's coverage of anniversaries has its origins in Soviet programmes that would never outlive themselves. One was *Moment of Silence*, a yearly special programme broadcast on 9 May, starting 1965.

Music as a social statement

If propaganda and war fully subverted the informative function of radio, the role of music as part of the entertainment function is another matter altogether. If we are to understand the revolution that the appearance of FM radio stations stirred up, we have to note that the Soviet Union's government-subsidized radio stations did not *rely* on music, but rather featured it in concerts and music programmes, or used it to fill airtime in between. The phenomenon of FM radio in Russia meant that radio stations dedicated predominantly to popular music would broadcast around the clock – something virtually unheard of in the Soviet Union.

On the other hand, the total absence of western music on Soviet radio spawned a flourishing and heavily politicized underground music culture in the 1970s and 1980s that was forced to essentially 'sell out' with the appearance of commercial radio after perestroika.

The underground music scene and the Leningrad Rock Club

One aspect of radio that both enhances the power of the radio journalist and serves as leverage in forging a propaganda machine is music. Much like television, in many cases radio is listened to not so much for its news as for its musical content. In the case of Soviet radio in the 1960s, 1970s and 1980s, what characterized its music policy was not what it broadcast, but what it didn't broadcast.

The fact that rock music was suppressed in the Soviet Union is no surprise. Ideologists on both sides of the Atlantic were keenly aware of its political potential, and since the western youth movements of the 1960s coincided with Brezhnev's leadership and, thus, a return of the Iron Curtain, it was inevitable that the Soviet government was particularly wary of any western musical influence.

Mainstream Soviet pop music of the day, the music of the 'establishment', was a mix of European-style chanson, ethnic folk and, when the influence of rock music became inevitable by the 1980s, elements of that genre. By the time perestroika opened up the borders, not only was western rock seeping in, but Soviet mainstream was leaking out. Here is how a *New York Times* article from that period described Russia's best-known superstar, Alla Pugacheva, who launched her career in the 1970s:

> Alla Pugacheva is a woman of many voices – delicate pop chirps, a clear rock mezzo-soprano, dramatic cabaret growls and sobs ... Mrs. Pugacheva tries to offer something for everybody, from rock and pop-funk to torchy ballads. The music, some of it written by Mrs. Pugacheva, looks westward for vocal styles, instrumentation (keyboards, electric guitars, trap drums), wardrobe, song forms and rhythms ... But even with American and European trappings, the songs have an unmistakable Slavic tone, conveyed not only by the hard consonants of the Russian lyrics but by a volatile, theatrical moodiness and the almost constant use of minor keys. Now and then a song would slow down and then quickly step up to double time like a Russian folk dance, rousing the staid audience to clap along.[9]

This review, from 1988, describes the perestroika pop scene. In fact, when Pugacheva was starting out, her songs were a far cry from the more subdued, often melancholy pop style that dominated the music scene. However much rock infiltrated the mainstream music scene, it was never accepted – to the point of not even being mentioned by name – officially.

The words of a composer and choir director, cited in an interview in *Health (Zdorovye)* magazine in 1977, reflect the general attitude towards 'loud' music:

> Some of our ensembles become hostage to imitating Western pop music groups that are far from the best, *too loud, too rhythmic* [emphasis added]. The ensemble is prone to competition of musicians. Each one tries to be louder than the next. The loud, cracking stream of sound masks lack of thought and the poor musical mastery of the performers.[10]

Another important component of both the mainstream and underground music scenes was the bard-poets. Epitomized by the more poetic Bulat Okudzhava and the outspoken chansonnier and actor, Vladimir Vysotsky, the poetry of the bards was in many cases deemed too subversive to allow it to be performed live or broadcast. But if the power, and hence danger, of the bards was essentially poetic, the 'loud music' inherent in rock was viewed as even more potent – even when the lyrics were in English. Given the power of the word in Russia, of the poet as being 'bigger than Russia', the possibilities for domestic rock were innumerable:

> Songs didn't necessarily contain a protest against the existing system, but the fact that they were in Russian was already enough for them to contain a certain danger for that system, because the word was the next step to ideology. And then the system took the only step it could in this situation – for those who didn't want to join [the Communist Youth League], a new youth organization was created in St. Petersburg: Leningrad Rock Club. The code that sweetened the medicine was the word 'rock.'[11]

This article, which tends to be sceptical of the club's authenticity, on the one hand reflects the club's origins, and on the other the widely publicized theories that it was the direct product of the KGB, which rightly assumed that the only way to control a subculture was to 'legalize' and regulate it themselves. While the extent of the role the KGB played in creating the club can be debated, the club's link to officialdom is practically inevitable, especially after the KGB theory was lent credibility by the Soviet rock icon Boris Grebenshchikov, who launched his music career first in the underground and then by joining the club. Whether or not the Rock Club was a spawn of the KGB is less important than the role it played for the musicians.

Officially created in 1981, it came against the backdrop of an underground rock-dissident culture that had been fomenting for at least a decade. It seems inevitable that once registered as a bona fide club, the organization would no longer be such an effective haven for dissidents. But in fact the budding artists, songwriters and performers who fought for a decade to give the club legal status had other motives in mind. In the Soviet Union, in order to perform or record music, an artist had to be officially 'registered' somewhere. Belonging to a club, however compro-

mised it was to the demands of officialdom, gave songwriters the chance
to be heard. But because it was such a potential hotbed of dissidence and
subculture, the club functioned for the first few years under the official
eye of the KGB, whose agents were persistent fixtures at its concerts.

The idea that the pressure of totalitarianism stimulates cultural revolution and development is not new. Thus it appears obvious that the official
and ideological stagnation of the 1970s would allow the youth subculture,
whose exposure to the cultural upheavals of the 1960s had been suppressed,
to flourish into a sophisticated counterculture. That counterculture of music
played a determining role where music tastes reflected jargon, literary styles,
political views and lifestyles in general. It was a counterculture that played
no small role in removing the Communist Party from power.

The revolution of FM radio and Russian radio today

In a dynamic series of events, the government's monopoly on radio was
broken practically overnight. Once commercial and private radio stations
became possible in 1990, within five years Russia's radio scene had
accomplished what it had taken decades to accomplish in the West.
Profitable FM radio stations flourished by providing access to the music
that young people just a decade before had craved so much but been denied.

In the early 1990s, two aspects put post-Soviet radio in an advanta-
geous position relative to other media. First of all, radio broadcasting is
technologically less expensive than television, and easier to distribute than
print. Second, budding radio stations could capitalize on an unexplored
market: by filling airtime with music, radio stations were both cheaper to
run and offered a more lucrative venue for advertisers. They were thus
able to bring in more revenue from the start. Even if the revenue for radio
is smaller than for television, the costs are lower still.

By the end of the 1980s, most Russian households would tune in to
radio via their three-programme cord radios, which were plugged directly
into the wall. Because Soviet radio used its own FM dial, FM radio in the
traditional sense simply did not exist. Soviet stations used MHz frequencies below the 80s, and this was the range that was initially populated by
up and coming stations. But with the increase in availability of western
and Japanese radios, more frequencies on the FM dial started to become
available to a wider range of Russians. This coincided with a geometric
growth of radio stations. If there were only three non-government radio
stations in Moscow in 1990, by 1991 there were 10, and by 1993 20.[12]

The first important independent radio stations were SNC radio and
Ekho Moskvy. If Ekho Moskvy, launched in June 1990, served to fill the
journalistic lacuna in independent broadcasting, then SNC went further.
By being the first to dedicate airtime to western and domestic rock, it
took independent broadcasting into a new realm. This music station went
on the air on 4 January 1991, and was the brainchild of musician Stas

Namin, who created it in tandem with city culture officials. It was the first station to air Russian rock, featuring groups like Aquarium, DDT, Kino and other members of the Leningrad Rock Club. Even more revolutionary was its decision to play forbidden western rock and heavy metal. Besides music, SNC featured a rather eclectic array of live performances by budding ensembles, various forms of previously unheard-of impromptu talk, and thematic programmes dedicated to everything from The Beatles to contemporary culture. SNC did not broadcast news or politics; nevertheless, together with Ekho Moskvy it was among the media outlets that were raided and temporarily shut down by the KGB during the failed coup of August 1991. Lacking finance, the station was ultimately closed in September 1992. Its role was therefore to create a breakthrough, to form a path that others could follow.

Ekho Moskvy, however, survives to this day, and for telling reasons. According to L. Bolotova, its most attractive feature was its interactivity and a dialogue with listeners. As the radio's chief editor, Alexei Venediktov said, 'It's impossible to do radio without a host, without names, without people who are present in your home ... These should be friends, family, familiar voices, familiar intonations'.[13]

If SNC took the first steps in laying a path towards FM radio (even though it broadcast over AM waves), the next steps were more professional and less impromptu. French and American businessmen invested in the first FM stations. French capital helped to create Evropa Plus, Nostalgie and M-Radio, while US funds and know-how helped launch Radio Maximum. According to Rita Mitrofanova, who has been a voice of Radio Maximum since 1993, if SNC took a truly revolutionary stance, henceforth FM radio developed along a predictable trajectory: it wholeheartedly exported the US radio formula. Even though a number of stations were created with French capital, the know-how, says Mitrofanova, was predominantly American.[14]

But even with US broadcasting formulas, in order to satisfy the demand for contemporary music (which was practically never broadcast on Soviet radio), the concept of genre remained virtually non-existent for many years. Radio producers fashioned a mixed flow of music whose only unifying quality was that it was an alternative to Alla Pugacheva and Soviet mainstream. Reflecting a similar situation in other media, radio producers were guilty of taking their newfound freedom to the other extreme, and catering to exceptionally marginal tastes. One arguable result – and something particularly characteristic of the print media during the mid-1990s – was the alienation of Russia's mainstream.

Radio, however, proved more versatile than print. In the summer of 1995, domestic producers launched Russkoye Radio, which would become the most popular music station in Russia (and the second most popular station overall, after the state-owned, universal radio station, Radio Russia). Its distinguishing feature – and the driving force behind its success – was a strict adherence to one single rule: all songs were in Russian. If the new FM stations of the early 1990s catered to a sophisticated, young class that preferred the 'forbidden' fruit of late-Soviet rock, then Russkoye Radio adopted a penchant of catering to the lowest common denominator. In that context of mass-produced Russian pop, Alla Pugacheva's lasting popularity proved to be on the upper end of the pop spectrum.

> The whole American formula collapsed. The Americans, after all, had certain clear-cut instructions. But they should have taken the so-called 'Russian soul' into account. After all, even our surveys can't be explained logically. Whatever side of the bed a person got up from, whatever his mood – that's what determines what music will be played. Tomorrow it can be entirely different.[15]

Against the backdrop of the success of Russkoye Radio, other radio stations sprouted up, sticking to the less formulaic, more eclectic approach that had been an underlying feature of Russian music radio from the start. In the latter half of the 1990s, these were stations like Silver Rain and Moscow's Radio Seven.

Today, after some years of experience, radio producers are reinventing format and thus catching up, to an extent, with their western counterparts. But these attempts, for the most part, have revolved around background music – thus the emergence of easy-listening, no live-talk Radio Jazz and Relax FM, stations that Mitrofanova describes as 'sound wallpaper'. If Russia has Radio Retro, it still lacks more sophisticated differentiation that separates the 1950s and 1960s ('oldies') from the 1980s. Two rock stations, meanwhile, remain eclectic on the one hand and alternative on the other.

One area of Russian radio broadcasting that has been making unique strides is talk radio. Talk was a constant and important feature of early FM stations (as a relic of Soviet radio), and the success of Ekho Moskvy proved that it was in demand. In the last decade, however, as radio stations began moving away from mixed format and towards greater stratification and genre differentiation, the demand for talk radio began manifesting itself in new stations.

If the state currently has a de facto monopoly on news television in Russia, the radio market for informational stations is far more lenient. An interesting example is, again, Ekho Moskvy. Once an asset of Vladimir Gusinsky's Media-Most empire and an important part of the vocal opposition, today Ekho Moskvy belongs to the state giant Gazprom, and yet has lost none of its propensity for dissent as it continues to be regarded as an 'independent' medium. It remains a leader of informational radio, staking 28.5 per cent in the informational radio market. It is closely followed by the state-run Radio Russia, at 25.1 per cent, and the state-owned Mayak, at 22 per cent. Together, information stations – or talk radio – make up over 20 per cent of the radio market.[16]

If one looks at statistics that compare the influence and pervasiveness of media and radio stations (see Chapter 1), it isn't difficult to understand the advantages of radio, and particularly talk radio, in reaching out to society. If critics complain that the Kremlin dominates Russia's evening news, even state-owned radio stations like Mayak have a myriad of venues for criticism and connection to their listeners at their disposal. A typical weekday evening programme could be a half-hour chat with a real estate lawyer about housing reform, or with an economist about inflation and how it will affect buyers – both perennially hot topics for the population, and ones that far outweigh the more politicized concerns like human rights, Chechnya, Yukos and media freedom, which are frequently presented in the West as Russia's most pressing issues. Programmes such as these will field live questions from listeners wanting to know how local governments can be forced to renovate their apartment buildings and what legal mechanisms can help residents rebuild communities. Another advantage is that such programmes link Muscovites with Russians in the regions: a typical setting involves a Moscow resident sitting in traffic on his way home from work and listening to a caller from Yekaterinburg who has essentially the same questions as one from St Petersburg.

The recent radio market has reflected this demand. The last decade witnessed the launch of three independent talk radio stations: Citi-FM and RSN in 2006, and Business-FM in 2007. Citi-FM, which describes itself as an all-news 24/7 station, has taken a nonchalant approach towards its listeners. The typical 'listener', in fact, stands carved out of cardboard in the studio, reminding anchors and journalists who they have to keep in mind when they create their programmes. According to the station's director general, Mikhail Eidelman,

> The typical Citi-FM listener is easy to understand. His name is Andrei Gavrilovich, he is a cardboard cutout and has lived in our studios since Feb. 1, 2006. Today we know everything about Andrei Gavrilovich: where he works, how he gets around Moscow, what he does on weekends, who his wife and children are, and how he feels about his boss or the traffic police. Our Andrei Gavrilovich is a Muscovite aged 30–49, he usually has a higher education, he works in a commercial or government company, and he has long ago adapted to contemporary Russia's economic realities.[17]

With hours of news and talk, Citi-FM frequently airs laid-back conversations about nothing in particular. The journalist, writer and TV anchor Dmitri Bykov uses his Sunday night slot for chats with experts, writers and simply friends. Sometimes unstructured and lacking a specific topic, the show fields random questions from callers. As such, it is more reminiscent of evening tea sessions in the kitchen than an 'influential' talk show. But as to connecting and informing people, it is precisely this approach that bridges gaps more effectively than the print media. This kind of attitude on budding talk radio stations, coupled with a trend towards segmentation, already points to a medium that seems to be overcoming some of the more perennial problems of elitism that plague the printed press.

7 THE INTERNET, BLOGGING AND THE MEDIA OF THE FUTURE

> • **The birth of RuNet and its success**
> • **Online media today: shortcomings and potential**
> • **The blogosphere**

As the youngest medium, the internet from the start managed to combine some of the best and worst aspects of Russia's journalistic legacy – from the thick literary journals of the nineteenth century to the sway of politicized capital in journalism. Like an embryo, in a short span of about 15 years it managed to represent each stage of development in Russia's media. The reason was that the birth of the Russian internet coincided with the birth of a new, post-communist Russia – arguably, a completely new country which launched its own, unique, media by starkly severing ties with its Soviet legacy.

This coincidence may be behind both the failures and successes of RuNet, so named for the .ru domain. It is also behind the defining feature that differentiates Russian online journalism from its western counterparts. If the American internet boasts a handful of popular original content publications, most notably Slate.com and Salon.com, much of its online news and journalism centres around secondary content sites like those of newspapers, television stations and wires. The origins, therefore, are in print media – even if newspapers are struggling to survive and relying ever more on their online versions. In Russia during the 1990s, the situation was starkly different. By the second half of the decade, when there were enough internet users for the web to become eligible as a bona fide 'mass medium', existing outlets, newspapers and news agencies were in no hurry to grab domains and set up online versions. Instead, the internet became a venue for Russia's young intelligentsia. E-magazines that were set up more in the tradition of thick literary journals quickly transformed into revenue-generating news providers – and then flourished as independent news services. In fact, they were the ones that laid the foundations and encouraged more established outlets in the traditional media to start staking out territory on the web in the last decade.

If RuNet witnessed a surge of original content sites (much like the internet in western countries prior to the dot com collapse), that direction has somewhat changed, although a large number of original sites continue to thrive. The stake is no longer in original publications, but in developing online versions of outlets – reflecting a general trend towards conglomeration and holdings. The appearance of a vibrant blogosphere via Livejournal has led media developers to make aggressive attempts to capitalize on blogs – either for commercial or political purposes. But blogs are also becoming increasingly interactive – not just with users via mobile phones, but with traditional print publications. Thus the trend towards interactivity – whether with users or with other media outlets – looks as if it will continue.

The birth of RuNet and its success

The first technological evidence of the new medium was visible as early as 1991. In the Soviet Union, the Kurchatov Institute of Nuclear Physics had already developed a computer network, and this early 'web' went untouched when the KGB tried to seize independent media during the August coup. In fact, much like in the early days of radio, tens of thousands of reports about the 1991 coup were 'broadcast' through these early internet channels. For the first half of the 1990s, however, the development of the internet was limited to a small, closed, cliquish subculture, a majority of which resided abroad, near universities in the USA, Europe and Israel.

The first online mass media were registered with the government in 1996. These included one of the chief success stories of post-Soviet news agencies – Rosbusinessconsulting, launched exclusively from the internet. But according to Anton Nossik, the founder of some of the most successful internet media outlets in the country, any meaningful use of the internet as a mass medium in Russia occurred no earlier than 1998, when the number of internet users in Russia reached 1 million.[1] Those users were drawn from the ranks of the educated elites, reflecting not just the audience of the content, but its creators.

In the autumn of 1996, a group of young Russian fringe intellectuals gathered around the table in the cramped kitchen of Eugene Gorny, the unemployed but revered philologist. Out of those wine-soaked conversations came Zhurnal.ru (The Journal), the first Russian online publication of its sort: a portal offering young, professional Russians news and essays on the political atmosphere of the day, culture, and intellectual entertainment.

Funding came from grants amassed by Dmitri Itskovich, an up-and-coming entrepreneur who would go on to launch a successful chain of fringe cafés and nightclubs. Yet Zhurnal.ru proved so successful among Moscow's literary clique that it spawned Polit.ru – publishing political essays and media criticism – and sparked a whole slew of similar sites. Oligarchs were eager to finance these projects, which were relatively inexpensive and offered a lot of promise. In 1999, Anton Nossik used funding from the Foundation of Effective Politics, a pro-Kremlin think tank, to launch the Gazeta.ru project. Gazeta was later sold to the Yukos oil company for $1 million, and split into two entities – Vesti.ru, with its news analysis, features and reviews, and Lenta.ru, which offered a wide range of readers hard news compiled from wire services. Sites like these quickly became a magnet for Russia's emerging young professional middle class.

While more in-depth sites like Vesti.ru offered a degree of journalistic prestige, news-only sites that split from them, like Lenta.ru, provided the first opportunity for Russian readers to keep abreast of news from around the world with hourly updates in their own language.

One important feature of this budding media landscape – and something that remains an important characteristic to this day – was that most of the future editors and contributors who formed the Russian internet all met each other in the editorial offices of Zhurnal.ru. These founding fathers of the RuNet had no formal journalistic training. Gorny, for example, was a scholar, and Nossik started his adult life as a urologist. In a sense, though, the 'hippies' of the post-perestroika early 1990s suddenly became yuppies by the end of the decade. There was a sea of opportunity in Russia around 1995, and young talents like Nossik had returned from abroad and wanted to try their journalistic hand online.

On RuNet, there was no escaping politics. 1997 saw the launch of *Russky Zhurnal,* a journal of cultural criticism accompanied by a monthly print version (after the financial crisis of 1998, the print version was discontinued). Funding came from the Foundation for Effective Politics, headed by the political scientist, Gleb Pavlovsky, who was known to invest in cultural and journalistic ventures with little chance of profitability.

While today's Vesti.ru is an online site of the television news programme *Vesti, Russky Zhurnal* still exists, albeit as a conservative-leaning, often pro-Kremlin intellectual e-zine. Given its historical loyalty, one must remember that being pro-Kremlin in 1997, when Boris Yeltsin was in office, poised to appoint a liberal prime minister, was very different from being pro-Kremlin in 2008. In fact, the 'pro-Kremlin' elite of 1997 makes up today's liberal opposition.

Apart from the political significance of these online magazines, Lenta.ru, which succeeded in becoming a profitable news source, is striking in itself. This offshoot has no news correspondents of its own, no cultural essays or reviews, yet managed, practically from the start, to attract up to 900,000 unique visits every day. Nossik then saw it as Russia's answer to Yahoo.com as well as a leading resource for Russians all over the world who wanted easy access to Russian news. Initially without its own reporting staff, Lenta.ru employed dozens of editors who compiled news from news services such as RIA Novosti, Interfax and ITAR-TASS, the top Russian news agencies, as well as AP, Reuters and the BBC.

Internet journalists and experts attributed this early success to the fact that Russians preferred to read news in their own language, and in the late 1990s they simply had few other places to turn to. Prior to RuNet, readers would go to Yahoo and the BBC for foreign news, and read

Moscow newspapers for local news. News agencies like ITAR-TASS hadn't yet made their foreign source news available to the people. What gave these new sites the upper hand when competing with existing print publications was their ability to cater to a new, albeit small, professional intellectual class by offering fast-paced news and analysis – something that existing print publications couldn't keep up with. Simply put, they offered a faster and more accessible way to get across to readers, and readers a faster way to respond.

Another reason behind the relatively rapid proliferation of internet technologies was lack of legislation regulating intellectual property. The authorities practically ignored the distribution of unlicenced audio and video recordings, not to mention word-processing and HTML-processing software, which could be purchased for the equivalent of just a few cents.[2] Internet use among Russians, meanwhile, skyrocketed in 1998 for another logical reason: the financial crisis of August that year left a large number of Russia's budding professional class seeking new sources of economic information after the collapse of numerous print publications. This demand pushed humour sites, chat sites, and other online entertainment into the background as RuNet came to be accessed predominantly for information.[3]

One of the chief success stories of the Russian internet was the Rosbusinessconsulting news agency – today a successful television channel. RBC.ru was launched in 1996 as a closed online resource, providing coveted information on stock rates and analysis for a subscription that cost a few hundred dollars a month. The financial crisis changed all that. In August 1998, its owners decided to try a daring, new step: they started offering free access to information that had previously cost hundreds of dollars. Having risked a great deal, they nevertheless made the right decision at the right time. Within weeks, RBC.ru became the leading site of the Russian internet, surpassing even Russian-language search engines in visits.[4]

It is interesting to note that Russia's internet, despite its relatively limited access, was flourishing and becoming profitable precisely at the time of the dot com collapse across the Atlantic. Its fast-paced development at the right time, and the fact that it took advantage of a number of social and economic factors, not only spelled out success but built the foundations for a medium with a unique potential for social change.

Online media today: shortcomings and potential

Approaching 2010, it is hard to recognize the RuNet of the late 1990s in Russia's quickly developing internet landscape. Vesti.ru is no longer a weekly e-zine. Instead the domain name belongs to the *Vesti* news programme, and the site offers news content from the television programme much in the manner of CNN.com or BBCnews.com. Political upheavals in the early 2000s also left their footprints on the internet. NTV.ru, initially developed with the help of Anton Nossik as a mirror site of the independent television network, with news content that reflected the channel's oppositionist slant, was swallowed up by the Gazprom empire, which took over NTV. The site itself was registered under a foreign domain, newsru.com, in some ways the only vestige of the independent NTV. Featuring predominantly secondary news content with no features or analysis, the site tends to report on news that was either ignored by other agencies or not given a lot of coverage, with a heavy focus on crime, corruption and, at times, sensationalism.

Gazeta.ru, launched together with Lenta.ru but offering original reporting, features, analysis and opinion, was part of the Yukos media empire. While Lenta.ru was sold to Rambler Media, a successful holding that centres around the popular Cyrillic search engine Rambler.ru, Gazeta.ru remained initially in the hands of Open Russia, a Yukos-controlled charity fund. After Yukos was taken over by the government and its top executives jailed, Gazeta.ru found its way into the hands of media tycoon Alisher Usmanov, one of Russia's richest men and the owner of the *Kommersant* business daily (whose previous owner was the outspoken Kremlin critic, Boris Berezovsky). More recently, it was bought by SUP, which controls Livejournal. As was the case with the oppositionist radio station Ekho Moskvy, which ended up in the hands of Gazprom Media, the fact that the owner of Gazeta.ru was a Kremlin-linked oligarch did not considerably affect the slant of its content. It remains to this day a moderately critical, liberal online newspaper, offering original content as well as news wires.

Lenta.ru, once a top news provider for internet users, now has to compete with a lot more than other secondary content news sites. Since it was launched, search engines have begun providing Russian-language news much in the manner of Yahoo, aggregated by popularity from Russia's top newspapers, television and online media. These are Rambler News and Yandex News, and can easily serve as an automatic gauge of the day's most important events and topics. These search engines can also categorize the most cited and popular topics in blogs. Moreover, in 2006 Google went Cyrillic and began providing its own Russian aggregate news. Obviously, had such services been available in the late 1990s, projects like Lenta.ru would never have had a chance of success. The fact that they coexist on the same internet landscape has meant that a number of adjustments have been made to Lenta.ru. Launched at a time when traditional media could not react efficiently enough to quickly developing news events, Lenta.ru, as a provider of secondary news in Russian, certainly filled a special niche and owed its success to the demand for quick, updated access to news in Russian. Today, however, these things are provided by a vast number of internet services. Lenta.ru acts as something of a news organizer, competing with search engine news, but offering two additional benefits – fast, wire-style development and news analysis pieces that provide background and put the story in perspective. Unlike other news sites like Gazeta.ru or the more tabloid, pro-Kremlin,

Dni.ru, Lenta.ru still lacks original reporting. But it remains a useful tool for understanding the story and putting it in context.

Initially, the Russian internet was characterized by three chief factors: centralization, reliance on secondary content among news media, and a relatively small pool of regular users. Today, these factors play a far less determining role than they did around the turn of the millennium, but are still present, to various extents, in today's internet landscape. While they could appear to be drawbacks at first, these factors in fact played an important role in giving the Russian internet the drive and potential it needed to flourish into an independent and powerful medium.

The centralizing aspect appears most interesting. Centralization, as we have seen, has historically been a defining factor of all Russian media, but the nucleus of that centralization has usually been the government. However, even as the government played only a minuscule role in the early days (we can only cite the involvement of Gleb Pavlovsky, the Kremlin's political strategist), the 'founding fathers' of the Russian internet appear to have taken on the centralizing pattern inherent to the development of other media as a blueprint. Moreover, there were apparently conscious efforts on the part of these 'founding fathers' towards this centralization, despite the fact that they represented a rather marginal, intellectual counterculture rather than a privileged, powerful elite.

One illustrative example of these efforts was Zhurnal.ru itself. In 1997, its creators categorized all popular and regularly updated internet publications into 'dailies' and 'weeklies', posted the bar of links on its page, and encouraged 'participants' – including writers and readers – to place the bar on their pages and use it regularly. Thus was born the first 'manifesto' of a union of internet portals. Fused with self-irony and reminiscent of the various avant-garde manifestos of the early twentieth century, the quirky language that was used to describe the history of the Russian internet says a lot about how exceptional its creators believed themselves to be. In this history of the early days of RuNet, aptly titled 'The project of the century from the view of its creator', Alexander Malyukov writes:

> On March 19, 1997 in the year of Our Lord, all of the above ideas were publicized on the Zhurnal.ru page – the main organ of the Russian Internet. The 'Dailies Manifesto' invited all those willing to join the project, while users were kindly encouraged to copy the bar on their home pages. This is the day that should be considered the birthday of dailies.[5]

These grassroots efforts at centralization appear all the more surprising when we consider that the technological base for internet connections – TCP-IP protocols and the possibility to connect modems to PCs – were facilitated circa 1991 by a handful of enthusiasts like Pavel Khodakov, one of the late founders of Zvuki.ru, Russia's most popular music portal and webzine. Indeed, while this is hard to understand from a western standpoint, the very breakthrough of the Russian internet was precisely the fact that individuals could connect to a powerful network of information without either obtaining a licence or getting 'permission' from any sort of state agency.

The centrifugal force that RuNet's creators adopted from the beginning appears to have had both a protective and fuelling effect. Today, after some of their projects have flopped while others have flourished into profitable assets, the key players in the Russian internet, with a few exceptions, still know each other from the early days of RuNet's creation, even if now they represent a multitude of various, and often warring, factions with various degrees of government involvement.

The issue of secondary content has already been discussed by media critics. As early as 2000, it was no secret that most popular online media suffered, in the words of Foundation for Effective Politics director Marina Litvinovich, from a 'crisis of secondariness'. All that was necessary to launch a project like Lenta.ru was a subscription to Interfax and a handful of literate editors to rewrite, update and post the news. This was indeed the case, but as Ivan Zassoursky points out, it was characteristic of all Russian media at that time, for reasons that included 'lack of direct access to information and the impossibility to influence the agenda'.[6] In fact, for a number of mid-sized print weeklies including *The Moscow News*, such 'secondary content' coupled with some news analysis was the prime product offered by the journalists.

Most of the concerns about the secondary nature of news content on the internet were voiced around the turn of the millennium, when blogging had not yet become such a powerful phenomenon across the world. In hindsight, as we have seen, a number of media have successfully managed to overcome this drawback either by introducing more original reporting or by offering other features. Most importantly, however, the advent of blogging and the demise of print news has proved that for the reader, originality, exclusivity and the 'you heard it first' attitude that characterized some veteran reporters of the last generation is not the main priority when it comes to staying informed and getting entertainment. While newspapers are struggling to find a way to capitalize on this just to stay alive, online media are already finding new, original ways of engaging the reader. Primary news portals and secondary sites like Kommersant.ru are doing this not just by providing original news, but by joining forces with bloggers, introducing cross-posting options and allowing bloggers to shape the news agenda more and more.

Unfortunately, however, the third factor noted above, which involves limited access to the internet among Russians, has also proved to be a lasting one, and one that still undermines the potential described above. As we noted in Chapter 1, a striking 76 per cent of those polled in 2006 by the All Russian Centre for Public Opinion Research said they do not use the internet. Among those who did, just 19 per cent said they used it as a source of news, while 9 per cent said they used it predominantly to socialize/chat and 4 per cent said they used it for social networking (and, presumably, blogging). Given these numbers, we see that while the internet is a potentially powerful and influential medium, it did not get far ahead of serious, quality newspapers in terms of its ability to reach out to the Russian population as a whole. Even this, however, is rapidly changing in Russia's oil-fuelled economy, as more people are getting access to new technology, and as blogging and social networking sites proliferate and become more popular.

The blogosphere

In a typical Moscow newsroom in the middle of the last decade, it was not uncommon to observe half the staff logged on to Livejournal, or, as it was commonly known in Russian, ZheZhe (Zhivoi Zhurnal). The unprecedented popularity of this American blog-hosting service in Russia was at one point so massive that it inspired the service's US-based owners to sell Livejournal to a Russian company in 2007. For a few years, as the spearhead of the blogging explosion, Livejournal indeed appeared to be one of the most promising platforms for a genuine civil society.[7] But since it was, from the start, more of a social networking service than a blogging service, Russia's Livejournal offered more than just an alternative to mainstream media.

The Russian-language community on Zhivoi Zhurnal got off to a typically Russian and intellectualized start in early 2001, when Roman Leibov, a literary scholar and social critic, launched the first Russian-language blog. His initial entry was, 'Let's try this in Russian. What a funny little thing …'. By February 2007 there were more than 12 million users on LiveJournal, some 700,000 posting in Cyrillic, making them second only to English speakers. ZheZhe is no longer the only blog service, but remains very popular.

Livejournal founder Brad Fitzpatrick first visited Moscow in October 2006 when his company, Six Apat, announced a partnership with the Russian media company SUP-Fabrik, which would service the enormous Cyrillic sector. What struck him was the social magnitude of ZheZhe and the serious content of its journal entries. According to him, in America, 'Livejournal is lots of people writing to ten people [each, and] reading each other', whereas the Russian Livejournal magnifies into thousands of readers. What for Americans is an electronic diary accessible to a few chosen acquaintances became, for Russians, a platform for forging thousands of interconnected virtual 'friends'. Fitzpatrick believes it has potential as a tool for activism because of its use as a political platform. Anatoly Vorobey, a Russian programmer who blogs in English and Russian out of his home in Jerusalem, worked on the Livejournal team while being one of its best-read bloggers. For him, a big part of ZheZhe's uniqueness lay in the maths: even a user who doesn't have a thousand friends will read, on average, 50 to 60 people – more than an American user. 'Now multiply that by hundreds of thousands of people, and that leads to the unique media sphere that we are witnessing today,' he said in an interview in February 2007.[8]

When Livejournal bloggers draw an audience of th
the inevitable question that arises is: What is the
blog and a publication? In Russia, where anything that ௦
'media' is regulated and watched, this circumstance has aௗ
eye of legislators. In 2008, there was talk of making it manௗ
register a blog with a thousands-strong audience as a bona fide ௗ
outlet – with all the legal responsibilities that this entailed. There is ௗ
wonder that these discussions are being taken seriously – after all, such
blogs are no less powerful than traditional media in organizing the public
– perhaps more so.

Thousands-strong street protests organized by political opposition
leaders using Livejournal are just the start. A more telling incident was
that of Alexandra Ivannikova, a woman accused in 2005 of killing an
Armenian cab driver who was allegedly trying to rape her. In a campaign
organized on ZheZhe, right-wing organizations flocked to her defence,
sparking a heated debate on illegal immigration, ultranationalism and the
right to bear arms (Ivannikova's weapon was a kitchen knife). She was
unexpectedly cleared of all charges in a retrial. Today, those on both sides
of the Ivannikova issue admit that it showed how powerful ZheZhe could
be as a grassroots tool.

While most experts dismiss the possibility of direct government
involvement, Russian Livejournal has been vulnerable to political influence. Some of the more founded rumours claim that some influential
political bloggers are no strangers to kickbacks from the government or
other powerful interests. Some bloggers close to the government have
admitted that in order to ensure that certain news is spun a certain way,
or that certain items get leaked, money does change hands. Ivan Zassoursky, who worked as a marketing director at SUP-Fabrik, summarized it
this way in a personal interview: 'Can you give someone money to
organize a demonstration? Sure you can. So why can't you give someone
money to write something on ZheZhe?'.

As a cultural phenomenon, Livejournal permeates various other
spheres, beyond the media. According to Eugene Gorny,

> Russian LiveJournal (RLJ) community shows a considerable devia-
> tion from average blogging patterns both on the level of individual
> blogs and on the level of the blogging community. These differences
> are as follows: (1) an older average age of users; (2) the predomi-
> nance of adult professionals; (3) the content of personal journals
> often consists of serious topics of discussion; (4) a greater degree of
> interconnection between individual journals expressed in a larger
> number of 'friends' of the average user as well as in the phenomenon
> of RLJ celebrities with the audience of hundreds and even thousands
> 'friends of" (readers); (5) the higher significance of reading other
> posts, which sometimes exceeds the desire to keep one's own
> journal; (6) an influence upon online and offline media. To summa-
> rize, RLJ seems to be older, more serious and more communal
> than LJ on average.[9]

While Livejournal remains one of the most popular blogging sites in Russia, more recently it has become evident that it is no longer alone, nor is intellectual blogging, criticism or political organizing as big a component of the community as it used to be. Livejournal was undoubtedly the first to introduce social networking to Russia, but as social networking is becoming more in demand by increasingly tech-savvy young users, it is being overshadowed by other sites geared to socializing rather than expressing opinions.

One is Odnoklassniki.ru, a spin-off of the US-based social networking site Classmates.com. Launched in 2005, by 2007 it had 7 million registered users, with 2.5 million logging in each day. Another is Vkontakte.ru, an answer to Facebook.com. According to Albert Popkov, Odnoklassniki's creator, his site is predominantly used by adults, while Vkontakte.ru is popular among students.[10]

The appearance of such sites shows that the Russian internet is increasingly shifting its dominant orientation towards entertainment, thus catching up with its western counterparts. But as entertainment means more social involvement, not less, this trend only compliments rather than undermines the potential of Russia's blogosphere. Given how small a percentage of Russians use the internet today, it appears that diversification, specialization and profitability are driving today's RuNet towards better engaging the population. The historic failure of Russia's media in doing this, coupled with the ongoing, worldwide transformation in media culture as it increasingly shifts towards interactivity, point to RuNet as one of the pioneers in bridging the gap between the media and the people.

CONCLUSION

- **Towards a new media paradigm**
- **Bridging the gap**

We have set out to raise questions about whether Russia has ever really had a free press and about the meaning of that freedom for Russians. After seven chapters that have detailed the many failures of the media to forge lasting freedoms, the outlook of a strong media system that can play a central role in creating democracy in Russia may appear dismal.

Where Russia's future and its democracy is concerned, it would be wrong to end on such a note. Besides the failures, we have also seen the unique directions being taken by traditional media like radio and some major innovative tendencies that are unique to Russia – such as its internet. These media, as well as new telecommunications solutions, hold immeasurable potential that can be combined with a uniquely Russian penchant for dialogue, criticism and ideology to forge lasting and powerful media institutions that can prove themselves independent both from the government and from politicized capital.

The chief reason it would be wrong to suggest that post-Soviet Russian media has failed in its quest to freedom, independence and sustainability has to do with processes that are going on all over the world. The Russian media embarked on its new course in the last decades just as the traditional power and influence of newspapers was beginning to wane in the West. In this way, Russia's newspapers reflect, to a large extent, global processes that are exacerbated by uniquely Russian traits such as elitism and a history of government control. They are partly declining for the same reasons that readerships are declining all over the world.

What, then, could hold the keys to a revival of the Russian media, and how will that revival play into a global media transformation?

Whether it is free or not, the emergence of a post-Soviet media coincided with new communication technology that has endowed it with unprecedented potential for fundamental transformation. With the growing popularity of the blogosphere in the West and in Russia, it is evident that that transformation has already begun.

Towards a new media paradigm

The structure of this book has examined the Russian press medium by medium, exploring newspapers, television, radio and the internet as if each were a separate entity. Instead of setting out from the financial point of view of a media holding or from tenets of media theory, we looked at how the general population regards its information sphere – how it uses television, newspapers, radio and the internet, and to what extent it trusts each medium as a source of reliable news, information and analysis.

The motive behind this audience-oriented approach lies in the basic questions that this book sought to ask: is the Russian media free, what progress has it seen in transforming into a mediator between the people and the government, and how has it emerged as an independent, popular voice that can impact policy? With each medium developing at different points in history, taking with them the particular nuances of the day, we chose to examine them in separate chapters. While viewed as occupying different niches, each medium elicited the same questions: the potential of each medium for independence and its power to shape society.

Merging media

Organizing the Russian media into four different segments, however, is only a symbolic necessity. So far, it may create the illusion that each media sphere functions independently from the others. Not only has this never been the case, but in the information age any separateness is increasingly becoming obsolete.

The medium, in other words, is no longer the message. Today, even such a stationary medium as television has not only become interactive, but is increasingly bridging the gap with other media. Television talk-shows field calls from viewers, with whole programmes based on news events that callers tell anchors about live. (A good example of this was one of the longest running 'people's news shows', *Vremechko*, which took calls from viewers and then sent crews to investigate their concerns, which were broadcast during the next programme. *Vremechko* was however stopped in 2008, and it was unclear whether it would resume.) Analytical shows offer digests of the printed media, while printed articles frequently become news events in themselves. Newspapers are launched in tandem with radio stations (like Business FM), while internet-based news agencies like Rosbusinessconsulting launch print newspapers.

The internet has made the boundaries between traditional genres murky. What, exactly, defines television? Is it necessarily something one watches in one's living room via antenna or cable? Are live news reels available over the internet classified as TV media or internet media? What category does YouTube fall into? Many internet users read newspapers and magazines exclusively online – does this speak of the internet genre or the print media? Most radio stations have been available over the internet for years.

Newspapers, which have been struggling with declining readerships around the world, have been the first to capitalize on the blogging phenomenon, and this is not unique to Russia. Most star columnists boast blogs that are advertised in the print versions, and even news agencies like

RIA Novosti are busy promoting a blog-savvy image with its chief analysts and political experts hosting blogs. As editor of *Moskovskie Novosti*, Vitaly Tretyakov launched a much-discussed blog on Livejournal, printing excerpts in every edition of his newspapers.

Perhaps a uniquely Russian take on this phenomenon involves the near-merging of social networking sites and traditional media. A case in point is the *Kommersant* business daily and SUP, the Russian company that purchased Livejournal from its American creators in 2006. The friendship between *Kommersant* general director Demian Kudryavtsev (who is no stranger to Boris Berezovsky, either) and SUP head Anton Nossik certainly helped matters when, in May 2007, the *Kommersant* site began letting bloggers registered on Livejournal post on *Kommersant's* forums *precisely* as Livejournal bloggers – in other words, retaining their identity and disposing of the need to register *again*. Given the near-superstar status of some Livejournal bloggers, this was an immensely important feature that, *Kommersant* hoped, would draw traffic from Livejournal's site. As of 2008, SUP had agreements with other news outlets – including RIA Novosti and the *Izvestia* newspaper – to allow Livejournal bloggers to post in a similar fashion.

Even more striking, however, is how this tendency is leading to something of a transformation of the whole idea of a media holding. Cross-posts on Kommersant.ru proved such a success that they led to an even closer partnership between SUP and the Kommersant Publishing House. In June 2008, the two traded shares in a near merger, with SUP getting the Gazeta.ru daily, and *Kommersant* getting a share of SUP stock. It was the first time that a company managing a social networking resource took over control of a bona fide (albeit online) media outlet. Experts estimated that Gazeta.ru was worth $10 to $15 million, while Livejournal could be worth as much as $40 million.[1]

There was no talk that the purchase would affect Gazeta.ru content, although the newspaper was planning to take advantage of closer ties with Livejournal. However, the purchase, by increasing SUP's capitalization, makes it attractive for other media holdings. This, in turn, opens doors to completely new spheres of media business.

Mobile media

The proliferation of mobile phones is transforming – and transcending – the very meaning of media genres. If Russian internet users – though one of the fastest-growing groups in the world – still make up just a fraction of the population, Russia is fast becoming a nation of mobile phone users. In September 2008, Apple signed a contract with three of the largest mobile operators in Russia – MTS, Vimpelcom and MegaFon, Russia's largest mobile phone operator, to offer licenced iPhones. Russia, where the popular Apple brand was available for years on the grey market, became the first country where a company made deals with all the largest mobile operators, reflecting the huge demand for the phone.

But even without iPhone, use of mobile phones in Russia represents not only a communication tool, but a powerful emerging new media. By 2008, nearly three out of four Russians (69 per cent) were using a mobile phone, according to a January 2008 study by the Levada Centre, which polled over 2000 people. Not only does this figure demonstrate the comparatively powerful scope of mobile phone use to internet use, it also shows that mobile phone use is growing exponentially: between 2005, when only 32 per cent of Russians used mobile phones, and 2008, the figure has more than doubled.

With internet access over mobile phones becoming ever easier, the mobile phone itself is being redefined as a medium. Newer brands make it possible to download RSS feeds, send emails, browse the internet, write blog postings and listen to the radio. Meanwhile, a TNS Gallup poll conducted in the summer of 2008 found that some 7 million Russians access the internet from their mobile phones at least once a month (28 per cent of the total internet audience). While not all internet users get their news online, most people who use their mobile phones to get on the web do so for news, stories, weather or blogging. Meanwhile, in remote places across the country mobile phones are reportedly used to access the internet simply because it is the only way to do so. Thus, while in the last chapter we noted the currently limited possibilities of the internet given the small proportion of Russians who use it, it should be stressed that this is the most dynamically developing sphere of the Russian media which can drive an ever increasing number of Russians to read news and blogs over their mobile phones.

Digital television is also becoming accessible via one's mobile phone – a development that will facilitate access to alternative television news stations and coverage. Starting in 2006, all major mobile providers began developing services that would allow subscribers to watch television on their mobile phones. Based on estimates by Sistema Mass-Media, a service provider owned by AFK Sistema, which also controls MTS, the potential share of mobile television users could be as high as 30–50 per cent of mobile communication subscribers in Russia. In real terms, that is anywhere between 27.5 million and 45.8 million people, out of a population of over 140 million.[2]

Essentially, the mobile phone already has the potential to replace desktop and even laptop computers. While the actual replacement is unlikely to occur, the synergy between these technological tools means that the internet, blogs, radio, television and print media are no longer connected, through production and distribution, to any one single medium. The message – information – is being liberated from the medium.

Bridging the gap

It can be argued that Russia, in 2008, was blessed with a tech-savvy leader. President Dmitry Medvedev is widely seen as the protégé of

Vladimir Putin, who has continued to hold on to power in Russia through his post of prime minister. Even so, Medvedev, frequently seen using an iPhone, has been an outspoken defender of the new media, if only in words alone. He has maintained a regular video blog that is available on the presidential site, and has spoken repeatedly of the need to foster digital television and the internet *precisely because* these are areas that the government cannot control. In spring 2009, he even launched a blog on Livejournal.

His words, however, have not translated into any truly liberal tendencies in the press. During his first six months as president, in the summer and autumn of 2008, state-controlled television ignored the financial crisis that was gathering momentum in Russia, while prosecutors actually warned journalists to take extra care in their coverage of the financial turmoil – suggesting that publications could be prosecuted for exacerbating the situation. Another ironic incident was the closure of the *eXile*, a scandalous, English-language bi-weekly alternative tabloid that had survived in Russia since 1997 despite coming close to breaking numerous media laws, including pornography and defamation. In June 2008, an audit from the government press control watchdog forced the investor to withdraw funding, and the newspaper shut down. Editor Mark Ames relocated to New York, and what was left of the newspaper's online version relocated to a .com domain.

What this points to is that Medvedev's liberal rhetoric will not directly translate into liberal media policies. And that, ironically, may be an indicator that Russia's media is no longer developing according to its traditional, top-down model. New technologies and new media formats are driving the media from the ground up – an inherently new situation for Russia.

While social stratification and government control have limited the power of Russia's media to impact society and help form democracy, as we have seen in this book, the current global media transformation is playing to its advantage. While media conglomeration – with major holdings snapping up print media and television – continues to have a sinister ring, we should keep in mind what kind of opportunities this may hold for new format media holdings like SUP. There is no question that there will be even more movement towards this kind of interaction in the future, and that the new possibilities for informing and interacting that this will open up are untold.

What does this bode for Russia? If newspapers are struggling in the West precisely because they have managed to forge themselves as lasting, independent institutions, Russia has a completely different landscape, with different problems, limitations and advantages. Just as the new freedoms of the early 1990s coincided with the flourishing of the internet, the inherently 'nascent' status of the Russian media as a free and independent institution means, in a word, that it has nowhere to go but up.

RuNet today doesn't have nearly as much influence on a social scale as television, nor do any other media. That, however, is likely to change as a younger, savvier generation grows up and begins demanding serious news content that it will want to access in a more mobile way: via laptops and mobile phones. As the blogging phenomenon has already shown, this will open up inherently new dimensions for the way content is presented.

As newspapers wane, traditional news agencies still stand strong – partly because their on-the-minute supply of breaking news is still in demand. While an appetite for news is not likely to change, what readers are looking for more and more is contextualized, commented news analysis – preferably in the accessible, interactive format that blogs have made possible. There is nothing in Russia that inherently hampers these new developments in exchanging information. In fact, it is precisely the absence of influential, well-established media institutions that will drive the search for new media formats in Russia. If the gap between social strata has yet to be bridged in Russia, the emergence of new media technology that is not regulated by the government, the role that social networking is increasingly playing in blogs and news media, and the fact that Russia today boasts one of the fastest-growing media in the world – may all mean that its media is well on the way to bridging that gap.

NOTES

Introduction

1 Yevtushenko, Y., 'Prayer before the poem' (1964), reprinted in Russian in *Medlennaya Lyubov, Domashnyaya biblioteka poezii*, Moscow, Exmo-press, 1998.
2 Attributed to Joseph Stalin, who first used it in a speech given to Soviet writers on 26 October 1932, in the home of Maxim Gorky. Since the speech was noted by several writers, there is controversy whether Stalin was the first to coin the term, and some claim the original line belonged to writer Yuri Olesha, while Stalin later attributed it to the writer.
3 Lenin, V.I., 'Party organization and Party literature', *Novaya Zhizn*, No. 12, 13 November 1905.
4 Not to be confused with the modern-day *Vedomosti*, a business daily published by the Independent Media publishing house in partnership with *The Wall Street Journal*.
5 'Situatsia so svobodoi SMI ne luchshe I ne khuzhe, chem v drugikh strankakh, polagaet president' ('Press freedom is no better or worse off than in other countries, said the president'), *Rossiyskaya Gazeta*, 23 December 2004.
6 This version appeared in a talk show on mass media hosted by media scholar Anna Kachkayeva, which aired on Radio Svoboda (Radio Liberty) on 27 June 2007 (www.svoboda.org/programs/tv/2005/tv.062705.asp).
7 Minkin, A., 'Who is Mr. Putin?', *Moskovsky Komsomolets*, 10 February 2006.
8 Pfanner, E., 'On advertising: Russia rises to the top in ad world', *International Herald Tribune,* 23 May 2005.
9 'Review of the Russian media scene', TNS Gallup, presented by Ruslan Tagiev at the World Association of Newspapers Congress, held in Moscow on 5 June 2006.

Chapter 1

1 Law of the Russian Federation, 'On mass media', No. 2114–1, 27 December 1991, as of 8 December 2003.
2 Gurevich, S.M., *Ekonomika otechestvennikh SMI*, Moscow, Aspekt Press, 2004.
3 Fomicheva, I.D., 'Auditoriya pechatnykh SMI', *Sredstva massovoi informatsii*, Moscow, Aspekt Press, 2006.
4 Based on a survey conducted in 2006 by the All-Russian Center for Public Opinion Research. Used with permission.

5   Resnyanskaya, L.L., 'Obshcherossiyskiye izdaniya', *Sredstva massovoi informatsii*, Moscow, Aspekt Press, 2006, p. 226.
6   Ibid., p. 230.
7   Source: Comcon, rating of printed publications, top 50, Russian index of target groups, TGI-Russia. The poll included Russians 10 years of age and older residing in cities with a population of at least 100,000.
8   TNS Gallup National Readership Survey of daily newspapers by region (Russia, Moscow and St Petersburg), conducted between September 2007 and February 2008 (www.tns-global.ru/rus/data/ratings/press/index.wbp).
9   Fomicheva, I.D., 'Auditoria pechatnykh SMI', *Sredstva massovoi informatsii v Rossii*, Moscow, Aspekt Press, 2006, p. 211.
10 Pew Research Center for the People and the Press, report: *Key News Audiences Now Blend Online and Traditional Sources*, released August 2008.
11 Based on a survey conducted in 2006 by the All-Russian Center for Public Opinion Research.
12 Source: Comcon, rating of television stations, top 50, Rossiyski index tselevykh grup TGI-Russia. The poll included Russians 10 years of age and older residing in cities with a population of at least 100,000.
13 Daily radio audiences, 12+, Comcon-2, September, 2007, www.comcon-2.ru/default.asp?artID=1742.
14 'Radio as a channel for political communication', research based on a survey conducted in 2006 by the All-Russian Center for Public Opinion Research.
15 Bolotova, L.D., 'Otechestvennoye radioveshchaniye v nachale XXI veka: novyie realii I stariye problemy', *Teleradioefir, istoriya i sovremennost*, edited by Y.N. Zassoursky, Moscow: Aspect Press, 2005, p. 156.
16 A survey by ROMIR Monitoring, conducted among 1500 respondents over the age of 18 in 76 cities and residential areas across Russia in 2003.
17 Based on a survey conducted in 2006 by the All-Russian Center for Public Opinion Research.
18 Allan, S., *News Culture*, Open University Press, 2004, 2nd edn, p. 18.
19 Kozlova, M., 'Istoria otechestvennykh sredstv massovoi informatsii', Ulyanovsk, State Technical University of Ulyanovsk, 2000.
20 McReynolds, L., 'Autocratic journalism: the case of the St Petersburg Telegraph Agency', *Slavic Review*, Vol. 49, No. 1 (spring 1990), pp. 48–57.
21 Ibid.
22 Taken and translated from a history and mission statement of the paper posted on its site, www.kommersant.ru/about.aspx.

Chapter 2

1   Zassoursky, Y. (ed.), *Sredstva massovoi informatssii rossii*, Moscow, Aspekt Press, 2006, p. 158.

2 'My ne byli trubadurami marksizma-lenininzma', *Moskovskie Novosti*, No. 38, 30 September 2005.

3 Zassoursky, Y., *Iskusheniye svobodoi, Rossiyskaya zhurnalistika, 1990–2004*, Moscow, Moscow State University Press, 2004, p. 229.

4 Ibid., p. 222.

5 Ibid.

6 Kachkayeva, A., 'Transformatsia Rossiyskogo Televideniya', Chapter 4, *Sredstva Massovoi Informatsii v Rossii*, Moscow, Aspekt Press 2006.

7 Ovsepyan, R., *Istoria noveishei otechestvennoi zhurnalistiki*, Moscow, Moscow State University Press, 1999, p. 264.

8 Zassoursky, I., *Rekonstruktsiya Rossii, Mass-media I politika v 90e*, Mosscow, Moscow State University Press, 2001, p. 212.

9 Ovsepyan, R., *Istoria noveishei otechestvennoi zhurnalistiki*, Moscow, Moscow State University Press, 1999, p. 265.

10 Kachkayeva, A., 'Transformatsia Rossiyskogo Televideniya', Chapter 4, *Sredstva Massovoi Informatsii v Rossii*, Moscow, Aspekt Press 2006, p. 300.

11 Borodina, A., 'Pervyie knopki Rossii' ('First buttons of Russia'), *Kommersant-Vlast*, 4 April 2005.

12 Belyavsky, Y., 'Sergei Blagovolin: Peizazh posle bitvy', ('After the battle'), *Kultura*, No. 25, 15 July 1998.

13 Zassoursky, I., *Rekonstruktsiya Rossii, Mass-media I politika v 90e*, Mosscow, Moscow State University Press 2001, p. 214.

14 Ibid.

15 Kachkayeva, A., 'Transformatsia Rossiyskogo Televideniya', Chapter 4, *Sredstva Massovoi Informatsii v Rossii*, Moscow, Aspekt Press 2006, p. 305.

16 Jack, A., *Inside Putin's Russia*, London, Granata Publications, 2005, pp. 147, 149.

17 Kachkayeva, A., 'Transformatsia Rossiyskogo Televideniya', Chapter 4, *Sredstva Massovoi Informatsii v Rossii*, Moscow, Aspekt Press 2006, p. 302.

18 Ibid., p. 300.

19 Zassoursky, I., *Rekonstruktsiya Rossii, Mass-media I politika v 90e*, Mosscow, Moscow State University Press 2001.

20 *The President in 1996: Scenarios and Technologies of Victory*, Foundation for Effective Politics report, March 1996.

21 Kachkayeva, A., 'Transformatsia Rossiyskogo Televideniya', Chapter 4, *Sredstva Massovoi Informatsii v Rossii*, Moscow, Aspekt Press 2006, p. 300.

22 Jack, A., *Inside Putin's Russia*, London, Granata Publications 2005, pp. 142–3.

23 Karatsuba, I., Kurukin, I., Sokolov, N., *Vybiraya Svoyu Istoriyu. Razvilki na puti Rossiyi: ot ryurikovichei do oligarkhov*, Moscow, Kolibri 2005, p. 619.

24 Ibid., p. 605.

25 Zassoursky, I., *Rekonstruktsiya Rossii, Mass-media I politika v 90e*, Mosscow, Moscow State University Press 2001.
26 Karatsuba, I., Kurukin, I., Sokolov, N., *Vybiraya Svoyu Istoriyu. Razvilki na puti Rossiyi: ot ryurikovichei do oligarkhov*, Moscow, Kolibri 2005, p. 620.
27 Zassoursky, Y., *Iskusheniye svobodoi, Rossiyskaya zhurnalistika, 1990–2004*, Moscow, Moscow State University Press, 2004, p. 229.
28 Tretyakov, V., 'Journalists-politicians', *Nezavisimaya Gazeta*, 22 September 2000.
29 Tretyakov, V., 'Defense against Putin', *Nezavisimaya Gazeta,7* September 2000.
30 Shkondin, M.V. 'Sistemniye Kharakteristiki SMI', *Sredstva Massovoi Informatsii Rossii*, edited by Y.N. Zassoursky, Moscow, Aspekt-Press 2006, pp. 180–1.
31 Zassoursky, Y., *Iskusheniye svobodoi, Rossiyskaya zhurnalistika, 1990–2004*, Moscow, Moscow State University Press, 2004, p. 229.
32 According to figures from the Association of Communication Agencies in Russia.
33 Vartanova, E.L., 'Ekonomicheskiye Ossobenosti SMI v Rossii', *Sredstva Massovoi Informatsii Rossii*, edited by Y. Zassoursky, Moscow, Aspekt Press 2006, p. 141.
34 Zassoursky, I., *Rekonstruktsiya Rossii, Mass-media I politika v 90e*, Mosscow, Moscow State University Press 2001.
35 Tretyakov, V., 'Sootnosheniye lichnykh, professionalnykh, korporativny interesov zhurnalista i natsionalnykh interesov', *Kak stat znamenitom zhurnalistom*, Moscow, Ladomir 2004, pp. 252–3.
36 Zassoursky, I., *Rekonstruktsiya Rossii, Mass-media I politika v 90e*, Mosscow, Moscow State University Press 2001.
37 Zassoursky, Y., *Iskusheniye svobodoi, Rossiyskaya zhurnalistika, 1990–2004*, Moscow, Moscow State University Press, 2004, p. 201.

Chapter 3

1   Committee to Protect Journalists, www.cpj.org/attacks06/europe06/rus06.html.
2   www.rsf.org/article.php3?id_article=8247.
3   Zhirkov, G.V., *Istoria Tsenzury v Rossii*, Moscow, Aspekt Press 2001.
4   Ibid.
5   Ibid.
6   Ibid.
7   Pushkin, A.S., Puteshestviye iz Moskvy v Sankt Peterburg, in *Complete Anthology of Works*, Leningrad, Nauka 1978, vol. 7, p. 207.
8   Zhirkov, G.V., *Istoria Tsenzury v Rossii*, Moscow, Aspekt Press 2001.
9   The 1826 censorship statute, as quoted by G.V. Zhirkov.
10 Zhirkov, G.V., *Istoria Tsenzury v Rossii*, Moscow, Aspekt Press 2001.
11 Ibid.
12 Vasilyev, M.V., *Zlo vsei pressy*, St Petersburg, 1904.

13 By comparison, in 1910 an average factory worker earned about 245 rubles a year, *Pravda* No. 86, 9 August 1912, from *Lenin Collected Works*, Progress Publishers, Moscow, 1975 Vol. 8, pp. 258–9.

14 Cited in Zhirkov, G.V., *Istoria Tsenzury v Rossii*, Moscow, Aspekt Press, 2001.

15 Sorokin, P.A. Cited in Zhirkov, ibid.

16 'Zhurnalist', *Pechat i revolutsiya*, January 1923, No. 3.

17 Lenin, V.I., *Sochineniya*, 4th edn, Vol. 32, p. 480.

18 Zhirkov, G.V., *Istoria Tsenzury v Rossii*, Moscow, Aspekt Press 2001.

19 Ibid.

20 Stalin, I.V., 'Beseda s inostrannymi rabochimi delegatsiyami', 5 November 1927, *Sochineniya*, Moscow, OGIZ State Publishing House for Political Literature 1949, pp. 206–38.

21 'The 20 journalists who have lost their lives in Putin's Russia', *The Independent*, 11 March 2007.

22 Jack, A., *Inside Putin's Russia*, London, Granata Publications 2005

23 'In Moscow, second Klebnikov murder trial starts tomorrow', Committee to Protect Journalists, *News Alert 2007*, www.cpj.org/news/ 2007/europe/russia14feb07na.html.

24 'Analysis: a conversation with Russian media activist Oleg Panfilov', RFE/RL, 3 August 2004, www.rferl.org/featuresarticle/2004/08/ 3cf8dcc1–48dd-4474-b1f7–33bffda8cb8c.html.

25 Law of the Russian Federation, 'On mass media', No. 2124–1 of 27 December 1991, as of 8 December 2003, Chapter 1, Article 3.

26 Ibid., Article 4.

27 Arutunyan, A., 'Informatsionny golod', *Novy Mir*, No. 10, 2005.

28 Ibid.

29 Androunas, E., *Soviet Media in Transition: Structural and Economic Alternatives*, Westport, CT, Praeger 1993.

30 Arutunyan, A., 'Informatsionny golod', *Novy Mir*, No. 10, 2005.

31 Zassoursky, I., *Rekonstruktsiya Rossii, Mass-media I politika v 90e*, Mosscow, Moscow State University Press 2001, p. 93.

32 Jack, A., *Inside Putin's Russia*, London, Granata Publications 2005.

33 'Otvetsvennost' sredstv massovoy informatsii', *Nezavisimaya Gazeta*, 14 June 1997.

Chapter 4

1 *Vedomosti*, 2 January 1703, *Bychkov*, 1855, pp. 1–4.

2 Kozlova M.M., *Istoria otechestvennikh sredstv massovoi informatsii, Uchebnoye posobiye*, Ulyanovsk, Ulyanovsky Gosudarstvenny Tekhnichesky Universitet (Ulyanovsk State Technical University) 2000.

3 Yesin, B.I., *Istoria russkoi zhurnalistiki (170 –1917), uchebno-metodichesky komplekt*, Moscow, Nauka, 2000.

4 Mironov, B.N. 'Gramotnost v Rossii 1797–1917: Poluchenie novoi istoricheskoi informatsii s pomoshchyu metodov retrospektivnovo prognozirovaniya', *Istoria SSSR*, 1985, No. 4, pp. 127–53.

5 Cressy, D., *Literacy and the Social Order: Reading and Writing in Tudor and Stuart England*, Cambridge, Cambridge University Press 2006, p. 51.
6 Yesin, B.I., *Istoria russkoi zhurnalistiki (170 –1917), uchebno-metodichesky komplekt*, Moscow, Nauka 2000.
7 Danilevsky, I.N., *Istochnikovedenie: Teoria, Istoria, Metod*, Moscow, Russian State University for the Humanities 2000, p. 460.
8 'Severnaya Pchela', *Abridged Literary Encyclopedia in 9 Volumes*, Vol. 6, Moscow, Sovetskaya Entsyklopedia 1971.
9 Chernyshevsky, N., 'Noviye periodicheskiie izdaniya', first published in *Sovremennik*, 1861, No. 1.
10 *Golos,* 1 January 1863, No. 1.
11 McReynolds, L., *The News Under Russsia's Old Regime: The Development of a Mass-Circulation Press*, Princeton, NJ, Princeton University Press 1991, p. 36.
12 Ibid., pp. 99–100.
13 Ibid.
14 Inikova, S.A., 'Gazeta Russkoye Slovo i tsenzura', *Problemy istorii SSSR,* 13th edn, Moscow, MGU Press 1985.
15 Konovalova, A.V., 'K voprosyu ob istorii gazety Birzhevye vedomosti', *Ekonomicheskaya istoria, Obozreniye*, edited by L.I. Borodkina, 6th edn, Moscow 2001, p. 111.
16 Lenin, V., 'Party organization and party literature', *Novaya Zhizn*, No. 12, 13 November 1905.
17 Pietlainen, J., *The Regional Newspaper in Post-Soviet Russia*, Tampere, University of Tampere 2002, p. 103.
18 Reisner, L.M., ‚Kazan-Sarapul', *Izvestia*, 16 November 1918.
19 'Frantsuzki proletariat privetstvuyet sovetsky soyuz', *Izvestia,* 4 December 1930.
20 Nikitin, A., 'Etot "malchishka" Adjubei', *Izvestia*, 12 December 2005.
21 Frolova, T.I., 'Informatsionnyie agentstva', *Sredstvo massovoi informatsii Rossii,* edited by Y.N. Zassoursky, Moscow, Aspekt Press 2006.
22 McReynolds, L., *The News Under Russia's Old Regime: The Development of a Mass-Circulation Press*, Princeton, NJ, Princeton University Press 1991.
23 Juskevitz, S., *Professional Roles of Russian Journalists At the End of the 1990s, A Case Study of St Petersburg Media*, Tampere, University of Tampere 2002, p. 15.
24 Taken and translated from a history and mission statement of the paper posted on its site, www.kommersant.ru/about.aspx.
25 Kharatyan, K., 'Dostali Sovetami' (an interview with Kommersant founder Vladimir Yakovlev), *Vedomosti*, No. 9, 16 March 2007.
26 Tumakova, I., 'Otchim ubil pedofila, spasaya rebenka', *Izvestia*, 29 January 2008.
27 Balashova, E., 'Gazetny rynok vstupil v tyazhely period', an interview with Vladimir Sungorkin, editor and general manager of the *Komsomolskaya Pravda* publishing house, *Kurier pechati,* No. 47, 2005.

28 Perekrest, V., 'Chemodan, vokzal, Big-Ben', *Izvestia,* 29 June 2007.
29 Rostovsky, M., 'Sami s USAmi, *Moskovski Komsomolets,* 29 February 2008.
30 Resnyanskaya, L.L., 'Obshcherossiiskiye izdaniya', *Sredstva massovoi informatsii,* Moscow, Aspekt Press 2006, p. 228.
31 Zassoursky, I., *Rekonstruktsiya Rossii, Mass-media I politika v 90e,* Mosscow, Moscow State University Press 2001, p. 285.
32 *Moskovsky Komsomolets* editorial independence during perestroika is attested to by correspondents who worked for the paper at the time and by people who regularly read both *Moskovsky Komsomolets* and *Moskovskie Novosti* at that time.
33 From an interview with Julia Bakhareva given to the author.
34 Ibid.
35 'YLC Subotnik November 12', *The Moscow News,* 5 November 1933.
36 Arutunyan, A., 'A paper of pioneers and purges', *The Moscow News,* 24 April 2009.
37 Borisov, Sergei, 'My ne byli trubadurami marksizma-leninizma', (an interview with Yakov Lomko), *Moskovskie Novosti,* No. 38, 30 September 2005.
38 From an interview given to the author.
39 Arutunyan, A., 'Waking Up Russia', *The Moscow News,* 8 May 2009.
40 'Putin oznakomilsya s rabotoi redaktsionnogo kompleksa RIA Novosti I RT', *RIA Novosti,* 24 February 2009, www.rian.ru/politics/20090224/163054597.html.

Chapter 5

1 Vertov, D., 'Three songs of Lenin and Kino-Eye', Kino-Eye, The Writings of Dziga Vertov, translated by Kevin O'Brien, Berkeley, CA, University of California Press 1984, p. 123.
2 Ibid.
3 Kuznetsov, G., Mesyatsev, N., 'Zolotye gody otechestvennogo televidenia. 1957–1970', Ocherki po istorii rossiyskogo televidenia, Moscow, Voskresenye 1999.
4 Sappak, V., Televidenie i My, Moscow, Aspekt Press 2007, p. 53.
5 Yegorov, V.V., Televidenie: Stranitsy istorii, Moscow, Aspect Press 2004.
6 Muratov, S.A., 'Vladimir Sappak – utopist ili proritsatel?', Teleradioefir, Istoria I sovremennost, edited by. Y.N. Zassoursky, Moscow, Aspekt Press 2005, p. 59.
7 Kachkayeva, A., 'Noveishaya istoria rossiyskogo televidenia', Teleradioefir, Istoria I sovremennost, edited by Y.N. Zassoursky, Moscow, Aspekt Press 2005, p. 36.
8 Golovanov, V., 'Televorot, Gosteleradio v period putcha 1991 goda', Teleradioefir, Istoria I sovremennost, edited by Y.N. Zassoursky, Moscow, Aspekt Press 2005, p. 125.

9   McNair, B., 'Media in post-Soviet Russia: an overview', European Journal of Communication, 1994, No. 9, p. 115.
10 'Rossiyskoye TV vykhodit v efir, A Kravchenko bolshe ne chlen soyuza zhurnalistov', Vlast, No. 15, 8 April 1991.
11 Zassoursky, I., Rekonstrukstiya Rossii, Mass Media I politika v 90e, Moscow, MGU 2001, p. 58.
12 'Genprokuratura prodolzhayet presledovat NTV', Kommersant, No. 161, 2 September 1995.
13 Zassoursky, I., Rekonstrukstiya Rossii, Mass Media I politika v 90e, Moscow, MGU 2001, p. 65.
14 Zassoursky, Y.N. (ed.), 'Nuzhno li obshchestvu televidenie?' in Teleradioefir, Istoria I sovremennos, Moscow, Aspekt Press 2005. p. 9.
15 Ibid.
16 'Russia: Elections   of   the   Absurd',   Index   on   Censorship, www.indexoncensorship.org/?p=128.
17 Samedova, Y., 'Abros obros REN TV', Gazeta, No. 67, 13April 2007.
18 Digital Television in Russia, report, edited by Groteck Co., Lfd for the European Audiovisual Observatory, Moscow 2008, p. 53, www.obs.coe.int/online_publication/reports/digitaltv_groteck.pdf.en.
19 'Nuzhno li obshchestvu televidenie?' Teleradioefir. Istoria I sovremennost, edited by Y.N. Zassoursky, Moscow, Aspekt Press 2005, p. 15.
20 Solntseva, A., 'Rossiyskoye televidenie: vsego lish biznes?' Vremya Novostei, 26 February 2007.
21 Finn, P., 'Russia pumps tens of millions into burnishing image abroad', Washington Post, 6 March.

Chapter 6

1   Zassoursky, Y.N., 'Samy otkrytyi istochnik informatsii', Teleradioefir, Istoria I Sovremennost, Moscow, Aspekt Press 2005, p. 145.
2   Sherel, A.A. (ed.), Radiozhurnalistika, Moscow, Moscow University Press 2000, p. 18.
3   Hale, J., 'Radio power', as cited in G.S. Jowett, and V. O'Donnell, Propaganda and Persuasion, Thousand Oaks, CA, Sage 2006, p. 124.
4   Jowett, G.S. and O'Donnell, V., Propaganda and Persuasion, Thousand Oaks, CA, Sage 2006, p. 125.
5   Sherel, A.A. (ed.), Radiozhurnalistika, Moscow, Moscow University Press 2000, p. 24.
6   Levitan, Y., 'Govorit Moskva!', Yunost, No. 12, 1966, pp. 62–3.
7   Ibid.
8   Vernadsky, V.I., as quoted in A.A. Sherel, (ed.), Radiozhurnalistika, Moscow, Moscow University Press 2000, p. 48.
9   Pareles, J., 'Alla Pugacheva's moody, ardent Soviet pop', The New York Times, 25 September 1988.
10 Okunev, Ilya, 'Muzyka muzyki rozn', interview with V.S. Levashov, Zdorovye, 9 June 1977, pp. 23–4.
11 Gakkel, V., 'Yesli by ne bylo rok-kluba?', Spetsialnoye radio, 26 February 2007.

12 Belyayev, S., Korobitsyn, V., Radiostantsyii Rossii, Gosudarstvennoye i nezavisimoye veshchaniye, Moscow 1995. publisher?

13 Venediktov, A., as quoted in 'Otechestvennoye radioveshchaniye v nachale XXI veka: novyie realii i stariye problemy', L. D. Bolotova, Teleradioefir, istoriya I sovremennost, ed. Y.N. Zassoursky, Moscow, Aspect Press 2005, p. 157.

14 Rita Mitrofanova in an interview with the author.

15 Ibid.

16 Source: TNS Gallup, April 2007.

17 Volkova, T., 'Radio dlya vzroslykh', Izvestia, 20 June 2007.

Chapter 7

1 Nossik, A., Kuznetsov, S. (eds) Internet dlya zhurnalista, Moscow, Mediasoyuz 2001, p. 9.

2 Zassoursky, I., Rekonstruktsiya rossii, Mass media i politika v 90-e, Moscow, MGU 2001, p. 161.

3 Nossik, A., Kuznetsov, S. (eds) Internet dlya zhurnalista, Moscow, Mediasoyuz, 2001, p. 10.

4 Ibid., p. 11.

5 Malyukov, A., 'Proekt veka glazami sozdatelya', Zhurnal.ru, www.zhurnal.ru/7/malukoff.html.

6 Zassoursky, I., Rekonstruktsiya Rossii, Mass media i politika v 90-e, Moscow, MGU 2001, p. 180.

7 Arutunyan, A., 'In Russia's blogosphere, anything goes', The Nation, 13 March 2007, www.thenation.com/doc/20070312/arutunyan.

8 From an interview given to the author, February 2007.

9 Gorny, E., Russian LiveJournal: national specifics in the development of a virtual community, version 1.0 of 13 May 2004, www.ruhr-uni-bochum.de/russ-cyb/library/texts/en/gorny_rlj_2.htm.

10 Arutunyan, A., Cooper, N., 'Odnoklassniki: Russians connect to their student days', The Moscow News, 27 December 2007, www.mnweekly.ru/national/20071227/55299953.html.

Conclusion

1 Alexeeva, A., 'Sup "syel" gazetu', Expert, 30 June 2008.

2 Digital Television in Russia, Groteck Co., Ltd for the European Audiovisual Observatory, 2008, p. 93.

BIBLIOGRAPHY

Allan, S. (2004) *News Culture*, 2nd edn. Maidenhead: Open University Press.

Androunas, E. (1993) *Soviet Media in Transition: Structural and Economic Alternatives*. Westport, CT: Praeger.

Arutunyan, A. (2005) Informatsionny golod, *Novy Mir*, 10.

Arutunyan, A. (2007) In Russia's blogosphere, anything goes, *The Nation*, 13 March.

Bolotova, L. D. (2005) Otechestvennoye radioveshchaniye v nachale XXI veka: novyie realii I stariye problemy, in Y. N. Zassoursky (ed.) *Teleradioefir, istoriya I sovremennost*. Moscow: Aspect Press.

Cressy, D. (2006) *Literacy and the Social Order: Reading and Writing in Tudor and Stuart England*. Cambridge: Cambridge University Press.

Jack, A. (2005) *Inside Putin's Russia*. London: Granata.

Jowett, G., Garth, S. and O'Donnell, V. (2006) *Propaganda and Persuasion*. Thousand Oaks, CA: Sage.

Juskevits, S. (2002) *Professional Roles of Russian Journalists At the End of the 1990s: A Case Study of St. Petersburg Media*. Tampere: Tampere University.

Lenin, V. (1905) Party organization and party literature, *Novaya Zhizn*, 12, 13 November 1905.

McNair, B. (1994) Media in post-Soviet Russia: an overview, *European Journal of Communication*, 9: 115.

McReynolds, L. (1990) Autocratic journalism: the case of the St Petersburg Telegraph Agency, *Slavic Review*, 49(1).

McReynolds, L. (1991) *The News Under Russia's Old Regime: The Development of a Mass-Circulation Press*. Princeton, NJ: Princeton University Press.

Ovsepyan, R. (1999) *Istoria noveishei otechestvennoi zhurnalistiki*. Moscow: Moscow State University Press.

Pietlainen, J. (2002) *The Regional Newspaper in Post-Soviet Russia*. Tampere: University of Tampere.

Sherel, A. A. (ed.) (2000) *Radiozhurnalistika*. Moscow: Moscow University Press.

Yegorov, V. V. (2004) *Televidenie: Stranitsy istorii.* Moscow: Aspect Press.

Yesin, B. I. (2000) *Istoria russkoi zhurnalistiki (1703–1917), uchebno-metodichesky komplekt.* Moscow: Nauka.

Zassoursky, I. (2001) *Rekonstruktsiya Rossii. Mass-media i politika v 90e.* Moscow: Moscow University Press.

Zassoursky, Y. (2004) *Iskusheniye svobodoi: Rossiiskaya zhurnalistika, 1990–2004.* Moscow: Moscow University Press.

Zassoursky, Y. (ed.) (2005) *Teleradioefir: Istoria i sovremennost.* Moscow: Aspekt Press.

Zassoursky, Y. (ed.) (2006) *Sredstva massovoi informatssii rossii.* Moscow: Aspekt Press.

Zhirkov, G.V. (2001) *Istoria Tsenzury v Rossii.* Moscow: Aspekt Press.

TIMELINE

1447 Invention of the Guttenberg printing press.

1551 The Stoglav compilation adopted in Russia as the first censoring document. It consisted of 100 decrees dictating Church affairs and establishing rules for book printing and manuscript editing.

1556 Republic of Venice publishes *Notizie Scritte*, one of the first newspapers in Europe. It cost a small coin called a *gazetta*.

1605 First modern newspaper, *Relation*, published in Germany.

1621 Russian government begins releasing an internal, handwritten newsletter, *Kuranty*.

1682 Decree issued in Russia forbidding the distribution of any literature on religious themes by anyone except Church clerics. All printing presses were required to have special permission from the Moscow patriarch to publish. Peter the Great ascends the throne at the age of 10.

1701 Peter issues a decree forbidding Church clerics to 'wield pen and ink', thus ending the Church's monopoly on censorship.

1702 Peter founds *Vedomosti,* the first printed newspaper in Russia.

1703 St Petersburg, Russia's northern capital, founded by Peter.

1721 Peter proclaims himself emperor of Russia, thus transforming his *czardom* into an empire.

1759 Poet Alexander Sumarokov launches the *Trudolyubivaya Pchela* (*The Hardworking Bee*), the first privately-run periodical in Russia. It was shut down just months later for its criticism of the government of Empress Elizabeth.

1762 Catherine the Great becomes empress of Russia. Her reign, which ended in 1792, saw a number of reforms.

1769 Catherine launches *Vsyakaya Vsachina* (*This and That*), a literary magazine that was controlled by the state and used to mould public opinion.

1783 Catherine establishes the right to create private printing presses in Russia.

1796 Catherine issues a decree establishing preliminary censorship – all manuscripts must first undergo screening by a censorship organ.

1838 *Severnaya Pchela* (*Northern Bee*) launched as the first privately-owned daily newspaper. Although private, it was stringently loyal to the government of Nicholas I.

1861 Alexander II abolishes serfdom in one of his most famous reforms. Others included mass education campaigns and political reforms.

1905 The first revolution, albeit failed, eventually leads to the establishment of parliament (the State Duma), a multi-party system, and the Russian constitution of 1906. In 1905, Nicholas II passes a number of decrees, one of which eliminated preliminary censorship in Russian cities.

1917 The February Revolution overthrows the czar and ushers in a liberal provisional government headed first by Prince Georgy Lvov and then by Alexander Kerensky. The Bolshevik October Revolution ultimately brings communist Bolsheviks to power. While the February Revolution effectively abolished censorship, it would creep back soon after the Bolsheviks took power, even though they, too, had initially proclaimed an end to censorship.

1921 The implementation of the New Economic Policy (NEP), which introduced elements of a free market and allowed for some open discussion.

1922 The establishment of the Glavlit – the Central Directorate for Affairs of Literature and Publishing – lays the cornerstone of the Soviet censorship apparatus. Beyond censorship, it also controlled propaganda.

1928 The end of the NEP. Stalin comes to power, ushering in an era of rigid censorship.

1939 World War II breaks out in Europe; Russia joins the war against Germany in 1941.

1945 Russia celebrates victory over fascist Germany at the end of World War II.

1953 Nikita Khrushchev comes to power as general secretary of the Communist Party after the death of Joseph Stalin. He ushers in 'de-Stalinization', and other policies that would come to be known as the 'thaw'.

1964 Khrushchev removed from power and replaced by Leonid Brezhnev. The later years of the Brezhnev era in the 1970s would come to be known as a time of stagnation.

1985 Mikhail Gorbachev becomes general secretary, ushering in per-estroika and glasnost.

1990 Gorbachev signs a law that in effect liberates the press for the first time in Russian history; censorship is abolished and private individuals are given the right to establish publications.

1991 The hardliner coup in reaction to Gorbachev's reforms ultimately ends in the collapse of the Soviet Union. Russia becomes a federation.

1993 Yeltsin's move to dissolve parliament results in the opposition storming the White House, then the seat of parliament, leading to an armed standoff with Yeltsin's forces. Afterwards, the Supreme Soviet was abolished, replaced with the much less powerful, two-chamber parliament, the Federal Assembly.

1996 Yeltsin re-elected president after a powerful media campaign orchestrated by pro-Yeltsin oligarchs hypes up a 'communist scare'.

1999 Yeltsin resigns on New Year's Eve, handing over the presidency to Prime Minister Vladimir Putin, who is elected president in a landslide in March 2000.

2000 NTV, one of Russia's most popular television stations, is taken over by the state-owned Gazprom gas monopoly in the summer, formally over debt. It is widely believed that the takeover was politically motivated.

2004 Putin re-elected president.

2008 Dmitry Medvedev, Putin's 'anointed' successor, is elected president in March.

GLOSSARY

authoritarianism: a form of government characterized by highly centralized power structures, a repressive political system, lack of rule of law, flawed elections, self-appointed leadership, lack of civil society, lack of civil liberties, lack of free media and a suppressed opposition. The Soviet Union was best associated with this type of governance. Post-Soviet Russia, particularly under President Vladimir Putin, has shown several elements of an authoritarian government. However, the extent of the centralization of power in the Russian Federation can be questioned; although regional governors are appointed rather than elected, some Russian political analysts have questioned to what extent various regions are under the control of the Kremlin. Moreover, while Russia has had flawed elections under both Presidents Boris Yeltsin and Putin, its leadership is not fully self-appointed.

'For order' article, *see* **jeans**

fourth estate: the hallowed role of the press as an institution of social power. It has been attributed to Edmund Burk, who, following the French Revolution, referred to the three estates in parliament and the fourth estate in the reporters' gallery, which he termed the 'more important' one. The first estate is the clergy, the second is the nobility and the third estate consists of the commoners. In Russia's exceedingly more centralized political system, there was hardly room for autonomous estates, much less a fourth estate. For this reason, the idea that its press could and should become a fourth estate arose only during perestroika in the late 1980s. The vague meaning of the term as an institution in Russia kept it from realizing its potential to create social change.

glasnost: a policy of openness, publicity, transparency and freedom of information that the Soviet Union's last leader, President Mikhail Gorbachev, tried to introduce into the government institutions of his country after coming to power in 1985. The core of Gorbachev's glasnost policy was freedom of information. The mass media were encouraged to uncover what had been previously suppressed by the Soviet government, and institutions were urged to be more open in providing factual information. Although Gorbachev was trying to revive the moral standing of the Soviet government, one result of glasnost was that the state came under even more criticism from inside the country. It has been argued that rather than raising the moral standing, glasnost, by uncovering the flaws of the Soviet government, ultimately brought it down.

Gosteleradio: the state committee that controlled all radio and television broadcasts in the Soviet Union. The full name of this body was the State Committee for Television and Radio. It was established in 1931, when it was called the All-Union Committee for Radio Broadcasting, and was part of the People's Commissariat of Postal and Telegraph Services. This agency, which owned and controlled all stations and was responsible for censorship, answered to the Soviet cabinet of ministers rather than the Communist Party. With the breakup of the Soviet Union, part of its functions and assets became the Ostankino broadcasting company (later known as Channel 1), and part of it became a government agency. The government agencies responsible for press and media have undergone many transformations in recent years.

Iron Curtain: the name given to the symbolic and physical boundary that separated the communist bloc from the rest of Europe from the end of World War II in 1945 to the demise of the Soviet Union and the end of the Cold War in 1991. The first use is attributed to the Nazi propaganda minister Joseph Goebbels in 1945, but it was more famously used by Winston Churchill the same year. Although it had physical shape in the form of border defences between eastern and western Europe and later the Berlin Wall, the Iron Curtain usually refers more to the various degrees of political, economic and cultural isolation shared by countries in the Soviet bloc. In Russia that isolation was more prevalent than in countries like Czechoslovakia or Yugoslavia, where citizens had access to a wider range of western goods and ideas.

jeans (*dzhinsa*): Russian slang for articles that have been paid for by certain interest groups, whether public or private. Otherwise known as 'hidden advertising', these articles are written by staff reporters, promoting a certain slant and advertising a product or a particular point of view. However, because of the generally subjective style of Russian reporting and the murky nature of finances in journalism, the prevalence of *dzhinsa* in mainstream Russian journalism is widely exaggerated. Rather, the term has become a derogative one, used to question the credentials of a journalist or an entire publication. It is virtually impossible, however, to establish whether actual cash changed hands in relation to the appearance of a particular article.

lede: also written as 'lead', it is the first sentence of a journalistic article, and the most important structural element in western-style printed journalism. The concept, devised to draw a reader's attention and introduce the topic, was virtually non-existent in Russia until western news formats were introduced in the late 1980s and 1990s. The Russian journalistic style often sought to catch a reader's attention with a quote or a *bon mot* that in some cases had little to do with the article's topic. In other cases, the first sentence would state an opinion that the rest of the article would uphold with facts or incidents.

loans for shares: a programme adopted by the Russian government in 1995 to raise money. The government pawned off lucrative industrial assets in exchange for loans from prominent bankers and businessmen. Because the government was unable to pay off the loans, the properties and state companies came under the ownership of private businessmen. Yukos, Norilsk Nickel, LUKoil, Sibneft and Mechel were among the assets that came under private ownership. Proposed by Vladimir Potanin, the programme propelled bankers like Potanin and Mikhail Khodorkovsky to the forefront of the business elite by allowing them to buy major production assets on the cheap. This was beneficial for the assets themselves – oil companies like Yukos began operating more efficiently, and, hence, bringing in more profits. However, the government 'sell-out' worsened the image of the Yeltsin administration and demonized the new class of oligarchs in the public mind.

nationalization: the transfer of ownership of private assets into government hands. After the privatization of the early 1990s, some companies were taken over by the government. In 1998, the state began seizing parts of the Gazprom natural gas monopoly, citing back-taxes. Since then, the government has obtained a controlling share in the company. Back-taxes were the most common pretext by which the Russian government would partially or fully take over a company in the later years. Yukos, whose chief, Mikhail Khodorkovsky, was jailed on fraud and tax evasion, was nationalized in this way. After the financial crisis in the autumn of 2008, the government began buying up assets of struggling companies to keep them afloat, in a symbolic reversal of the state's relations with business in the early 1990s.

New Economic Policy (NEP): a temporary policy of free market elements proposed by Vladimir Lenin to revive the new Soviet economy in 1921. Under the new conditions, the government continued to control banks, foreign trade and industry, but permitted private ownership of business and the sale of goods by farmers and individuals. The policy re-introduced money and cash payments and put an end to grain sequestering. In 1928, Joseph Stalin ended the policy and launched collectivization in order to raise money for the government's industrialization plans.

ocherk: a literary sketch, a uniquely Russian journalistic genre that combined elements of classic reportage, the essay and short fiction. Prevalent from the nineteenth century onwards, it gave serious, quality dailies such as *Izvestia* a literary air, and reached a peak in popularity during the thaw of the 1950s and 1960s. In a journalistic environment that was still tightly censored, the *ocherk* proved popular because it allowed the layperson to read between the lines. Among the most acclaimed writers of the *ocherk* genre was *Izvestia*'s Anatoly Agranovsky, who wrote under the editorship of the paper's most liberal chief, Alexei Adjubei.

oligarch: the classical definition refers to a member of an oligarchy, a form of government where political power is held by a small, wealthy elite. In Russia, however, the word has come to refer to any business magnate regardless of whether he or she actually holds political power. The demise of the Soviet Union led to a situation where a near-bankrupt government was in some cases less powerful than a growing class of business tycoons who had gained their assets in the sweeping privatizations after 1991. (During the Soviet Union there was no private property, apart from personal property that could be used as long as it did not create an income for the user.) Throughout the 1990s, the economic situation was such that business magnates were de facto close to the government – businessmen had to depend on the government for access to deals, while the government depended on the businessmen for financing. This situation was exacerbated in the loans for shares programme in 1995. Because the oligarchs were initially positioned so close to the government, a number of them, most notably Boris Berezovsky, did in fact acquire a great deal of political influence and even power. Meanwhile, officials who occupied government posts would go on to acquire state assets – including media holdings – throughout the 1990s.

'paid for' article, *see* **jeans**

perestroika: a series of political and economic reforms launched by Mikhail Gorbachev in June 1987. The word literally means 'rebuilding' in Russian. Among his political reforms, Gorbachev pushed for the reduction of Party control of the government apparatus (including the Council of Ministers), the separation of the government apparatus from the Party at a regional level, and the introduction of multi-candidate elections for the ruling Communist Party and the parliament. In 1988, the Supreme Soviet, the country's parliament, was reduced and transformed into the Congress of People's Deputies, the precursor to Russia's modern-day two-chamber parliament, the Federal Assembly. Coupled with Gorbachev's policy of glasnost, this new parliament allowed deputies to speak out for the first time against the Soviet government and Gorbachev himself. Economic reforms included the Law on Cooperatives, which permitted private ownership of business for the first time since the NEP, allowing foreigners to invest in the Soviet Union through joint ventures and drastically reducing the power that the Foreign Trade Ministry held over industrial and agricultural sectors. These economic policies did not stop (and, in some cases, helped hasten) the demise of the Soviet economy, and the Soviet Union as a whole.

privatization: the transfer of property or business from the government (or the public sector) to the private sector. Following the breakup of the Soviet Union, the new government proceeded with sweeping privatization reforms, putting state-owned industrial assets and property into private ownership. In the Soviet economy, private ownership of enterprises was illegal, while the legal concept of private ownership for other things, such as property, for all intents and purposes, did not exist. Personal property, such as a car, an apartment or a summer home could be 'owned' or 'used indefinitely' so long as the owner did not make any income from the asset through sale or lease. The privatization of the early 1990s was a step from the planned economy of the Soviet Union towards a market economy. It occurred in several stages. In 1988, before the breakup of the Soviet Union, Gorbachev passed new legislation that partially transferred property rights of enterprises from the government to the employees and management. This 'spontaneous privatization' involved several thousand enterprises, including several newspapers – most notably, *Izvestia* and *Moskovskie Novosti*. Voucher privatization was a method, institutional-ized in 1992, by which the Russian government could sell off all its assets. To avoid concentration of former government assets in the hands of criminalized groups and the former elite, the government decided on free voucher privatization, by which every citizen got a share of national wealth in the form of a voucher, which they could invest or sell. However, insiders managed to get their hands on most of the assets, while average citizens opted to sell the vouchers for money rather than investing them. Ultimately, this facilitated the rise of the oligarch class. After 1995, a cash-strapped government went on to sell off the rest of its assets through the loans for shares programme.

shock therapy: the fast-paced implementation of pro-market reforms which occurred in Russia during the early 1990s. Orchestrated by key economists in Boris Yeltsin's government such as Yegor Gaidar and Anatoly Chubais, it involved full trade liberalization, withdrawal of state subsidies and the release of price controls. Proponents argued that it was the best way to transform the planned economy of the Soviet Union into a free market, even though it would have temporary side-effects such as inflation. But the economists underestimated the extent of the inflation, which was 3000 per cent by 1993. While successful in some eastern European countries, shock therapy proved devastating for Russia. News-papers were among the enterprises that were affected by price liberaliza-tion; the newly-established, privately-owned media outlets could not afford the cost of paper, printing and distribution.

thick journal: a type of journal prevalent in Russian journalism and characterized by its thickness. Among existing publications, the monthly *Novy Mir* best typifies this genre: it is literally thick, with no illustrations, and publishes long essays, short stories, novellas, poetry and other fiction. During the nineteenth century, this form of publication dominated Russian journalism because over 90 per cent of the population was illiterate, while newspapers, because of censorship, were powerless to report on political and daily events in an objective manner. This helped breed a highbrow culture of journalism where polemic was possible only when it pertained to literary issues – hence the popularity of the thick journal among intellectuals as the only venue to discuss anything, from the literary to the political. Prominent thick journals of the nineteenth century were *Vremya* and *Sovremennik*; they published writers like Fyodr Dostoevsky and Nikolai Chernyshevsky.

westernizer: a supporter of western values as opposed to historic Russian and Slavic traditions. This line of thought originated in the nineteenth century, although Peter the Great can be considered a 'westernizing' czar because of his policies. Westernization embraced liberal political thought, industrialization and economic reform.

INDEX

THE MEDIA IN ITALY

Matthew Hibberd

The Italian media – the press, cinema, radio and television – is one of the largest and most controversial media industries in mainland Europe. In this introductory text Matthew Hibberd explores the key historical processes and events in the growth and development of Italy's main media and considers it in the context of the economic, political, socio-cultural and technological movements that have affected Italy.

Featuring a timeline of key Italian events, the book begins with the Unification – or Risorgimento – of Italy in 1861, and charts the rise of Italy from a fragmented and rural-based society through to a leading industrialised and urbanised world power. It details Fascism's reliance on the exploitation of the mass media, analyses Italy's remarkable post-war recovery, the development of democratic institutions and the contribution that a pluralistic media has made to this. Finally, it examines Silvio Berlusconi's rise to high political office and questions whether the involvement of Italy's leading media mogul in politics has harmed Italy's international reputation.

The Media in Italy addresses key themes that show how the Italian state and Italian media operate, such as:

- How governing parties and individuals have been able to assert influence over media intuitions
- Why there is a close relationship between political elites and media professionals
- The lack of consensus over key media reforms
- The importance of the Catholic Church in the development of the Italian media
- How a unique Italian media system has been shaped by issues of citizenship, democracy and nation-state

The Media in Italy is key reading for students on media, journalism, politics, and modern language courses.

Contents: *Acknowledgements – Map of Italy – Introduction – The media and the Unification of Italy – The liberal years, 1861–1922 – The media in Fascist Italy – The First Italian Republic: cinema and the press in the postwar years – The First Italian Republic and 'Mamma RAI' – Broadcasting and the Wild West years – The Second Italian Republic: cinema and the press since 1992 – Silvio Berlusconi – Moving towards digital: Italian media in the new millennium – Conclusion – Timeline of political events in Italy, 1861–2007 – Notes – Bibliography – Index.*

2007 192pp

978-0-335-22285-8 (Paperback) 978-0-335-22286-5 (Hardback)

MEDIA AND THEIR PUBLICS

Michael Higgins

This accessible and thought-provoking book provides a critical insight into the relationship between the media and the public. It examines the way in which the public is represented, referred to and portrayed in the media, and how the media acts or speaks on the public's behalf.

The first part explores the political side of the relationship between the media and the public. This includes interesting discussion of advocacy in political interviews and the discursive arrangement of political discussion programmes.

The second part of the book examines a range of discourses outside of the political realm. Michael Higgins looks at the construction of ordinariness, authenticity and public legitimacy, the relationship between institutional and media expertise, and the exercise of public decency. He argues that what unites the relationships between media and forms of public are their concern with wider issues of politics, governance, and cultural influence.

The author offers a range of illustrative examples of broadcasting from US, Australian and British contexts, providing students with a rage of engaging international examples with which to draw comparisons and compare their own media experiences. Each chapter includes recommended texts for further reading and questions for discussion.

The Media and Their Publics is an essential text for students and researchers in media studies, cultural policy and political communications.

Contents: *Acknowledgements – Issues of the public – The construction of the political public – The political public and its advocates – The political public take the stage – The construction of the cultural public – Cultural publics and participation – The construction of expertise in the media – Rethinking media publics – Key figures and their thoughts – References – Index.*

2008 192pp

978-0-335-21929-2 (Paperback) 978-0-335-21930-8 (Hardback)

THE MEDIA IN LATIN AMERICA
Jairo Lugo-Ocando (ed)

'Ably edited, this volume offers an unusually wide-ranging collection of well-informed chapters by experts from across the region. For those who want to understand the current realities that shape media performance from the Gulf of Mexico to the Tierra del Fuego, here is the ideal starting-point.'
Professor Philip Schlesinger, University of Glasgow, UK

'For those of us in the area of Latin American studies, this text comes to fill a gap in the field, both in terms of teaching and research.'
Charles Jones, Centre of Latin American Studies,
University of Cambridge, UK

'More than an introduction, it provides a comprehensive insight into the modern Latin America media landscape.'
Ramesh Jaura, Chairman of the Global Cooperation Council
and Euro-Mediterranean coordinator of the IPS News Agency

The media's role as a mechanism of control throughout Latin America has become increasingly sophisticated. Many repressive elements of the dictatorship periods have remained in place or have mutated into more subtle means of censorship and control. Media owners and political elites are more than keen to use the media's increasingly prominent role in framing politics in the region, in order to pursue their own agenda and interests.

This book provides a comprehensive and critical overview of some of the most important media systems in Latin America. Drawing on original and critical essays from some of the most prominent authors in the field, the author approaches the subject with a country-by-country analysis, exploring the most relevant aspects of the media in each society. The essays cover:

* Media history
* Organisation
* The interrelationship of the media and the state
* Media regulation and policy and ownership
* Broadcast media
* Film, music, advertising and digital media

The Media in Latin America is valuable reading for students of media and journalism studies.

Contents: The contributors – Acknowledgements – An introduction to the maquilas of power: media and political transition in Latin America – The media in Argentina: democracy, crisis and the reconfiguration of media groups – The media in Bolivia: the market-driven economy, 'shock therapy' and the democracy that ended – The media in Brazil: an historical overview of Brazilian broadcasting politics – The media in Chile: the restoration of democracy and the subsequent concentration of media – The media in Colombia: beyond violence and a market-driven economy – The media in Costa Rica: many media, scarce communication – The media in Castro's Cuba: every word counts – The media in Mexico: from authoritarian institution to hybrid system – The media in Nicaragua: an escape valve for a dysfunctional democracy – The media in Paraguay: from the coverage of political democracy to the obsession with violence – The media in Peru: the challenge of constructing a meaningful democracy – The media in Venezuela: the revolution was televised, but no one was really watching – Beyond national media systems: a medium for Latin America and the struggle for integration – References.

2008 296pp

978-0-335-22201-8 (Paperback) 978-0-335-22202-5 (Hardback)